Learning
TRS-80
BASIC

Another publication from the CompuSoft® Learning Series

by David A. Lien

COMPUSOFT PUBLISHING®
A Division of Compusoft®, Inc.
Box 19669 • San Diego, California 92119 USA

International Standard Book Number: 0-932760-08-2

Library of Congress Catalog Card Number: 81-70768

10   9   8   7   6   5   4   3   2

A Personal Note From the Author

In 1977 I wrote the original TRS-80 Level I Users Manual. It was supplied with each Level I computer (both Models I and III) and helped make the TRS-80 the world's best selling computer. That book was translated into French, Spanish and German and received critical acclaim around the world. Also distributed through Radio Shack stores and computer centers, it is probably the world's best selling full-length computer book.

The Model I TRS-80 with Level I BASIC opened the frontier, guiding untold thousands into computing. When it was upgraded to Level II BASIC, I wrote *Learning Level II* to teach BASIC's advanced features. CompuSoft Publishing distributed *Learning Level II* around the world and it too became a best seller.

Learning TRS-80 BASIC combines the best of both earlier books. . .plus much more, updated to include Models I, II, III and 16. It is written for the average person who has no experience with a computer. The style is light and non-threatening since we have no insecurities to pass along. Learning should be fun, not intimidating . . .

And why shouldn't Learning be fun. . ?

Sit back, relax, read slowly as though savoring a good novel, and above all, let your imagination wander. I'll supply all the routine facts and techniques you need. The real enjoyment begins when *your* imagination starts the creative juices flowing and the computer becomes a tool in *your own* hands. *You* become its master — not the other way around. At that time it evolves from just a box of parts into an extension of your own personality!

Enjoy your TRS-80!

Dr. David A. Lien
San Diego — 1982

Acknowledgements

This comprehensive book is the result of work by many people over a number of years. At the risk of missing a few, my thanks go to the following who made major contributions:

Dave Waterman, Technical Director, CompuSoft Publishing

Dave Kater, Writer, CompuSoft Publishing

Dave Lunsford, Writer, CompuSoft Publishing

Mike Hunter, Researcher, CompuSoft Publishing

Dave Gunzel, Director of Publications, Radio Shack

Lance Leventhal, Author

Rich Barnes, Cartoonist, The Printers, Inc.

And last, but not least, to Radio Shack for their kind permission to quote freely from my original best selling Level I book. Portions of the material contained herein were originally created by the author for Radio Shack in support of the TRS-80 computer.

Introduction

Learning TRS-80 BASIC is organized into five major sections:

A. Fifty chapters which teach how to use the many capabilities of your TRS-80. . .in small enough bites so you won't choke. Many chapters include check points and examples.

At the end of most chapters are Exercises. If you're studying alone, use them to test yourself and exercise your creativity. If you're studying with a class, your instructor may use them to supplement his own.

B. A section with the Answers to the Exercises.

C. A section with some User's Programs — examples of interesting and practical programs ready to type right in and use. (Some are for fun, some for business, some for education, etc.).

D. A section with Appendices which provide specialized information about Models I, II, III and 16.

E. An Index, for easy reference after you've learned it all, but forgotten where you learned it.

The computer assists you to learn. . .a sort of "Computer Aided Instruction".

Although it doesn't matter which of the 4 Models of TRS-80 you use, we had to pick one on which to center this book. For a number of reasons we chose the Model III. Fear not! The manuscript has been repeatedly tested on the other Models. This book doesn't know which Model you have.

We hope you have as much fun *Learning TRS-80 BASIC* as we did preparing it.

Contents

TRS-80 BASIC Tutorial

Part I

Getting Started

CHAPTER 0

A Glance at History

"Level II BASIC" is used on all four TRS-80 systems covered here (as well as several work-alike systems) but each "dialect" of BASIC is slightly different.

Historically, here's how we got to where we are:

The Model I was first introduced with LEVEL I BASIC, a so-called "tiny" BASIC, which did a fine job for its time and price. We will not address Level I BASIC here since it is completely covered in my original Radio Shack Manual published under these names:

USERS MANUAL For Level I
BASIC Computer Language
USERS MANUAL, Level I, For Model III

The Model I was then upgraded with the so-called "Level II" BASIC, very similar to our current "TRS-80 BASIC". Besides encompassing numerous additional standard BASIC features, it added provisions for using floppy disks.

The Model II TRS-80 followed with its BASIC, a somewhat diminished version of Level II BASIC. Until this book, there has been no comprehensive tutorial available for Model II users.

The Model III TRS-80 is a redesign and repackaging of the original Model I, and is available with either the original Level I BASIC or a somewhat improved version of Level II BASIC.

The Model 16 is a substantial upgrade of the Model II. As of this printing, a special BASIC has not been written specifically for the Model 16, so it uses the same version of BASIC as the Model II.

The four Models have far more in common than they have differences. TRS-80 BASIC today is essentially the same on Models I and III, and very similar on the Model II/16.

The physical differences between the systems and variations in features require us to insert special notes and comments throughout the book. We address BASIC here as it is implemented on the Model III, and include notes and remarks as necessary for Model I, II and 16 users. BASIC on all three machines is called "TRS-80 BASIC".

In order to help the maximum number of users, this book is written to simple non-disk systems. **If you are learning on a disk system, skip immediately to Appendix A for special instructions and meet the rest of us at Chapter 1 in a few minutes.**

Everyone else move straight ahead to Chapter 1.

Computer Etiquette

From the moment we turn it on, our TRS-80 follows a well-defined set of rules for coping with us, the "master". This makes it an easy computer to use. To a large extent, all we have to do is say the right thing (via the keyboard) at the right time. Of course, there are lots of "right things" to say; putting them together for a purpose is called *programming*.

> The rules are permanently stored in the computer in two programs, called the *monitor* and the *interpreter*.

In this chapter we'll start a conversation with our TRS-80 and teach it some simple social graces. At the same time, you'll learn the fundamentals of computer etiquette. You'll even write. . .wonder of wonders. . .your first TRS-80 computer program!

Getting "READY"

Hook up the computer as shown in its manual, and turn it ON. Allow the video tube a few seconds to warm up.

The word:

```
Cass?
```

will appear in the upper left-hand corner.

On Models I and II/16 Cass? does not appear.

Press ENTER and watch it say:

```
Memory Size?
```

Press ENTER again and after some propaganda we are finally:

```
READY
>
```

On Model I cursor doesn't flash; READY on Model II.

Press the ENTER key several times to produce a column of > signs. The computer is trying to tell us something:

"I'm ready — it's your turn to do something!"

ENTER is a *monitor* Command. It tells the computer to look at whatever is typed on the screen. We haven't typed in anything yet, so the computer just responds with another >.

To make sure you start off with a clean slate — erasing all traces of prior programs or tests — type NEW and press ENTER. The computer will respond by erasing the screen and printing:

```
READY
>
```

at the top of the screen.

Now type in PRINT MEM and ENTER. This is a very simple test to see that the computer "powered up" properly. The display should read:

```
READY
>PRINT MEM
 15314
READY
>
```

> If your TRS-80 has 4K of memory, the number should be about 3026. If it's a disk system the numbers may vary widely. Model II 64K will be 33608 and Model III 48K (disk system) will be 48082. It will always be some value less than the full 48K, 32K, 16K or 4K.

> If the number is not 15314 (or whatever is reasonable for your system), turn the computer OFF. Wait for about 10 seconds and turn it ON again. Repeat the test and verify that the number is in the ball park. If not, it's off to the repair center.

Don't use the shift key — letters are always *capital* unless we change them.

Just What Is a Computer Program?

A program is a sequence of instructions that the computer stores until we command it to follow (or "execute") it. Most programs for the TRS-80 are written in a language called BASIC, and its very name tells us how easy it is to learn!

Let's write a simple one-line program to let the TRS-80 introduce itself. Be sure the last line on the screen shows a > (which we call the "prompt"). The prompt is the computer's way of saying, "Go ahead — do something!"

Now type the following line, *exactly* as shown:

```
10 PRINT "HELLO THERE. I AM YOUR NEW TRS-80 MICROCOMPUTER!"
```

Do *not* hit the ENTER key yet!

We don't have to use the SHIFT key to get a capital letter. However, some of the keys *do* have two characters printed on them. Use the SHIFT key to get the upper characters — like the " marks and the exclamation point (!).

> Pressing SHIFT and 0 at the same time throws a "switch" inside the Model III and modified Model I so they can print both upper and lower case letters. Leave it alone for now as we have more important things to get tangled up with. Just wanted you to know now in case you hit it by accident!

If you made a typing error, don't worry — it's much easier to correct on the TRS-80 than on a regular typewriter. No rubber erasers or white paint to fuss with! Just use the backspace key ←. Each time you press this key, the rightmost character will be erased. If your error was at the beginning of the line, you'll have to erase your way back to that point and then retype the rest of the line. (If you hold the backspace key down longer than a second it will erase many letters very quickly. Not available on Model I.)

Model II use the **BACKSPACE** and **REPEAT** keys instead of back-arrow.

Now go back and examine *very carefully* what you have typed:

1. Did you enclose everything after the word PRINT in quotation marks?

2. Are there any extra quotation marks?

If everything's okay, press **ENTER** The >■ will reappear. The computer is telling us "Fine — what's next?"

If we press **ENTER** again, the screen will just say the same . . .>■.

As long as the bottom item on the screen is the >,. . . .you know it's "your turn".

See the flashing block (■) or the dash (−) that moves across the screen as you type in a letter? This is the "cursor". It tells us where the next character we type will appear on the screen. Pushing the space bar moves the cursor along one space without printing anything.

If It's Too Late

If you find an error after you've typed a line and pressed **ENTER** , the backspace key cannot correct it. Instead, retype the *entire* line correctly. As soon as you **ENTER** the line, it will replace the incorrect one. This is because they both share the same starting number (in this case, 1Ø), and the last one typed takes over. (In several chapters we'll learn how to "EDIT" out errors instead of retyping entire lines.)

"Allow Me To Introduce Myself"

Now we'll tell the computer to execute our program. The BASIC command for this is simple: RUN. So type:

```
RUN       ENTER
```

If you made no mistakes, the display will read:

```
HELLO!  I AM YOUR NEW TRS-8Ø MICROCOMPUTER!
```

If it doesn't work, try typing RUN again. If RUN still doesn't produce the greeting, there's something wrong in your program. Type NEW to clear it out and type in the one-line program again.

If it did work — let out a yell!

"HEY MA, IT WORKS!"

This is very important, because now that you have tasted success with a computer, it may be the last you are heard from in some time.

Note that the word PRINT was not displayed, nor were the quotation marks. They are part of the program's *instructions* and we didn't intend for them to be printed.

Type the word RUN again and hit `ENTER` .

Type RUN `ENTER` to your heart's content, watching the magic machine do as it's told, over and over. When you feel you've got the hang of all this, get up and stretch, walk around the room, look out the window — the whole act. You'll soon get hooked on computers and won't have time for such things.

Whether typing in a program, or giving direct commands like RUN, we have to hit `ENTER` to tell the computer to look at what we typed, and act accordingly.

Learned in Chapter 1

Commands	Statements	Miscellaneous
NEW	**PRINT**	> prompt
RUN	`ENTER`	▪ cursor
	`BREAK`	⇐ backspace
		" quotation marks

Commands are executed as soon as we type them in and press `ENTER`.

Statements are put into programs and are executed only after we type the RUN command.

We'll put a review list like this at the end of each chapter. Use it as a checkpoint to make sure you didn't miss anything.

Special message for people who can't resist the urge to play around with the computer and skip around in this book. (There always are a few!) It is possible to "lose control" of the computer so it won't give a READY message when you press ENTER. To regain control, just press BREAK, then ENTER. If that doesn't work, push the RESET button or switch. If that doesn't work, turn the computer OFF for 10 seconds, then turn it back ON again.

Disk users remove disks before turning computer OFF.

Expanded Program

We now have a program in the computer. (If you turned it off between chapters, fire it up agiain and type in line 1Ø from Chapter 1.) It's only a one liner, but let's expand it by adding a second line. In BASIC, every line in the program *must* have a number, and the program is executed in order from the smallest number to the largest. Type:

```
2Ø PRINT "YOU CALLED, MASTER. DO YOU HAVE A COMMAND?"
```

Check it carefully — especially the quote marks, then type: *Enter*

```
RUN   ENTER
```

If all was correct, the screen will read:

```
HELLO . I AM YOUR NEW TRS-8Ø MICROCOMPUTER!
YOU CALLED, MASTER. DO YOU HAVE A COMMAND?
```

If it ran OK, answer the question by typing:

```
YES   ENTER
```

Oh — sorry about that! It "bombed", didn't it? The screen said:

```
?SN Error  (or ?SN ERROR or SYNTAX ERROR or Syntax Error)
```

We deliberately "set you up" to demonstrate the computer's ERROR troubleshooter. The computer is smart enough to know when we've made a mistake in telling it what to do, and it prints a clue as to the nature of the error. In this case, the ? tells us that it doesn't understand what we are saying. SN stands for the word "syntax" (an obscure word that refers to the pattern of words in a language). ERROR means we have made one. The computer is expecting a new program line or a BASIC command. Later we'll learn how to make the computer accept a "YES" or "NO" and respond accordingly.

Model II has 66 ERROR codes.

There are dozens of possible errors we can make, and in good time we will learn the built-in "ERROR codes". Meanwhile, there is just one other important ERROR situation which we should be able to recognize to pry ourselves out of accidental trouble. Let's retype line 2∅ and deliberately make a spelling error:

```
2∅ PRIMT "YOU CALLED, MASTER. DO YOU HAVE A COMMAND?"
```

and RUN.

Again we get an ERROR message:

```
?SN Error in 2∅
```
(or its equivalent),

but after READY instead of a prompt we get:

```
2∅ ▪
```

This tells us that the error is in line 2∅. By pressing the ENTER key, line 2∅ will be printed in full so we can look for the error. (Shhh! If you know what else it will let us do don't say anything yet. We don't want to confuse anyone with too much too soon.)

Retype line 2Ø to correct the misspelling in PRIMT before continuing on.

Have you noticed that we use Ø for the number zero — so we can distinguish between the letter O and number 0? The Video Display does it this way — and it's standard throughout computerdom.

And the Program Grows

It is customary, traditional, and all that to space the lines in a program 1Ø numbers apart. Note that our two-line program has the numbers 1Ø and 2Ø. The reason. . .it's much easier to modify a program if we leave room to insert new lines in between the old ones. There is no benefit to numbering the lines more closely (like 1,2,3,4). **Don't do it.**

Look at the Video Display. Let's decide we'd rather not have the two lines so close together, but would like to have space between them. Type in the new line:

```
15 PRINT
```

Then:

```
RUN  ENTER
```

It should now read:

```
HELLO. I AM YOUR NEW TRS-8Ø MICROCOMPUTER!

YOU CALLED, MASTER.   DO YOU HAVE A COMMAND?
```

Looks neater, doesn't it? But what about line 15??? It says PRINT. PRINT what???? Well — print *nothing*. That's what followed PRINT, and that's just what it printed. But in the process of printing nothing it automatically inserted a space between the printing ordered in lines 1Ø and 2Ø. So *that's* how we insert a space.

Didn't that room between lines 1Ø and 2Ø come in handy?

Another important statement is REM, which stands for REMark. It is often convenient to insert REMarks into a program. Why? So you or someone else can refer to them later, to help you remember complicated programming details, or even what the program's for and how to use it. It's like having a scratch-pad or notebook built into our program. When we tell the computer to execute the program by typing RUN and [ENTER], it will skip over any numbered line which begins with the statement REM. A REM statement has no effect on the program. Insert the following:

```
5 REM *THIS IS MY FIRST COMPUTER PROGRAM*    [ENTER]
```

then:

```
RUN
```

The run should read just like the last run, totally unaffected by the presence of line 5. Did it?

> You might be wondering why the asterisks(*) in line number 5? The answer is . . . they're just for decoration. Let's give this operation some class! Remember, anything that is typed on a line following REM is ignored by the computer.

Well, this programming business is getting complicated and I've already forgotten what is in our "big" program. How can we get a listing of what our program now contains? Easy. A new BASIC command. Type:

```
LIST
```

The screen should read:

```
5 REM *THIS IS MY FIRST COMPUTER PROGRAM*
10 PRINT "HELLO. I AM YOUR NEW TRS-80 MICROCOMPUTER!"
15 PRINT
20 PRINT "YOU CALLED, MASTER. DO YOU HAVE A COMMAND?"
```

You can call for a LIST any time the prompt appears on the screen.

Where Is the END of the Program?

The end of a program is, quite naturally, the last statement we want the computer to execute. Many computers require us to place an END statement after this point, so the computer will know it's finished. But with our TRS-

80, an END statement is optional — we can put it in or leave it out. Remember, though, if we want to run our BASIC programs on fussier computers, we'll probably need the END statement.

When we get into more complex programs, you'll want to use END statements to *force* the computer to stop at specified points. So actually, END comes in very handy even with the TRS-80.

Let's take a close look at END. By the rules governing its use, most dialects of BASIC which require END insist that it be the last statement in a program, telling the computer "That's all, folks." By tradition, it is given the number 99, or 999, or 9999 (or larger), depending on the largest number the specific computer will accept. Our TRS-80 accepts line numbers up to 65529.

Let's add an END statement to our program. Type in:

```
99 END      ENTER
```

then:

```
RUN    ENTER
```

The sample run should read:

```
HELLO.   I AM YOUR NEW TRS-80 MICROCOMPUTER!
YOU CALLED, MASTER. DO YOU HAVE A COMMAND?"
```

"Why didn't the word END print?" Answer: Because nothing is printed unless it is the "object" of a PRINT statement. So how could we get the computer to print THE END at the end of the program execution? Think for a minute before reading on.

```
98 PRINT "THE END"
```

We're assuming that line 98 is the last PRINT statement in your program.

Erasing Without Replacing

Just for fun, let's move the END statement from line 99 to the largest usable line number, 65529. This requires two steps.

The first is to erase line 99. Note that we're not just making a change or correcting an error in line 99 — we want to completely eliminate it from the program. Easier done than said:

Type:

99

Then [ENTER]

The line is erased. How can we be sure? Think about this now. Got it? Sure, "pull" a LIST of the entire program by typing:

LIST   [ENTER]

The screen should show the program with lines 5, 1∅, 15, 2∅, and 98. 99 should be gone. Any entire line can be erased the same way.

The second step is just as easy. Type:

65529 END   [ENTER]

. . .and the new line is entered. Pull a listing of the program to see if it was. Was it? Now RUN the program to see if moving the END statement changed anything. Did it? It shouldn't have.

Other Uses For END

Move END from number 65529 to line number 17, then RUN.

What happened? It ENDed the RUN after printing line 1∅ and a space. RUN it several times.

Now move END to line 13 and RUN. Then to line 8 and RUN. Do you see the effect END has, depending where it is placed (even temporarily) in a program? Feel like you are really gaining control over the machine? You ain't seen nothing yet!

Learned in Chapter 2

Commands	Statements	Miscellaneous
LIST	PRINT (space)	Error messages
	REM	line numbering
	END	

The EDITor — First Semester

An extraordinarily valuable capability of our BASIC is a feature called the
EDITor. Its purpose is as simple as its name. It lets us "EDIT", or make
changes, in a program. The TRS-80 uses a so-called "line EDITor" since it
EDITs letters and numbers in only one line at a time. It is so easy to use but
so powerful you'll never again want to use a computer without one.

Clear out the current program with NEW. Then type in this line (errors and
all):

```
10 PRINT "THIS HEAR ARE SHORE A FLOXY CONFUSER."
```

    . . .and RUN.

It should RUN just fine, and if that's the way you usually talk you're
probably wondering what all the fuss is about. If, on the other hand, you
wish to change the sentence to something like:

```
THIS IS SURE A FOXY COMPUTER.
```

then we need to do some EDITing in line 10.

In the first two chapters we would just retype the entire line, hoping we didn't make more mistakes than we eliminated. This particular example has so much to change it might be just as easy to retype it, but our purpose is to "exercise" the EDITor, so type:

EDIT 10   ENTER

and see what happens.

Hokay. . .we get

10 ∎

a good (but not perfect) sign it's in the EDITor mode.

To get out of this situation we could just hit ENTER. Being in EDITor isn't like being in BASIC. We only use ENTER when we are *done* EDITing and want to *return* to BASIC. The EDITor is *not* part of BASIC. It's a special feature we call up from BASIC using the word EDIT.

Hit the L Key.

The screen now shows:

```
10 PRINT "THIS HEAR ARE SHORE A FLOXY CONFUSER."
10 ∎
```

By typing L we LISTed the line being EDITed. Then the cursor returned back where we started — still in EDITor.

Since we want line 10 to read **THIS IS SURE A FOXY COMPUTER**, let's first get rid of the word HEAR. Tap the space bar slowly and watch it print one new character each time. When you get to

```
10 PRINT "THIS
```

press the letter D (which stands for Delete) five times. It will add to the screen:

```
! !!H!!E!!A!!R!
```

\   \\H\\E\\A\\R\ on the Model II

Between each pair of exclamation marks is the letter or space which was deleted. Press L again and let's list the line to see what it looks like now. But pressing L once just LISTs the rest of the line. Pressing it a second time lists the entire line as it now exists after EDITing. Shore enuf, the word "HEAR" and the space which preceded it are gone.

By the way, here are two additional ways to space forward and backward while still in the EDIT mode.

1. To space forward five spaces (or any other number), you can type five and then press the space bar.

2. To backspace five spaces (or any other number), you can type 5 ⬅

5 `BACKSPACE` on Model II.

Let's now change the word ARE to IS, and learn another EDITing trick in the process. The EDIT letter S stands for Search. Instead of using the space bar and tapping over to the A in ARE, let's let the computer Search for the letter A. As we look at line 1Ø from left to right, we see that the A in ARE is the first A in the line, so type:

SA   (meaning, search for the first A),

and

1Ø PRINT "THIS■

is displayed.

Now we just learned that we can get rid of ARE by typing D (for Delete) three times in a row, but it's quicker and easier to just type:

4D   (do it), meaning "Delete the next four characters" (ARE and the space following it).

The line now reads:

```
10 PRINT "THIS  !ARE !
```

\ARE\ on Model II.

Let's type a couple of L's to see what we have now:

```
10 PRINT "THIS SHORE A FLOXY CONFUSER."
```

We know we have to insert the word IS between THIS and SHORE. Worded another way, we have to insert a new word between the first two "S's". Any ideas? How about searching for the 2nd S? We won't print it — just search for it.

Type:

```
2SS (search for the 2nd S)
```

and the screen reads:

```
10 PRINT "THIS
```

Now we can use the Insert feature. Very carefully, and *only once* (since nothing will show on the screen), type I.

You have activated Insert. Type the letters:

```
IS
```

and press the space bar once.

The screen now reads:

```
10 PRINT "THIS IS
```

We've inserted the IS and a space following it, but must now *leave* the Insert mode. We can always completely bail out of the EDITor at any time by hitting ENTER, but since we have a lot more work to do on this line, we instead press SHIFT and the ⬆ key at the same time. As with pressing I, nothing shows on the screen. Now press L to see what we've got left.

Model II, use the `ESC` key instead of `SHIFT` `↑` .

```
1Ø PRINT "THIS IS SHORE A FLOXY CONFUSER."
1Ø ▪
```

If it seems like we're going slowly, you're right! The EDITor is so important but so simple we may as well learn it right the first time. You know the old story, "there's never time to do it right the first time, but always time to do it over."

Forging onward. . .let's use the next feature called C (for Change, or ex-change). We can change the word SHORE to SURE if we delete the H and change the O to a U.

So, let's type:

2SH (to SEARCH for the 2nd H).

```
1Ø PRINT "THIS IS S▪
```

and D to Delete it.

This permits us to change the next letter to some other letter or character. Type:

UC

Very carefully, type a single U. (It will not show on the screen.)

and then

L twice to get a fresh new line to see what's left.

```
1Ø PRINT "THIS IS SURE A FLOXY CONFUSER."
1Ø ▪
```

Think for a moment. How can we change FLOXY to FOXY?

How about:

    SL   to Search for the first L, then

    D   to Delete it, then

    L   twice to see what the line now looks like.

```
1Ø PRINT "THIS IS SURE A FOXY CONFUSER."


1Ø ▮
```

Only one more word to change. Should we go into the word CONFUSER and delete the N and F and insert M and P? Would it be easier to just change those letters instead? What about the S? Think about it.

Of course! It takes fewer steps to change than to delete and then insert, so we always change when possible. Perform this sequence:

    2SN   Search for the second N (the first one is in PRINT)

    2C   prepare to Change the next two letters

    MP   the two new letters

    SS   Search for the next S

    C   prepare to Change one letter

    T   the new letter

    L   finish Listing the line so we can look at it.

Whew! Finally done. But wait — we're still in the EDITor. Press `ENTER`, see the prompt, and know that we're back in BASIC. RUN it to be sure.

Despite our taking each EDITing task one step at a time, it is possible to make all these EDITing changes in only one pass through the line. The purpose of an EDITor *is to save time.*

Since you're now the "ace of the base" when it comes to flying this EDITor, let's type:

```
NEW
```

and type in old line 1Ø again, then EDIT it in one pass.

```
1Ø PRINT "THIS HEAR ARE SHORE A FLOXY CONFUSER."
```

Follow with me now, step by step. If you blow it, start all over by retyping line 1Ø.

>EDIT 1Ø `ENTER`

L   to LIST it

2SH   Search for 2nd H

8D   Delete next 8 characters

I   prepare for Insert

IS   the new letters

`SHIFT` ⬆ terminate Insert

> `ESC` on Model II.

SH   Search for next H

D   Delete the H

C   Change next character

U   the new character

SL   Search for the next L

D   Delete it

SN   Search for the next N

2C   Change next 2 characters

MP   the new characters

SS   Search for the next S

C   Change next character

T   the new character

LL   to LIST the EDITed program for inspection

ENTER to leave the EDITor mode.

Pretty slick, huh? With some practice it will take you less than 30 seconds. From here on, you should always use the EDITor for changes, especially in long lines. Compare the time it would take to change only one letter or number in a very long line by retyping that line, with the speed of doing it with the EDITor.

EXERCISE 3-1: Use the EDITor to change:

```
10 PAINT "WE CAN TAKE CREDIT FOR CONSUMER PROGRESS."
```

to:

```
10 PRINT "WE CAN EDIT COMPUTER PROGRAMS."
```

You'll find sample answers in Section B, along with further comments.

Learned in Chapter 3

Commands	Statements
EDIT	EDITing Features

AUTOmatic Line Numbering

They laughed when I sat down at the computer to play!

As the artist approaches a blank canvas with only a gleam in his eye, so you approach your empty computer and type:

`AUTO` `ENTER`

Type NEW if your computer isn't empty.

The screen returns:

`10` ∎

Are we in EDITor? It looks like it! But we're not. We are in an AUTOmatic line numbering mode. Type:

`PRINT"WHAT IS GOING ON HERE?"` `ENTER`

and

`20` ∎

pops up on the screen.

Type:

```
PRINT"THIS IS RIDICULOUS."  ENTER
```

and

```
30
```

appears.

Well, it's obvious at this point that we're being fed the new line numbers as fast as we need them. Hit the ENTER key a few more times and watch them jump. Okay. . .how do we get *out* of AUTO? Hit the BREAK key.

The Model II shows a ?UL ERROR when you hit enter. But, no harm done.

Type LIST and see that only those line numbers you actually used (1∅ and 2∅) contain anything.

Type NEW, then:

```
AUTO 1000,200
```

Hit the ENTER key a half dozen times or so and the pattern becomes immediately clear. The "1∅∅∅" established the beginning line number, and the "2∅∅" determined the spacing between lines.

Hit BREAK and type NEW again, then

```
AUTO 1000
```

and ENTER a few times.

BREAK out of AUTO and start again with:

```
AUTO 3000,1
```

and a few ENTERs. Very handy with very big numbers.

Press `BREAK`.

How about:

```
AUTO 17,4
```

You get the idea. It is even possible to use AUTO as a statement in a program, though I can't think of any reasonable excuse for putting it there. Can you?

Unless you specify otherwise, AUTO will always begin on line 1Ø and always space the lines 1Ø numbers apart.

One important caution. Whenever you get fooling with something that's automatic, a degree of personal control is lost. Enter this quickie:

```
1Ø PRINT"NOW WHAT ARE YOU UP TO?"
2Ø PRINT"BEATS ME!"
99 END
```

Then type:

```
AUTO  ENTER
```

. . .oh, oh! What does the 1Ø* mean?

The asterisk means that there is already a line number 1Ø, and if we hit `ENTER` it will erase the existing line 1Ø. That's fine if it's what we want. Otherwise, we *must* `BREAK` in order to escape.

The AUTO command is not just for the lazy, it can be a real time saver (and save mental energy as well). For the touch typist who doesn't have to look at the screen when typing fast, it's a real delight.

`AUTO.` starts the automatic line numbering with the current line number, similar to the EDIT. feature.

Learned in Chapter 4

Commands	**Miscellaneous**
AUTO	Automatic line numbering
AUTO.	

Part II

Speak To Me,
Oh Great Computer

"WELL I DON'T KNOW ABOUT THE COMPUTER,
BUT HAVING ONE IN THE HOUSE SURE
HAS MADE THE KIDS MULTIPLY!"

Math Operators

"But Can It Do Math?"

Yes, it can. Basic arithmetic is a snap for the TRS-80. So are highly complex math calculations — when we write special programs to perform them. We'll learn how in this book.

BASIC uses the four fundamental arithmetic operations, plus a fifth which is just a modification of two of the others.

1. ADDITION, using the symbol +.

2. SUBTRACTION, using the symbol − (See, nothing to this. Just like grade school. I wonder whatever happened to old Miss. . .well, ahem . . .anyway).

3. MULTIPLICATION, using the special symbol * (Oh drat, I knew this was too easy to be true!).

4. DIVISION, using the symbol / (Well, at least it's simpler than the old ÷ symbol).

5. NEGATION (meaning "multiply times minus one"), using the − symbol.

Of course, we also need that old favorite, the equals sign (=). But wait — the BASIC language is particular about how we use this sign! Math expressions (like 1 + 2* 5) can only go on the *right-hand side* of the equals sign; the left-hand side is reserved for the "variable name". This is the name we give to the result of the math expression. (This all may seem a little strange, but it's really very simple, as we'll discover in the next few pages.)

Now that wasn't too bad, was it?

Be careful. We *cannot* use an "X" for multiplication. Unfortunately, a long time ago a mathematician decided to use "X", which is a letter, to mean multiply. We use letters for other things, so it's much less confusing to use a "*" to specify multiplication. Confusion is one thing a computer can't tolerate.

So, to computers, "*" is the only symbol which means multiply. After using it a while, you too, may feel we should do away with X as a multiplication symbol.

Putting all this together in a program is not difficult, so let's do it. First, we have to erase the "resident program" from the computer's memory.

"Resident program" is computer talk for "what's already in there".

Type the command:

```
NEW    ENTER
```

Then type:

```
LIST    ENTER
```

to check that there's nothing left in memory. The computer should come back with a simple:

```
READY
>
```

Model II: Ready.

Putting The Beast To Work

We will now let the computer do some very simple problem solving. That means using equations (oh − panic). But then, an equation is just a little statement that says what's on one side of an equals sign amounts to the same as what's on the other side.

That can't get too bad (it says here).

We're going to use that old standby equation,

> "Distance traveled equals Rate of travel times Time spent traveling."

If it's been a few years, you might want to sit on the end of a log and con-template that again.

To shorten the equation, let's choose letters (called variables) to stand for the three quantities. Then we can rewrite the equation as a BASIC statement ac-ceptable to the TRS-80. Type in:

```
4Ø    D = R * T
```

Remember, we have to use the * for multiplication.

What's that number 4Ø doing in the equation? That's a program line number. Remember, every line in a BASIC program has to have one. We chose 4Ø, but another number would have done just as well.

The extra spaces in the line are there just to make the equation easier for us to read; the TRS-80 ignores them. Later, when we write very long programs, we may want to eliminate extra spaces, because they take up memory space. For now, they may be helpful, so leave them in.

Here's what line 4Ø means to the computer: "Take the values of R and T, multi-ply them together, and assign the resulting value to the variable D. So until further notice, D is equal to the result of R times T.

We can use any of the 26 letters from A through Z to identify the values we know as well as those we want to figure out. Whenever we can, it's a good idea to choose letters that remind us of the things they stand for − like the D, R, and T in the Distance, Rate, Time equation.

We *could not* reverse the equation and write: R*T=D. This has no meaning for the computer. Remember, the left-hand side of the equation is reserved for the *result* of a mathematical computation. The right-hand side is where the ingredients of the computation are placed — numbers, operators, and known variables.

To further complicate this very simple example, we'll point out now that there's an optional way to write the equation, using the BASIC statement LET:

```
4Ø   LET D = R * T
```

This use of LET reminds us that making D equal R times T was *our* choice, rather than an eternal truth like 1 + 1 = 2. Some computers are fussy, and always require the use of LET with equations. Our TRS-80 says, "Have it your way".

Ask your accountant, "How much is 1 + 1?". If he says, "How much would you like it to equal?" he's a good choice.

Okay. . .let's complete the program.

Assume:

Distance (in miles) = Rate (in miles per hour) multiplied by Time (in hours). How far is it from San Diego to London if a jet plane traveling at an average speed of 500 miles per hour makes the trip in 12 hours?

(Yes, I know you can do that one in your head but that's not the point!)

Type in the following:

```
1Ø REM * DISTANCE, RATE, TIME PROBLEM *   ENTER
2Ø R = 5ØØ  ENTER
3Ø T = 12   ENTER
4Ø D = R * T   ENTER
```

Remember AUTO?

Check the program carefully, then:

RUN ENTER

Hum de dum. . .ho-hum. . .(this sure is a slow computer).

READY

All it says is READY. *The computer doesn't work!*

Yes it does. *It worked just fine.* The computer multiplied 500 times 12 just like we told it, and came up with the answer of 6000 miles. But we forgot to tell it to give *us* the answer. Sorry about that.

> *EXERCISE 5-1:* Can you finish this program without help? It only takes one more line. Give it a good try before reading on for the answer. That way, the answer will mean more to you.
>
> (Hint: We've already used PRINT to PRINT messages in quotes. What would happen if we said 5Ø PRINT "D"? No, we want the *value* of D, not "D" itself. Hmmmm, what happens when we get rid of the quotes?)

Don't read beyond this point until you've worked on the above exercise!

Well, the answer of 6000 is correct, but its "presentation" is no more inspiring than the printout from a hand calculator. This inevitably leads us back to where we first started this foray into the unknown — the PRINT statement.

Note that we said 5Ø PRINT D. There were no quotes around the letter D like we had used before. The reason is simple but fairly profound. If we want the computer to PRINT the *exact words* we specify, we enclose them in quotes. If we want it to PRINT the *value* of a variable, in this case D, we leave the quotes off. That simple message is worth serious thought before continuing on.

Did you think seriously about it? Then on we go!

Now suppose we want to include both the *value* of something *and* some *exact words* on the same line. Pay attention, as you will be doing more and more program designing yourself, and PRINT statements give beginners more trouble than any other single part of computer programming. Type in the following:

```
5Ø PRINT "THE DISTANCE (IN MILES) IS", D  ENTER
```

Then:

(REMEMBER: Typing in a statement with a line number that already is in use erases the original line — and that's what we want to do here.)

The Display should show:

```
RUN  ENTER
```

How about that! The message enclosed in quotes is PRINTed exactly as we specified, and the letter gave us the value of D. The comma told the computer that we wanted it to PRINT two separate items on the *same* line. We can PRINT up to four items on the same line by simply inserting commas between them.

Model II — five items per line.

With this in mind, see if you can change line 5Ø so the computer finishes the program with the following message:

```
THE DISTANCE (IN MILES) IS              6ØØØ
```

ANSWER: Break up the quoted message into two parts, and put the variable in between them on the same PRINT line. (Use the EDITor.)

```
THE DISTANCE IS     6ØØØ              MILES.
```

How about all that extra space on both sides of the 6ØØØ in the PRINTout? The reason for it is that the computer divides up the screen width into four zones of 16 characters each.

Model II has five zones of 16 characters each.

```
5Ø PRINT "THE DISTANCE IS",D,"MILES."
```

When a **PRINT** statement contains two or more items separated by commas, the computer automatically **PRINTs** them in different **PRINT** zones. Automatic zoning is a very convenient method of outputting tabular information, and we'll explore the subject later.

It's possible to eliminate all that extra space in the output from our Distance, Rate, Time program. EDIT the last version of line 5Ø, substituting semicolons (;) for commas throughout the line.

(Careful — don't replace the period with a semicolon.)

RUN `ENTER`

The Display should read:

`THE DISTANCE IS 6000 MILES.`

Look carefully at line 5Ø. There is no unused space between the S in IS, the D, and the M in *miles*. But in the display, there *is* a space between IS and 6000, and another space between 6000 and MILES. How come?

REASON: When a number is PRINTed from a numeric variable (like D), spaces are reserved in front of and behind the number. As we do more programming, this point will become increasingly important and we will discuss it in more detail.

WHEW!

Well, we have already covered more than enough Commands, Statements and Math Operators to solve myriads of simple problems.

Math Operators? They're the =,+,−, *, and / symbols we mentioned earlier.

Now let's spend some time actually writing programs to solve problems. There is no better way to learn than by doing, and *everything* covered so far is fundamental to our success in later chapters. So don't jump over these exercises — it's the best way to get into the thick of programming.

EXERCISE 5-2: Write a program which will find the time required to travel by jet plane from London to San Diego, if the distance is 6000 miles and the plane travels at 500 MPH.

```
10 REM * Time Solution Knowing Distance and Rate *
20 D = 6000
30 R = 500
40 T = D/R
50 Print "The time Required is"; T; "Hours."
```

EXERCISE 5-3: If the circumference of a circle is found by multiplying its diameter times π (3.14), write a program which will find the circumference of a circle with a diameter of 35 feet.

```
10 Rem * Circumference Solution *
20 P = 3.14
30 D = 35
40 C = P * D
50 Print "The circles circumferce is"; C; "Feet."
```

EXERCISE 5-4: If the area of a circle is found by multiplying π times the square of its radius, write a program to find the area of a circle with a radius of 5 inches.

```
10 Rem * Circular area Solution *
20 P = 3.14
30 R = 5
40 A = P * R * R
50 Print "The circle's area is"; A; "square inches"
```

EXERCISE 5-5: Your checkbook balance was $225. You've written three checks (for $17, $35 and $225) and made two deposits ($40 and $200). Write a program to adjust your old balance based on checks written and deposits made, and PRINT out your new balance.

```
10  B= 225
20  C = 17 + 35 + 225
30  D= 40 + 200
40  N = B - C + D
50  Print "Your new balance is" ; N ;
```

Learned in Chapter 5

Statements	Math Operators	Miscellaneous
LET (OPTIONAL)		A - Z variables
	=	
	+	
	−	
	*	
	/	

Remember, we can use any of the 26 letters as variables, not just D, R, and T (they were just convenient for our problem).

Scientific Notation

Are There More Stars Or Grains Of Sand?

In this mathematical world we are blessed with very large and very small numbers. Millions of these and billionths of those. To cope with all this, our computer uses "Exponential Notation", or "Standard Scientific Notation" when the number sizes start to get out of hand. The number 5 million-(5,000,000), for example, can be written "5E+06". This means, "the number 5 followed by six zeros."

Or technically, $5*10^6$, which is 5 times 10 to the sixth power: $5*10*10*10*10*10*10$.

If an answer comes out "5E-06", that means we must shift the decimal point, which is after the 5, six places to the *left*, inserting zeros as necessary. Technically, it means $5 \times 10(^{-6})$ *or 5 millionths, (.000,005).*

In our BASIC, that's 5/10/10/10/10/10/10.

It's really pretty simple once you get the hang of it, and a lot easier to keep track of numbers without losing the decimal point. Since the computer insists on using it with very large and very small numbers, we can just as well get in the good habit, too.

Type NEW before solving the following exercises:

EXERCISE 6-1: If one million cars each drove ten thousand miles in a certain year, how many miles did they drive altogether that year? Write and run a simple program which will give the answer.

Didn't forget the **ENTER** did you? Up till now we've been reminding you that you have to enter each line or command — but from now on, we'll assume you've got that little routine matter down pat.

```
10  Rem * Car Miles solution *
20  C = 1,000,000
30  D = 10,000
40  N = C * D
50  Print "The number of miles driven is"; N.
```

EXERCISE 6-2: Change lines 2Ø and 3Ø in the Car Miles Solution program (from Exercise 6-1) to express the numbers written there in exponential notation, or SSN (Standard Scientific Notation). Then RUN it.

Learned in Chapter 6

Miscellaneous

E — notation

(E stands for "exponent" and in our case it refers to the exponent of 10, i.e. the number of zeros to the right or left of the main number.)

( ) And The Order Of Operations

Parentheses play an important role in computer programming, just as they do in ordinary math. The computer uses them in the same general way, but there are important exceptions.

1. In BASIC, parentheses can enclose operations to be performed.

   Those operations which are within parentheses are performed before those *not* in parentheses.

2. Operations buried deepest within parentheses (that is, parentheses inside parentheses) are performed first.

If you want to be sure your formulas are calculated correctly, use ( ) around the operations you want performed first.

---

3. When there is a "tie" as to which operation the computer should perform first after it has removed all parentheses, it works its way along the program line from left to right performing the *Multiplication* and *Division*. It then starts at the left again and performs the *Addition* and *Subtraction*.

Recall the old memory aid, "My Dear Aunt Sally"? In math we are supposed to do Multiplication and Division first (from left to right), then come back for Addition and Subtraction (left to right). Our TRS-80 follows the same sequence.

Note: INT, RND and ABS functions are performed before multiplication and division. (We haven't talked about these yet, but just to be complete . . .)

   4. An operation written as (X)(Y) will *not* tell the computer to multiply. X*Y is the correct designation for multiplication.

Example: To convert temperature expressed in degrees Fahrenheit to Celsius (Centigrade), the following relationship is used:

   The Fahrenheit temperature equals 32 degrees plus nine-fifths of the Celsius temperature.

Or, maybe you're more used to the simple formula :

   $F° = 9/5 \ X \ C° + 32$

Assume we have a Celsius temperature of 25°. Type in this NEW program:

```
1Ø REM * CELSIUS TO FAHRENHEIT CONVERSION *
2Ø C = 25
3Ø F = (9/5)*C + 32
4Ø PRINT C; "DEGREES CELSIUS =";F;"DEGREES FAHRENHEIT."
```

   . . .and RUN.

SAMPLE RUN:

```
25 DEGREES CELSIUS = 77 DEGREES FAHRENHEIT.
```

Notice first that line 4Ø consists of a **PRINT** statement followed by four separate expressions — two variables and two groups of words in quotes called "literals" or "strings".

Remember what the semicolons are for?

Next, note how the parentheses are placed in line 3Ø. With the 9/5 secure inside, we can multiply its quotient times C, then add 32.

Now, remove the parentheses in line 3Ø and RUN again. The answer comes out the same.

Why?

1. On the first pass, the computer started by solving all problems within parentheses, in this case just one (9/5). It came up with (but did not PRINT) 1.8. It then multiplied the 1.8 times the value of C and added 32.

2. On our next try, without the parentheses, the computer simply moved from left to right performing first the division problem (9 divided by 5), then the multiplication problem (1.8 times C), then the addition problem (adding 32). The parentheses really made no difference in our first example because of the rules of Order Of Operation.

Next, change +32 to 32+ and move it to the front of the equation in line 3Ø, like this:

```
3Ø F = 32 + 9 / 5 * C
```

Run it again, without parentheses.

Did it make a difference in the answer? Why not?

ANSWER: Execution proceeds from left to right, multiplication and division first, then returns and performs addition and subtraction. This is why the 32 was *not* added to the 9 before being divided by 5. **Very Important!** If they had been added, we would of course have gotten the wrong answer.

EXERCISE 7-1: Write and RUN a program which converts 65 degrees Fahrenheit to Celsius. The rule tells us that:

"Celsius temperature is equal to five-ninths times what's left after 32 is subtracted from the Fahrenheit temperature."

$$C° = (F° - 32) * \frac{5}{9}$$

```
10 REM * Fahrenheit to Celsius Conversion *
20 F = 65
30 C = (F - 32) * (5/9)
40 Print F; "Degrees Farhenheit = ";C; "degrees Celsius
Run
```

EXERCISE 7-2:   Remove the first set of parentheses in the number 7-1 answer and RUN again.

EXERCISE 7-3:   Replace the first set of parentheses in program line 3Ø and remove the second pair of parentheses, then RUN. Note how the answer comes out — correctly!

EXERCISE 7-4:   Insert brackets in the following equation to make it follow the Order Of Operations and find the correct answer.   Write a program to check it out.

30 - 9 - 8 - 7 - 6 = 28

Learned in Chapter 7

Miscellaneous
( )
Order Of Operations

Relational Operators

If you liked the preceding chapters, *then* you're going to love the rest of this book!

Because we're really just getting into the good stuff. Like IF-THEN and GOTO statements that let your computer make decisions and take. . er, executive action. But first, a few more operators.

Relational Operators allow the computer to compare one value with another. There are only three:

1. Equals, using the symbol = (How'd you guess?)

2. Is greater than, using the symbol >

3. Is less than, using the symbol <

Example: A<B means A is less than B. To help distinguish between < and >, just remember that the *smaller* (pointed) part of the < symbol points to the *smaller* of the two quantities being compared.

Combining these three, we come up with three more operators.

4. Is not equal to, using the symbol <>

5. Is less than or equal to, using the symbol <=

6. Is greater than or equal to, using the symbol >=

By adding these six *relational* operators to the *math* operators we already know, plus two new *statements* called IF-THEN and GOTO, we create a powerful system of comparing and calculating that becomes the central core of everything else that follows.

The IF-THEN statement, combined with the six relational operators above, gives us the *action* part of a system of logic. Enter and RUN this NEW program:

```
10 A = 5
20 IF A = 5 THEN 50
30 PRINT " A DOES NOT EQUAL 5. "
40 END
50 PRINT " A EQUALS 5. "
```

The screen should display:

```
A EQUALS 5.
```

Now let's examine the program line by line.

Line 10 establishes the fact that A has a value of 5.

Line 20 is an IF-THEN statement which directs the computer to go to line 50 if the value of A is exactly 5 (skipping over whatever might be in between lines 20 and 50). Since A *does* equal 5, the computer jumps to line 50 and does as it says, printing:

```
A EQUALS 5.
```

Lines 30 and 40 are not used at all in this case.

Now, change line 1Ø to read:

```
1Ø A = 6
```

. . .and RUN.

The run should say:

```
A DOES NOT EQUAL 5.
```

Taking it a line at a time:

Line 1Ø establishes the value of A to be 6.

Line 2Ø tests the value of A. If A equals 5, THEN the computer is directed to GOTO line 5Ø. But "the test fails", that is, A does *not* equal 5, so the computer proceeds as usual to the next line, line 3Ø.

Line 3Ø directs the computer to PRINT the fact that A *does not equal* 5. It does not tell us what the *value* of A is, only that it does *not* equal 5. The computer proceeds to the next line.

Line 4Ø ENDs the program's execution. Without this statement separating lines 3Ø and 5Ø, the computer would charge right on to line 5Ø and PRINT *its* contents, which obviously are in conflict with the contents of line 3Ø. This is an example of using an IF-THEN statement with only the most fundamental relational operator, the equals sign.

Optional THEN

Not optional on Model II.

Both THEN and GOTO are optional in expressions which do not require GOing to a line number if the test passes. This can be useful in long PRINT lines, where PRINTing is the result if the test passes.

```
1Ø INPUT "X = ";X            (works)
2Ø IF X = Ø PRINT "X = Ø"
```

but

```
20 IF X = 0 100          (does not work)
99 END
100 PRINT "100 HERE"
```

Line 20 must read either:

```
20 IF X = 0 THEN 100
```

or

```
20 IF X = 0 GOTO 100
```

A comma can replace THEN as in 20 IF X = 0, 100 but it is highly *not* recommended. We've got enough problems without adding that kind of non-standard notation.

EXERCISE 8-1: Rewrite the resident program using a "does not equal" sign in line 20 instead of the equals sign. Remember we must change other lines to achieve the same results as the above Example.

EXERCISE 8-2: Change line 10 to give A the value of 6. Leave the other four lines from Exercise 8-1 as shown. Add more program lines as necessary so the program will tell us whether A is larger or smaller than 5 and RUN.

EXERCISE 8-3: Change the value of A in line 1Ø at least three more times, RUNning after each change to ensure that your new program works correctly.

No sample answers are given since you are choosing your own values of A. It will be obvious whether or not you are getting the right answer.

The IF-THEN statement is what is known as a *conditional branching* statement. The program will "branch" to another part of the program *on the condition* that it passes the IF-THEN test. If it fails the test, the program execution simply continues to the next line.

A statement called GOTO is known as an *unconditional branching* statement. If we were to replace lines 4Ø and 8Ø with GOTO 99, and add line 99:

```
99 END
```

. . .then whenever the computer hit line 4Ø or 8Ø it would *unconditionally* follow orders and go to 99, ENDing the RUN. While our TRS-80 is rather broad-minded when it comes to accepting various other BASIC dialects, many computers are not. For practice, change lines 4Ø, 8Ø and 99 as discussed above and RUN.

Did the program work OK as changed? Did you try it with several values of A? Be sure you do! We will find many uses for the GOTO statement in the future.

Learned in Chapter 8

Statements	Relational Operators	Miscellaneous
IF-THEN	=	Conditional Branching
GOTO	>	Unconditional Branching
	<	Optional THEN
	<>	
	<=	
	>=	

It Also Talks And Listens

Begin this chapter by typing in the sample answer program to Exercise 8-2:

By now you have probably gotten tired of having to retype line 1∅ each time you want to change the value of A. The INPUT statement is a simple, fast and much more convenient way to accomplish the same thing. It's a biggie, so don't miss any points.

Add the following lines to the RESIDENT program:

Resident — remember, that's the program now residing in the computer.

```
5 PRINT " THE VALUE I WISH TO GIVE A IS"
1∅ INPUT A
```

. . .and RUN.

The computer will print:

```
THE VALUE I WISH TO GIVE A IS
?▪
```

See the question mark on the screen? It means, "It's your turn — and I'm waiting. . ."

Enter a number and see what happens. It should be identical to what happened when you typed in the same number earlier by changing line 1∅. RUN the program several more times to get the feel of the INPUT statement.

Pretty powerful, isn't it?

Let's add a touch of class to the INPUT process by changing line 5 as follows:

```
5 PRINT " THE VALUE I WISH TO GIVE A IS";
```

Look at that line very carefully. Do you see how it differs from the earlier line 5? It is different — a *semicolon* is added to the END of the line.

Did you use the EDITor to add the semicolon?

Think back a few chapters. We used semicolons before in PRINT statements, but only in the *middle* to hook several of them together so they would PRINT close together on the same line. In this case, we put a semicolon at the END of the program line, so the *question mark* from line 1∅ will PRINT on the *same* line rather than down there by itself.

After changing line 5 as above, RUN. It should read:

```
THE VALUE I WISH TO GIVE A IS?
```

Please note that we cannot indiscriminately use a semicolon at the end of a PRINT statement. It is only meant to hook two lines together, both of which have PRINTing to be done. The INPUT line PRINTs a question mark. We shall see later where two long lines starting with PRINT can be connected together by the "trailing semicolon" so as to PRINT everything on the same line.

Your TRS-80 INTERPRETER is able to speak "The King's BASIC" as well as a variety of dialects. The first of the many "short-cut" dialects we will be exploring in upcoming chapters involves combining PRINT and INPUT into one statement.

> INTERPRETER — is a computer program which allows us to "rap" with the computer in the English language. We are studying BASIC, which stands for Beginners All-Purpose Symbolic Instruction Code.

Change line 5 to read:

```
5 INPUT " THE VALUE I WISH TO GIVE A IS";A
```

then delete line 10 by typing:

```
10
```

. . .and **RUN**.

> Sometimes the word "dialect" is used when talking about the different variations of a computer language. Just as with dialects in "human" languages, there are differences in word uses in BASIC. That's why I wrote *The BASIC Handbook, Encyclopedia of the BASIC Language* available at better computer and bookstores everywhere in English, and translated into French, German, Swedish, and Italian.

The results come out exactly the same, don't they? Here is what we have changed:

1. PRINT to INPUT.

2. Both statements on the same line.

3. Eliminated an extra line.

In the long programs which we will be writing, running and converting, this shortcut will be valuable.

Up to now, all our programs have been strictly one-shot affairs. We type RUN, the computer executes the program, PRINTs the results (if any) and comes back with READY. To repeat the program, we have to type RUN again. Can you think of another way to make the computer execute a program two or more times?

> No — don't enlarge the program by repeating its lines over and over again; that's not very creative!

We'll answer that question by upgrading our Celsius-to-Fahrenheit conversion program (Chapter 7). If you think GOTO is a powerful statement in everyday life, wait 'til you see what it does for a computer program!

Type in this NEW program:

```
10  REM * IMPROVED CELSIUS TO FAHRENHEIT CONVERSION PROGRAM *
20  INPUT "WHAT IS THE TEMPERATURE IN DEGREES CELSIUS";C
30   F = (9/5)*C + 32
40   PRINT C; "DEGREES CELSIUS = ";F; "DEGREES FAHRENHEIT."
50   GOTO 20
```

   . . .and RUN.

You'll have to hit `BREAK` to get out of the program loop.

The computer will keep on asking for more until we get tired or the power goes off (or some other event beyond its control). This is the kind of thing a computer is best at — doing the same thing over and over again. Modify some of the other programs to make them self-repeating. You'll find they're much more useful that way.

These have been 5 long and "meaty" lessons, so go back and review them all, repeating those assignments where you feel weak. We are moving out into progressively deeper water, and it is complete mastery of these *fundamentals* that is your life preserver.

Learned in Chapter 9

Statements

INPUT

INPUT with built-in PRINT

Miscellaneous

; Trailing semicolon

Calculator Or
Immediate Mode

Two Easy Features

Before continuing exploration of the nooks and crannies of our computer acting as a *computer*, we should be aware that it also works well as a *calculator*. If we *omit* the line number before certain commands, the computer will execute them, PRINT the answer on the screen, then erase the command we entered.

What's more, it will work as a calculator even when a computer program is loaded, *without disturbing that program.* All we need, to be in the calculator mode, is the prompt >.

EXAMPLE: How much is 3 times 4? Type in

```
PRINT 3*4
```

. . .the answer comes back:

```
12
```

EXAMPLE: How much is 345 divided by 123?

```
PRINT 345/123
```

. . .the answer is:

```
2.80488
```

Spend a few minutes making up routine arithmetic problems of your own, using the calculator mode to solve them. Any arithmetic expression we might use in a program can also be evaluated in the calculator mode. This includes parentheses and chain calculations like A*B*C.

Try the following problem:

```
PRINT (2/3)*(3/2)
```

The answer comes back:

```
1
```

Calculator Mode For Troubleshooting

Suppose a program isn't giving the answers we expect. How can we troubleshoot it? One way is to ask the computer to tell us the values of the variables used in the resident program.

Keep this handy tip in mind as we get into more complex programs.

EXAMPLE: PRINT X. The computer will PRINT the last value of X.

Another thought: *Something* is stored in every memory cell (even if *you* have not put anything there). Enter this instruction in the calculator mode:

```
PRINT A,B,C,D,E,F,G,H,I,J,K,L,M,N,O,P,Q,R,S,T,U,V,W,X,Y,Z
```

The answers depend on the values last given those variables — even from much earlier programs. If we turn the computer off, then on again, all variables will be reset to $\emptyset$. Typing RUN also "initializes" all variables to $\emptyset$.

We will probably get all zeros.

· The MEMORY Command

Since programs do occupy space in the computer's memory, and program size is limited to how much memory we have purchased, it may be important to know how much memory we are using for a given program. That's what the MEMORY Command is for.

This manual is meant to be for the computer operator and programmer, so we are studiously avoiding computer electronics theory — when possible.

The least amount of memory available for our TRS-80 is 4K. This means there are about 4,000 different memory locations to store and process programs. "4K" is just a shortcut phrase for the exact amount of memory, which is 4096. With "16K" of memory, the exact number is 16384.

The computer uses some of the memory for program control. To see the actual amount of memory available for our use, type:

```
NEW

PRINT MEM
```

. . .and the answer will be:

```
15314
```

NOTE: If you don't get this answer (for example, a very large number or one with a "−" in it), turn the computer's *power* off for at least 10 seconds and then turn it on again. Try PRINT MEM once more. (If your TRS-80 has 4K of RAM, expect 3026. Numbers for Model I and II computers will vary widely with factory changes and upgrades.)

With no program loaded, there are 15314 memory locations available for use. The difference in memory space between 15314 and 16384 is set aside for processing programs and overall management and "monitoring" of what the computer is doing.

Type in this simple program:

```
10 A = 25
```

then measure the memory remaining by typing:

```
PRINT MEM
```

. . .the answer will be:

```
15303
```

The program we entered took 15314 − 15303 = 11 bytes of space. Here is how we account for it:

> BYTE is the basic unit of storage for most computers; normally it is considered as a string of eight binary digits (bits). Thus a byte = eight bits. Our TRS-80 can use either eight or 16 bits, depending on the software.

1. Each line number and the space following it (regardless of how small or large that line number is) occupies four memory cells (or bytes). The "carriage return" at the end of the line takes one more byte, even though it does not PRINT on the screen. Thus, memory "overhead" for each line, short or long, is five bytes.

2. Each letter, number and space takes 1 byte. In the above program five bytes for overhead + six bytes for the characters = 11 bytes.

Now, type RUN, then check the memory again with PRINT MEM. It changed to 15296, seven more bytes! When RUN, a simple variable like the A takes up three bytes and the numerical value takes another four, totaling seven. We will be studying memory requirements in more detail later.

Obviously, the short learning programs we have written so far are not taking up much memory space. This will change quickly, however, as we move to more sophisticated programming. Make a habit of typing PRINT MEM when completing a program to develop a sense of its size and memory requirements.

Learned in Chapter 10

Commands

PRINT MEM

Miscellaneous

Calculator Mode
Memory
Byte

Using Cassette Tape and Disk

Note: Model II and disk users go directly to "'SAVE'ing and LOADing on Disk", found later in this chapter.

We will soon write and run long and powerful programs. It becomes tedious to type them in accurately just once, let alone each time we want to use them. Impressing your friends with this super-whazzoo computer is somewhat more difficult if they sit watching TV reruns of Star-Trek while you take an hour to type in a program. There has to be a better way.

The TRS-80 has a built-in "Cassette Tape Interface" which allows us to record and store any program on high quality cassette tape. A full "4K" of memory can be *DUMPed* onto tape or *LOADed* from tape, in under three minutes. Most programs are shorter and take even less time. That isn't enough time to get through the deodorant ads. Besides building up your own tape library of computer programs, you can exchange favorite programs with other TRS-80 owners by exchanging tapes.

DUMPed and LOADed are everyday terms used by computer people for "storing" and "playing back" computer programs.

Recording

Only a little practice is required. Follow the yellow brick road:

1. Obtain a Recorder (CTR-80A), Interconnecting Cable and cassette tape.

2. Connect the cable between the tape jack on the back of the TRS-80 and the Cassette Tape Recorder:

    a. The small gray plug goes into the REM jack on the recorder.

    b. The large gray plug goes into the AUX jack.

    c. The black plug goes into the EAR jack.

3. Type any program into the computer, preferably one that is at least several lines long. RUN it to be sure it is entered correctly.

4. Press the PLAY and RECORD buttons *at the same time* until they lock.

5. "DUMP" the program onto tape by typing the command:

```
CSAVE "A"
```

CSAVE stands for "Save on Cassette". "A" is the name assigned to the program.

The motor on the recorder will start and you'll be recording the computer's program onto tape.

Watch the video screen. When

```
READY
>
```

returns and the motor stops, the program is recorded on tape. It is also still in the computer's memory. It has only been "copied" out.

6. Rewind the tape, disconnect the plug from the EAR jack and play the tape so you hear what digital data sounds like. Sounds terrible, doesn't it? *You were expecting maybe Lawrence Welk?*

CLOAD?

We can compare a program on tape against the one in memory. That way we are sure of getting a good "LOAD" before erasing the memory.

After doing a CSAVE"A", rewind the tape. Set it up to play, and type:

```
CLOAD?"A"
```

and RUN.

Watch the blinking asterisks. It looks like we are LOADing in a program, but are actually just comparing program "A", character for character, against what's already there. We are not erasing or changing the memory. If they don't match up for any reason, the test will stop and the screen will read:

```
BAD
```

"BAD" means we'd better CSAVE the program again, maybe on a different tape.

If we type just

```
CLOAD?
```

without specifying the name of the program, it will check the first program on the tape against memory, and that's normally all we want to do.

LOADing

Reversing the process and LOADing (copying) the program from tape into the computer is just as easy.

1. Be sure the tape is fully rewound and the plugs are all in place.

2. Push down the PLAY button until it locks. Set the Volume control to about 6.

IMPORTANT: Too little volume will cause a bad "data load". Too much volume may result in distortion in the Tape Recorder and also goof-up the "LOAD".

---

3. Type NEW (to clear out any existing program).

4. Type the command

CLOAD

CLOAD stands for "Load from Cassette".

The tape recorder's motor will start and data will flow from the tape into the computer's memory.

As soon as the computer senses the data, it will flash a * on the screen; then, as it accepts each line of data, a second * will flash on and off.

The ** display (second one flashing) is the indication that data is being LOADed into the computer.

Watch the Video Display. The program is entered when:

READY

>

returns and the recorder motor stops.

If the recorder does not stop, press BREAK (Model III only) or the RESET button. This will take the computer out of the CLOAD or CSAVE mode and return control to the keyboard.

---

5. RUN the program to see that the data transfer was successful. In the event that it was not, repeat the above steps, being sure that all cables are properly connected, *the volume is set to 6,* and the tape recorder heads are clean. (Listen to the tape to be sure there is a program on it.)

Miscellaneous Tape Palaver

To minimize the chance of hitting a "soft spot" on a tape, where the oxide may be thin or have flaked off, experienced operators routinely do a "double DUMP" when copying from computer to tape. This simply means copying the program twice on the same tape — one recording right after the other. On long DUMPs, one is made in one direction, the cassette flipped over, and recorded in the other direction. For extra safety, very important programs are recorded on more than one tape. Your own experience should be your guide.

You may have noticed that specially wound computer tape has no plastic leader on the ends. This is because when you begin "DUMP"ing data from memory onto tape there must be real live tape there to record it.

> Normal audio tape has lead-ins on both ends (typically, non-magnetic mylar material). *You cannot record on the leader portion of tapes.* Advance the tape past the leader before recording a program.

If one little bit of data is lost the entire program can be lost. Computer tape is wound in shorter-than-usual lengths, with the C-10 being standard. It will record five minutes in each direction — far more than enough for most programs.

Experienced "computerists" have found that it is better to use a separate cassette (or at least a separate side) for each program rather than try to search through long tapes for a desired program. Since computer data on tape is not readable by the human ear, separate cassettes solve the problem.

> If you record programs on long audio cassettes, use the tape recorder's COUNTER to aid in locating programs.

When you are not using the Recorder for LOADing or recording, do not leave the RECORD or PLAY keys down (press STOP).

CAUTION!

Do not expose recorded tapes to magnetic fields.

Do not attempt to re-record on a pre-recorded computer data tape. Even though the new recording process erases the old recording, just enough information may be left to confuse the new recording. If you want to use the same tape a second or third time, use a bulk tape eraser to be sure all old data is erased.

If you want to SAVE a taped program permanently, break off the Erase Protect Tab on the cassette (see the tape recorder's manual). When the tab(s) has been broken off, you cannot press down the RECORD key (to keep from accidentally erasing that tape).

> Non-Disk Users GOTO the next chapter.

"SAVE"ing and LOADing on Disk

A big advantage of DISK BASIC over ordinary TRS-80 Level II BASIC is that programs can be SAVEd on or LOADed from disk much more quickly and reliably than with cassette. Type in this short BASIC program:

```
10 REM * DISK BASIC PROGRAM *
20 PRINT"HELLO THERE, DISK USER"
99 END
```

and type:

```
SAVE"PROGRAM1"
```

Well, something seemed to happen. Our little program is now SAVEd on the floppy disk under the name PROGRAM1.

On a one-drive system, the program is automatically SAVEd on the diskette in drive Ø, unless it has a write-protect tab on it. In multi-drive systems, the lowest numbered drive containing an unprotected diskette will receive the program.

Diskettes in drives 1 through 3 must be formatted before they are used. The master disk in drive Ø is, of course, already formatted. See your DOS Manual for use of the FORMAT command.

Let's recall the program from the disk. Type:

```
NEW
```

to clear the program out of memory. Check the situation with a:

```
LIST
```

to see that no trace remains. Good thing we SAVEd it on diskette. Hope it's really there. To copy the program from the diskette back into memory let's type:

```
LOAD"PROGRAM1"
```

and in it comes. How can we test to be sure it is really LOADed?

```
LIST
```

Yup, there it is.

Refer to the appropriate Appendix A, Part 2 at your leisure for additional information on determining what programs are on a diskette, and switching back and forth between DOS and BASIC.

Learned in Chapter 11

Commands

CLOAD
CSAVE

Miscellaneous

"loading"
"dumping"
**(program loading indicator)
SAVE
LOAD

FOR-NEXT Looping

FROM-TO, FOR-NEXT. . .Or Smart Loops

A major difference between the computer and a calculator is the computer's ability to do the same thing over and over an outrageous number of times, faster than a speeding bullet (to coin a phrase)! This one capability, more than any other, differentiates the two.

The FOR-NEXT loop is of such overwhelming importance in putting our computer to work, that few of the programming areas we will explore from this point on exclude it. Its simplicity and variations are the heart of its effectiveness, but its power is truly staggering.

Type in this NEW program:

```
10 PRINT "HELP ---- MY COMPUTER HAS GONE BERSERK!"
20 GOTO 10
```

. . .and RUN.

The computer will PRINT:

```
HELP ---- MY COMPUTER HAS GONE BERSERK!"
```

indefinitely, until we tell it to STOP. When you have seen enough, hit `BREAK`

We created what is called an "endless loop". (Remember our earlier programs which kept coming back for more INPUT?) Line 2Ø is an unconditional GOTO statement which causes the computer to cycle back and forth ("loop") between lines 1Ø and 2Ø forever, if not halted. This idea has great potential if we can harness it.

Let's modify the program to read:

```
8 FOR N = 1 TO 5
1Ø PRINT "HELP ---- MY COMPUTER HAS GONE BERSERK!"
2Ø NEXT N
3Ø PRINT "NO ---- IT'S UNDER CONTROL."
```

. . .and RUN it.

The line:

```
HELP ---- MY COMPUTER HAS GONE BERSERK!
```

was PRINTed 5 times, then:

```
NO ---- IT'S UNDER CONTROL.
```

The FOR-NEXT loop created in lines 8 and 2Ø caused the computer to cycle through lines 8, 1Ø, and 2Ø exactly 5 times, then continue through the rest of the program. Each time the computer hit line 2Ø it saw "NEXT N". The word NEXT caused the value of N to be increased (or STEPped) by exactly 1, and the computer "conditionally" sent back to the FOR N = statement that *began* the loop. Execution of this NEXT statement is conditional on N being less than or equal to 5, because line 8 says FOR N = 1 TO 5. After the 5th pass through the loop, the built-in test fails, the loop is broken and the program execution moves on. The FOR-NEXT statement harnessed the endless loop!

The STEP Function

There are times when it is desirable to increment the FOR-NEXT loop by some value other than one. The STEP function allows it. Change line 8 to read:

```
8 FOR N = 1 TO 5 STEP 2
```

   . . .and RUN.

Line 1∅ was PRINTed only 3 times (when N = 1, N = 3, and N = 5). On the first pass through the program, when NEXT N was hit, N was incremented (or STEPped) by the value of 2, instead of the default value of 1. On the second pass through the loop, N equaled 3. On the third pass N equaled 5.

FOR-NEXT loops can be STEPped by any decimal number, even negative numbers. Why we might want to STEP with a negative number might seem obscure now, but that too will be understood in time. Meanwhile, change the following line:

```
8 FOR N = 5 TO 1 STEP -1
```

   . . .and RUN.

Five passes through the loop stepping DOWN from 5 to 1 is exactly the same as stepping UP from 1 to 5. Line 1∅ was still PRINTed 5 times.

Change the STEP from −1 to −2.5 and RUN again. Amazing! It PRINTed exactly twice. Smart computer. Change the STEP back to −1.

Modifying The FOR-NEXT Loop

Suppose we wanted to PRINT both lines 1∅ and 3∅ five times, alternating between them. How would *you* change the program to accomplish it? Go ahead and make the change.

HINT: Try moving the *next* N line to another position.

Right − you moved line 2∅ to line 4∅ and the screen reads:

```
HELP ----- MY COMPUTER HAS GONE BERSERK!

NO ----- IT'S UNDER CONTROL.

HELP ----- MY COMPUTER HS GONE BERSERK!

NO ----- IT'S UNDER CONTROL.
```

. . .etc., 3 more times.

How would you modify the program so line 1Ø is PRINTed 5 times, and line 3Ø is PRINTed 3 times? Make the changes and RUN.

The new program might read:

```
8 FOR N = 1 TO 5
10 PRINT "HELP --- MY COMPUTER HAS GONE BERSERK!"
20 NEXT N
25 FOR M = 1 TO 3
30 PRINT "NO ---- IT'S UNDER CONTROL."
40 NEXT M
```

We now have a program with *two* controlled loops, sometimes called "DO" loops. The first DO-loop *does* something five times; the second one *does* something three times. We used the letter N for the first loop and M for the second, but any letters can be used. In fact, since the two loops are totally separate we could have used the letter N for both of them - not an uncommon practice in large programs where most of the letters are needed as variables.

RUN the program, being sure you understand the fundamental principles and the variations we have introduced.

FROM < TO Incrementing

There is nothing magical about the FOR-NEXT loop. In fact, you may have already thought of another (longer) way to accomplish the same thing by using features we learned earlier. Stop now, and see if you can figure out a way to construct a workable do-loop, substituting something else in place of FOR and NEXT.

ANSWER:

```
8 N = 1
10 PRINT "HELP ----- MY COMPUTER HAS GONE BERSERK!"
15 N = N + 1
```

```
20 IF N<6 THEN 10

30 PRINT "NO --- IT'S UNDER CONTROL."
```

We say that line 8 *initializes* the value of N, giving it an initial or beginning value of 1. Before initializing to the value we want, N could have been any number from previous program lines. Note that typing RUN automatically resets all the variables back to $\emptyset$ before the program executes.

Initializes: Gives a value to a variable.

Line 15 then *increments* it by 1, making N one more than whatever it was before. Line 1$\emptyset$ uses one of our relational operators (<) to see that the new value of N is within the bounds we have established. If not, the test fails and execution continues on the next program line.

Increments: STEPs (increases or decreases) values in specific steps: by 1's, 3's, 5's, or whatever.

Note that in this system of *incrementing* and testing we do not send the program back to line 8 as was the case with FOR-NEXT. What would happen if we did?

ANSWER: We would keep re-initializing the value of N to equal 1, and we'd be stuck in an endless loop.

The opposite of *incrementing* is *decrementing*.

To Decrement is to make smaller.

Change the program so line 15 reads:

```
15 N = N - 1
```

. . .then make other changes as needed to make the program work.

ANSWER: The changed lines read:

```
8 N = 6

15 N = N - 1

20 IF N>1 THEN 10
```

Putting FOR-NEXT To Work

It isn't very exciting just seeing or doing the same thing over and over, so there has to be a more noble purpose for the FOR-NEXT loop. There are many of them, and we will be learning new uses for a long, long time.

Let's suppose we want to PRINT out a chart showing how the time it takes to fly from London to San Diego varies with the speed at which we fly. Remember, the formula is D = R*T. Let's PRINT out the flight time required for each speed between 200 MPH and 1000 MPH, in increments of 100 MPH. The program might look like this:

```
10  REM * TIME VS RATE FLIGHT CHART *

20  CLS

30  D = 6000

40  PRINT "    L O N D O N    T O    S A N    D I E G O    "

50  PRINT

60  PRINT "RATE (MPH)","TIME (HOURS)","DISTANCE (MILES)"

70  PRINT

80       FOR R=200 TO 1000 STEP 100

90        T = D/R

100        PRINT R,T,D

110       NEXT R
```

ENTER the NEW program and RUN.

How about that ... ? Try doing that one on the old slide rule or hand calculator!

It is really solving the problem from Chapter 5 nine times in a row, for different values, and PRINTing out each result. Your screen should look like this:

```
L O N D O N    T O    S A N   D I E G O

RATE (MPH)              TIME (HOURS)           DISTANCE (MILES)

   200                     30                      6000

   300                     20                      6000

   400                     15                      6000

   500                     12                      6000

   600                     10                      6000

   700                     8.57143                 6000

   800                     7.5                     6000

   900                     6.66667                 6000

  1000                     6                       6000
```

Analyzing The Program

Look through the program and observe these many features before we do
some exercises to change it:

1. The REM statement indentifies the program for future use.

2. Line 2Ø uses the CLS (Clear Screen) statement to erase the screen so we
    have a nice clean place to write on. It allows us to write in a *top-down*
    manner. RUN the program later leaving out this line and see what is
    meant by the *scroll* mode. CLS is a very unfussy statement which you
    will want to use often just to make your PRINTouts neat and impres-
    sive.

> CLS in a program does the same thing as the **CLEAR** Key on the keyboard (but we
> can't use the **CLEAR** Key as part of a program). Model II does not have a **CLEAR** Key.

3. Line 3Ø *initializes* the value of D. D will remain at its initialized value.

4. Line 2Ø PRINTs a chart heading which is indented and double-spaced
    for appearance.

5. Lines 25 and 2Ø use blank PRINTs to insert spaces in the chart.

6. Line 3Ø PRINTs the chart column headings, and uses *automatic zone spacing* (the comma) to place those headings.

Remember zone spacing? The comma (,) in a PRINT statement automatically starts the PRINTing in the next 16-space PRINT zone.

---

7. Line 8Ø established the FOR-NEXT loop complete with a STEP. It says, initialize the rate (R) at 80 mph, and make passes through the "DO-loop" with values of R incremented by values of 80 mph until a final value of 800 mph is reached. Line 18 is the other half of the loop.

8. Line 9Ø contains the actual formula which calculates the answer.

9. Line 8Ø PRINTs the three values. They are positioned under their headings by automatic zone spacing (the commas).

8. Lines 9Ø and 8Ø are indented from the rest of the program text. This is a simple programming technique high-lighting the do-loop, and makes reading and troubleshooting easier. You will see it used increasingly as we move on. *Try to adopt good programming practices like this* as you do the exercises. Indenting does take up a little memory space, and on long programs in their final form it is sometimes omitted.

Take a deep breath and go back over any points you might have missed in this lesson. Copy the program onto Disk or Cassette Tape as we will use it in the next chapter, continuing our study of FOR-NEXT loops.

Learned in Chapter 12

Statements

FOR-NEXT
CLS
STEP

Miscellaneous

Increment
Decrement
Initialize
[BREAK] Key
[CLEAR] Key
"Top Down" display
"Scroll" display
"Do-Loop"

Son Of FOR-NEXT

This is heavy stuff. If we turned the computer off between chapters, LOAD in the program which we SAVEd in the last chapter.

Modify the program so the rate and time are calculated and PRINTed for every 50 mph increment instead of the 100 mph increment presently in the program.

____

____

____

    . . .and RUN .

ANSWER: 80 FOR R = 200 TO 1000

Trouble In The Old Corral

What a revolting development! The PRINTout goes so fast we can't read it, and by the time it stops, the top part is cut off. *Aught'a known you can't trust these computers!*

The entire printout fits on the Model II screen.

89

Solutions For Sale

Several solutions are available:

1. Pressing the [SHIFT] Key and the @ Key *at the same time* will halt program execution or a LISTing. Pressing most other keys will start it again. RUN the program a number of times, practicing stopping and starting it using [SHIFT] @.

Model II, use [HOLD] instead of [SHIFT] @.

There's another one you can try — press the [BREAK] Key. (To restart after a [BREAK], either type RUN to start the program all over again or CONT to continue execution at the 'break" point.)

---

2. If we want a classy display we can build a "pause" *into the program*. The screen will fill, halt a moment, and automatically continue, if we don't interrupt execution.

The Timing Loop

In order to learn about the *timer loop*, let's employ another sly trick. We're going to leave our "Flight Time" program in the computer, and put in a second program.

Start by typing:

```
9 END
```

We are going to use the space in lines 1 through 8 to write and experiment with a second little program, but want it to END without plowing ahead into the "Flight" program.

When LISTing a program that has more than 16 lines and the lines we want to see scroll off the top of the screen, we can use the [BREAK] key to stop the LISTing where we want it. (24 lines on the Model II/16.)

The Egg Timer

It takes time to do everything. Even this foxy box takes time to do its thing, though we may be awed by its speed. Type:

```
1 PRINT "DON'T GO AWAY"
```

```
2 FOR X = 1 TO 4000

3 NEXT X

4 PRINT "TIMER PROGRAM ENDED."
```

. . .and **RUN**.

> Remember back when we told you not to do this (number lines in close sequence)? Well. . .if we *hadn't* followed that rule we wouldn't have this nice space to demonstrate the point.

How long did it take? Well, it did take time, didn't it? About 10 seconds? The TRS-80 computer can do approximately 400 FOR-NEXT loops per second. That means, by specifying the number of loops, we can build in as long a time-delay as we wish.

> Execution rates of the Egg Timer program varies from computer to computer. Approximate rates are: Model I − 370 loops per second, Model II − 670 loops per second, Model III − 400 loops per second.

Change the program to create a 30-second delay. Time it against your watch or clock to see how accurate it is.

Answer:

```
2 FOR X = 1 TO 12000   (for Model III)
```

EXERCISE 13-1: Using the space in lines 1 through 6, design a program which:

1. Asks us how many seconds delay we wish

2. Allows us to enter a number, then

3. Executes the delay,

4. Reports back when the delay is over, and

5. How many seconds it took.

A sample answer is in Part B.

How To Handle Long Program Listings

We now have two programs in the computer. Let's pull a LIST to look at them. My, my. They are so long it won't all fit on the screen. Now what do we do?

Rather than wring our hands about the problem, type each of the following variations of LIST, and watch the screen very carefully as each does its thing:

`LIST 5Ø` (Lists only line 5Ø)

`LIST -5Ø` (Lists all lines up through 5Ø)

`LIST 5Ø-` (Lists all lines from 5Ø to end)

`LIST 3Ø-7Ø` (Lists all lines from 3Ø through 7Ø)

`LIST 4-85` (Note that these numbers are not even in the program)

`LIST.`   (Lists 8Ø, the last line number printed)

How's that for something to write home about?

Question: How would you look at the resident program through line 9?

Answer: Type LIST −9 (Talk about a giveaway!)

Is There No End To This Magic?

We have two separate programs resident in the computer. To RUN the first one — we just type RUN. To RUN the second one we have a foxy variation on RUN called:

`RUN ###`

The ###'s represent the number of the line where we want the RUN to start.

. . .and, as you might suspect, it is similar to LIST###. To RUN the program starting with line 1Ø type:

```
RUN 1Ø
```

. . .and that's just what happens.

Will wonders never cease? If there are 20 or 30 programs in the computer at the same time, we can RUN just the one we want, provided we know its starting line number. What's more, we can start any program in the middle (or elsewhere) for purposes of troubleshooting — a matter in which we will become more involved as our programs get longer and more complicated.

Try starting the program(s) at different numbers. As you do, different (but very predictable) results occur. Don't worry about the strange error messages. We'll be studying them in great detail as we need them.

Meanwhile, Back At The Ranch

We got into this whole messy business trying to find a way to slow down our RUN on the flight times from London to San Diego. In the process we found out a lot more about the computer and learned to build a timer loop. Now let's see if we can build a timer loop right into the distance program. First, let's erase the test program by typing:

```
DELETE 1-9
```

and

```
LIST
```

to see what happened.

Wow! How's that for power? It DELETEd those program sections right out, without having to type each individual line.

The variations of DELETE somewhat resemble LIST###, but only DELETE###, DELETE-###, and DELETE###-### will work.

Wrong Way Computer

One way to STOP the fast parade of information in our chart is to put in a STOP. Type in:

```
85 IF R = 600 THEN STOP
```

. . .and RUN.

We know R is going to increment to 600, and that's about half-way through the chart, so 600 is a good choice. See how the chart ran out to 550 mph, then hit the stop as 600 came racing down to line 85. Your screen should display the first part of the chart and:

```
Break in 85
```

This means the program is STOPped, or broken in line 85. We can now gaze at the top half of the chart to our heart's content. To restart the program merely type:

```
CONT
```

. . .and it will automatically pick up where it left off and PRINT the rest of the chart, or until it hits another STOP we may have placed.

CONT stands for CONTINUE.

At Last

Our ultimate plan is to build a timer into the program so as not to completely STOP execution, but merely delay it so we can study the display.   Type:

```
85 IF R<> 600 THEN 90
87 FOR X = 1 TO 4000
88 NEXT X
```

. . .and RUN.

Hey! It really works! As long as R does *not* equal 600 the program skips over the delay loop in lines 87 and 88. When R *does* equal 600, the test "falls through" and lines 87 and 88 "play catch" 4000 times, delaying the program's execution for about ten seconds.

Time For A Cool One

It's been a long and tortuous route with numerous scenic side trips, but we finally made it. We picked up so many smarts in these two lessons on FOR-NEXT, we must put them to work.

EXERCISE 13-2: Modify the resident program so that (MPH) appears below RATE, (HOURS) appears below TIME and (MILES) appears below DISTANCE. This one should be a breeze.

EXERCISE 13-3: Design, write and RUN a program which will calculate and PRINT income at yearly, monthly, weekly and daily rates, based on a 40-hour week, a 1/12th-year month, and a 52-week year. Do this for yearly incomes between $5,000 and $25,000 in $1,000 increments. Document your program with REM statements to explain the equations you create.

EXERCISE 13-4: Here's an old chestnut that the computer really eats up: Design, write and RUN a program which tells how many days we have to work, starting at a penny a day, so if our salary doubles each day we know which day we earn at least a million dollars. Include columns which show each day number, its daily rate, and the total income to-date. Make the program stop after PRINTing the first day our daily rate is a million dollars or more. (After that . . . who cares!)

Answers to these Exercises can be found in Section B.

The "Brute Force" Method (Subtitled: Get A Bigger Hammer)

Much to the consternation of some teachers, a great value of the computer is its ability to do the tedious work involved in the "cut and try", "hunt and peck" or other less respectable methods of finding an answer (or attempting to prove the correctness of a theory, theorem or principle). This method involves trying a mess of possible solutions to see if one fits, or to find the closest one, or to establish a trend. Beyond that, it can be a powerful learning tool by providing gobs of data in chart or graph form which would simply take too long to generate by hand. For example:

EXERCISE 13-5: You have a 1000-foot roll of fencing wire and want to make a *rectangular* pasture.

Using all of the wire, determine what length and width dimensions will allow you to enclose the maximum number of square feet? Use the brute force method; let the computer try different values for L and W and PRINT out the Area fenced by each pair of L and W.

The formula for area is Area = Length times Width, or $A = L*W$

EXERCISE 13-6: *Extra credit problem for "electronics types"*

As a further example (more complex and tends to prove the point better), try this final (optional) assignment. It involves a problem confronted by every electricity student who has studied SOURCES (batteries, generators) and LOADS (lights, resistors).

The *Maximum D.C. Power Transfer Theorem* states,

"Maximum DC power is delivered to an electrical load when the resistance of that load is equal in value to the internal resistance of the source."

And then the arguments begin. . .

"Use a HIGH resistance load because it will drop more voltage and accept more power."

"No, use a LOW resistance load so it will draw more current and accept more power."

"Use a load value somewhere in between."

Don't necessarily shy away from this problem if electricity doesn't happen to be your bag. Enough information is given to write the program. The principle, the optimizing of a value, is applicable to many fields of endeavor and is little short of profound.

With the values given in the schematic, design, write and RUN a program which will try out values of load resistance ranging from 1 to 20 ohms, in 1 ohm increments, and PRINT the answers to the following:

1. Value of Load Resistance (from 1 to 20 ohms)

2. Total circuit power (circuit current squared, times circuit resistance) $= I^2 * (10 + R)$

3. Power lost in source (circuit current squared, times source resistance) $= I^2 * 10$

4. Power delivered to load (circuit current squared, times load resistance) $= I^2 * R$

Note: Circuit current is found by dividing source voltage (120 volts) by total circuit resistance (load resistance +10 ohms source resistance). Everything follows Ohms Law $(V=I*R)$ and Watts Law $(P=I*V)$

GOOD LUCK! Don't look at the answer until you've got it whipped.

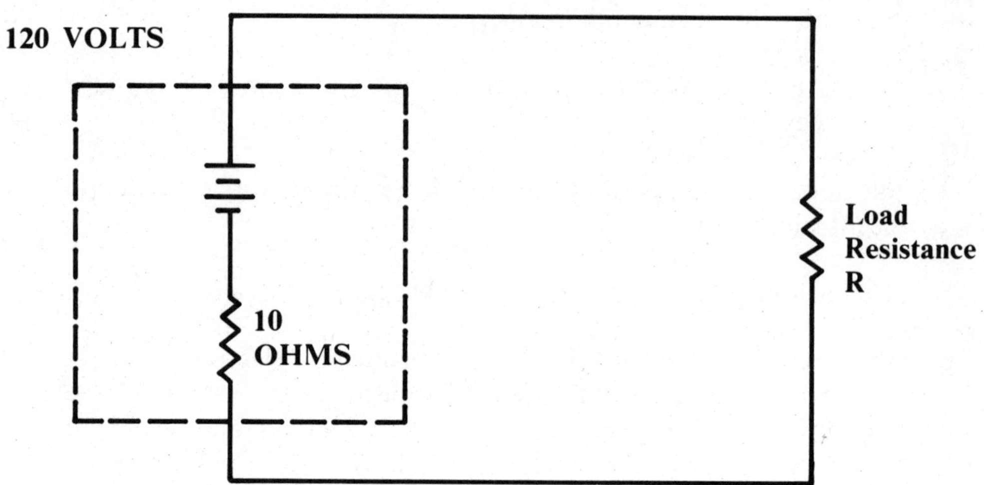

Learned in Chapter 13

Commands	Statements	Miscellaneous
LIST###	STOP	Timer Loop
RUN###		"Brute force"
DELETE###		
CONT		

Formatting With TAB

From > to TAB to LPRINT

After those last few chapters, it's *time out* for an easy one.

We already know three ways to set up our output PRNT Format.

We can:

1. Enclose what we want to say in quotes, inserting blank spaces as necessary.

2. Separate the objects of the PRINT statement with semicolons so as to PRINT them tightly together on the same line.

3. Separate the objects of the PRINT statement with commas to PRINT them on the same Line in the 6 different PRINT "zones".

A fourth way is to use the TAB Function, which is similar to the TAB on a regular typewriter. This is especially useful when the output is columns of numbers with headings. Type in the following NEW program and RUN:

```
10 PRINT TAB(5);"THE";TAB(20);"TOTAL";TAB(35);"SPENT"
20 PRINT TAB(5);"BUDGET";TAB(20);"YEAR'S";TAB(35);"THIS"
30 PRINT TAB(5);"CATEGORY";TAB(20);"BUDGET";TAB(35)"MONTH"
```

The Display will show:

```
THE                 TOTAL           SPENT

BUDGET              YEAR'S          THIS

CATEGORY            BUDGET          MONTH
```

EXERCISE 14-1: Write a program using the three PRINT Forms below:

```
1.  PRINT "          ","          ","          "
2.  PRINT "                                   "
    and
3.  PRINT TAB( );"          ";TAB( );"          ";TAB( );"          "
```

to set up the headings given in the prior example. Use Form #1 for the first line of the heading, Form #2 for the second line and Form #3 (the TAB Form) for the third line.

Hint: Since Form #1 uses automatic zone Formatting and is not adjustable, the other Forms have to be keyed to it.

Whether or not we follow TAB(##) with a semicolon makes no difference. In either case, the computer will start PRINTing ## spaces to the right of the left margin. However, it is important to remember that whenever numbers or numeric variables are PRINTed out, the computer inserts one space to the left of the number to allow for the − or + sign.

Type this NEW program:

```
10 A = 3
20 B = 5
30 C = A + B
40 PRINT TAB(10);"A";TAB(20);"B";TAB(30);"C"
50 PRINT TAB(10);A;TAB(20);B;TAB(30);C
```

> . . .and RUN.

A semicolon is traditionally used following TAB, as shown. Most later BASIC interpreters permit a blank, or even no symbol. Experiment to see which you like best.

It will appear:

```
A           B           C
   3           5           8
```

Note that the numbers are indented one space beyond the TAB(#). It's important to compensate when lining up (or indenting) headings and answers.

Change Line 20 to read:

```
20 B = −5
```

> . . .and RUN.

See why the indenting is necessary?

The Long Lines Division

Have you ever wondered what would happen if you wanted to PRINT a great number of headings or answers on the same line − but didn't have enough room on the program line to neatly type in all the TAB statements? You have? Really? You're in luck because it's easy. Type and RUN the following NEW program:

```
10 A = 1
```

```
20  B = 2
30  C = 3
40  D = 4
50  E = 5
60  F = 6
70  G = 7
80  H = 8
90  I = 9
100 J = 10
200 PRINT "A";TAB(5);"B";TAB(10);"C";TAB(15);"D";
210 PRINT TAB(20);"E";TAB(25);"F";TAB(30);"G";
220 PRINT TAB(35);"H";TAB(40);"I";TAB(45);"J";
300 PRINT A;TAB(5);B;TAB(10);C;TAB(15);D;TAB(20);
310 PRINT E;TAB(25);F;TAB(30);G;TAB(35);H;TAB(40);
320 PRINT I;TAB(45);J
```

It's the trailing semicolon (;) that does the trick. It makes the end of one **PRINT** line continue right on to the next **PRINT** line without activating a carriage return. The combination of **TAB** and trailing semicolon allows us almost infinite flexibility in formatting the output.

EXERCISE 14-2: Rework the answer to Exercise 13-3 in part 2 to include the *hourly* rate of pay in the PRINTout. Use the TAB Function to have the chart display all five columns side by side.

EXERCISE 14-3: (Optional) Rework the special program 13-6 in part 2 answer using the TAB Function so the PRINTout includes the internal resistance in a fifth column.

Chapter 14

Printing It All On The Line Printer

The Model II/16 and Model III computers have built-in printer interfaces.
Model I users need an external interface to use a line printer.

Ready to learn something else easy?

You have learned a lot of ways to print, but they have all been on the video screen. Now we'll show you how to print-out on a line printer. If you don't have a line printer, at least read over the rest of this chapter before going on.

Turn on your Printer and type this new one-line program:

```
10 LPRINT "THE LINE PRINTER WORKS!!!"
```

Notice that the first word is LPRINT — not PRINT. RUN the program.

Does it work? If your Printer did nothing, press BREAK to regain control of the computer. Check the connections again. Make sure the Printer is ON and ON-line. Try running the one-line program again.

Now, let's see how to print with a nice format. Erase your one-line program and type:

```
10 FOR X=1 TO 100
20 LPRINT X,
30 NEXT X
```

    . . .and RUN.

See how the Printer will format the printing into neat little columns. The comma with LPRINT works the same as it does with PRINT, except there may be a different number of columns on your Printer. (The number of columns depends on which printer you have.) The EPSON MX-Series Printers are highly recommended.

Try using a semicolon in line 20 rather than a comma. Type:

```
20 LPRINT X;
```

    . . .and RUN. The semicolon works the same on the printer as it

does on the video screen. Let's see how TAB works. Type NEW
and then type in this program:

```
10 LPRINT TAB(25) "TELEPHONE LIST"
20 LPRINT
30 LPRINT TAB(15) "NAME";TAB(45) "TELEPHONE NUMBER"
40 LPRINT
50 INPUT "TYPE A FRIEND'S NAME";A$
60 INPUT "PHONE NUMBER";B$
70 PRINT "THANK YOU"
80 LPRINT TAB(15) A$; TAB(45) B$
90 INPUT "IS THERE ANOTHER FRIEND (Y/N)#";Q$
100 IF Q$="Y" THEN 50
```

. . .and RUN it.

Yes, we know there are some new goodies in there. Just wanted to show off.
We'll get to the $s later.

If the paper size is larger or smaller than 8 ½- by 11-inches, you'll need to
use different TAB settings.

One more thing we want to learn. Type this command:

```
LLIST
```

and press **ENTER** . Now you have a permanent "hard copy" of this program.
It's a great feature, especially as our programs get longer.

Learned in Chapter 14

Print Modifiers	**Miscellaneous**
TAB	Trailing semicolon
	LPRINT
	LLIST

Grandson Of FOR-NEXT

The For-Next loop didn't go away for long. It continues more powerful than ever. Type this program:

```
1Ø FOR A = 1 TO 3
2Ø   PRINT "A LOOP"
3Ø    FOR B = 1 TO 2
4Ø     PRINT " ","B LOOP"
5Ø    NEXT B
6Ø NEXT A
```

. . .and RUN.

For legibility, add two blank spaces in line 2Ø before PRINT; three in line 3Ø before FOR; four in 4Ø before PRINT; and three in 5Ø before NEXT.

The result is:

```
A LOOP
              B LOOP
              B LOOP
```

```
A LOOP

            B LOOP

            B LOOP

A LOOP

            B LOOP

            B LOOP
```

This display vividly demonstrates operation of the nested For-Next loop. "Nesting" is used in the same sense that drinking glasses are "nested" when stored to save space. Certain types of portable chairs, empty cardboard boxes, etc. can be nested. They fit one inside the other for easy stacking.

When you write programs, be sure to indent lines to highlight nesting (or other lines you want to emphasize). This helps when reading programs — and is a great aid when debugging (troubleshooting) program problems.

Let's analyze the program, a line at a time:

Line 1Ø establishes the first For-Next loop, called A, and directs that it be executed 3 times.

Line 2Ø PRINTs "A Loop" so we will know where it came from in the program. See how this program line is indented a couple spaces to make it stand out as being nested in the "A loop"?

Line 3Ø establishes the second loop, called B, and directs that it be executed twice. It is indented even more so we can instantly see that it is buried even deeper in the "A" loop.

Line 4Ø PRINTs two items: First the blank shown between the two quote marks, then the comma kicks us into the next PRINT zone where "B Loop" is PRINTed. Makes for clear distinction on the screen between A loop and B loop, eh?

Line 5Ø completes the "B" loop and returns control to line 3Ø for as many executions of the "B" loop as line 3Ø directs. So far we have PRINTed one "A" and one "B".

Line 6Ø ends the first pass through the "A" loop and sends control back to line 1Ø, the beginning of the A loop. The A loop has to be executed 3 times before the program RUN is complete, PRINTing "A" 3 times and "B" six times (3 times 2).

Study the program and the explanation until you completely understand it. It's simple, but powerful, magic.

Okay, to get a better "feel" for this nested loop (or loop within a loop) business, let's play with the program. Change line 1Ø to read:

```
1Ø FOR A = 1 TO 5
```

   . . .and RUN.

Right! A was PRINTed 5 times, meaning the "A" loop was executed 5 times, and B was PRINTed 10 times — twice for each pass of the "A" loop. Now change line 3Ø to read:

```
3Ø FOR B = 1 TO 4
```

   . . .and RUN.

Nothing to it! A was PRINTed 5 times and B PRINTed 20 times. If you are having trouble counting A's and B's as they whiz by, you remember what to do. Just press the **SHIFT** and @ keys *at the same time* to STOP execution and temporarily freeze the display. Remember, **BREAK** and CONT also allows hands-off freezing, but inserts a **BREAK** note and otherwise messes up the display.

Model II use **HOLD** key to freeze the display.

How To Goof-Up Nested For-Next Loops

The most common error beginning programmers make with nested loops is improper nesting. Change these lines:

```
5Ø NEXT A
6Ø NEXT B
```

   . . .and RUN.

The computer says:

```
?NF Error in 60
```

Looking at the program we quickly see that the B loop is *not* nested within the A loop. We have the FOR part of the B loop inside the A loop, but the NEXT part is outside it. This doesn't work! A later chapter deals with something called "flowcharting", a means of helping us plan programs to avoid this type of problem. Meanwhile we just have to be careful.

> As disk BASIC users have already seen, their ERROR MESSAGES are the same but more elaborate: NEXT without FOR in 6∅.

Breaking Out Of Loops

Improper nesting is illegal, but breaking out of a loop when a desired condition has been met is OK. Add these lines:

```
50   NEXT B
55  IF A = 2 GOTO 100
60  NEXT A
99  END
100 PRINT "A EQUALED 2. RUN ENDED."
```

. . .and RUN.

As the screen shows, we "bailed out" of the A loop when A equaled 2 and hit the test line at 55. The END in line 99 is just a precautionary roadblock set up to STOP the computer from RUNning into line 1∅∅ unless specifically directed to go there. That would never happen in this simple program, but we will use protective ENDs from time to time to remind us that lines which should be reached only by specific GOTO or IF-THEN statements must be protected against accidental "hits".

We'll be seeing a lot of the *NESTED* For-Next loop now that we know what it is and how to use it.

EXERCISE 15-1: Re-enter the original program found at the beginning of this chapter. It contains a B loop nested within the A loop. Make the necessary additions to this program so a new loop called "C" will be nested within the B loop, and will PRINT "C LOOP" 4 times for each pass of the B loop.

EXERCISE 15-2: Use the program which is the answer to Exercise 15-1. Make the necessary additions to this program so a new loop called "D" will be nested within the C loop, and will PRINT "D LOOP" 5 times for each pass of the C loop.

Learned in Chapter 15

Statements

Nested For-Next loops

Miscellaneous

Protective END blocks

The INTeger Function

INTeger? "I can't even pronounce it, let alone understand it." Oh, come, come. Don't let old nightmares of being trapped in Algebra class *stop* you now. It's pronounced "in-teh-jur" and simply means a *whole* number like — 5, 0, or 3, etc. How difficult can that be? Come to think of it, some folks make a whole career of complicating simple ideas. We're here to do just the opposite.

The INTeger function, INT(X), allows us to "round off" any number, large or small, positive or negative, to an INTEger, or *whole* number.

Careful — we're not talking about ordinary rounding. Ordinary rounding gives us the closest whole number, whether it's larger or smaller than X. INT(X), on the other hand, gives us the *largest whole number which is less than or equal to X*. As you'll see in this chapter, this is a very versatile form of rounding — in fact, we can use it to produce the other "ordinary" kind of rounding.

Type NEW to clear out any old programs, then type:

```
30 X = 3.14159
40 Y = INT(X)
70 PRINT "Y= ";Y
```

. . .and RUN.

The display reads:

```
Y = 3
```

Oh — success is so sweet! It rounded 3.14159 off to 3. Change line 3Ø to read:

```
30 X = -3.14159
```

. . .and RUN.

Good Grief! It rounded the answer *down* to read:

```
Y = -4
```

What kind of rounding is this? Easy. The INT function *always* rounds *down* to the next *lowest whole number*. Pretty hard to get that confused! It makes a positive number less positive, and makes a negative number more negative (same thing as less positive). At least it's consistent.

Taking it a line at a time:

Line 3Ø sets the value of X (or any of our other alphabet-soup variables) equal to the value we selected, in this case π.

Line 4Ø finds the INTeger value of the above number and assigns it a variable name. We chose Y.

Line 7Ø PRINTs an identification label (Y=) followed by the value of Y.

Not Content To Leave Well Enough Alone

We can do some foxy things you probably never thought of with the INTeger function.

Change the program to read:

```
30 X = 3.14159
40 Y = INT(X)
50 Z = X - Y
```

```
60 PRINT "X = " ; X
70 PRINT "Y = " ; Y
80 PRINT "Z = " ; Z
```

    . . .and RUN.

SAVE this as "INT1". AHA! I don't know what we've discovered but it must be good for something. It reads:

```
X = 3.14159

Y = 3

Z = .14159
```

We've split the value of X into its Integer (whole number) value (called it Y), and its decimal value (called it Z).

Lines 60, 70, and 80 merely PRINTed the results.

There *is* a way to control the accuracy of our results. It involves artificially rounding the fraction to the desired number of decimal places, and then forcing the computer to PRINT out only those digits which are "properly rounded".

For example, suppose we need π to only three decimal places, (Of course, we can enter it as 3.142, but that's not the point.) Type NEW, then enter and RUN the following program:

```
10 X = 3.14159

20 X = + .0005

30 X = INT(X * 1000)/1000

40 PRINT X
```

Adding .0005 in line 20 gives our fraction a "push in the right direction". If this fraction has a digit greater than 4 in its 10-thousandths place, then adding .0005 will effectively increase the thousandths-place digit by 1. Otherwise, the added .0005 will have no effect on the final result. This results in what's called 4/5 rounding.

Try using other values for X. (Just make sure X*100 isn't too large for the INT function to handle.)

It's easy to change the program to accomplish rounding at a different point. For example, to round X off at the hundredths place (two digits to the right of the decimal point), change lines 2Ø and 3Ø to read:

```
1Ø  X = 3.14159
2Ø  X = X + .ØØ5
3Ø  X = INT(X * 1ØØ)/1ØØ
4Ø  PRINT X
```

  . . .and RUN, using several values for X.

This is useful when you're PRINTing out dollars and cents — it prevents $39.995-type prices.

HMMMM!!!

Do you suppose there is any way to separate each of the digits in 3.14159, or in any other number? Do you suppose we would have brought it up if there wasn't? After all. . .(mumble, mumble. . .)

It's really your turn to do some creative thinking, but we'll get it started and see if you can finish this idea. First, wipe out the resident program and retype or reLOAD INT1 as follows. It simply splits X into an INTeger and fractional parts.

```
3Ø  X = 3.14159
4Ø  Y = INT(X)
5Ø  Z = X - Y
6Ø  PRINT "X =   " ;X
7Ø  PRINT "Y =   " ;Y
8Ø  PRINT "Z =   " ;Z
```

We can go on taking the INT value of X over and over to try and split out the digits. Let's try it with Z:

```
9Ø  L = INT (Z)
1ØØ PRINT "L = ";L
```

  . . . and RUN.

Nope — that's a sure loser. We got ∅. The INTeger value of .14159 was that value rounded *down* to the next number, and the next number down was zero. Hmmm! Erase lines 9∅ and 1∅∅ and let's try again. Got any better ideas? No? Well, think some more.

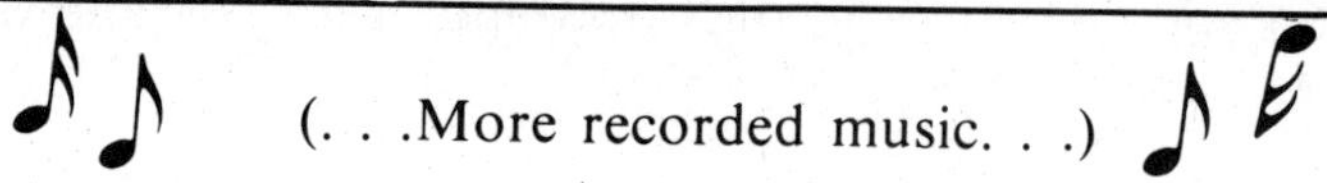

(. . .brief interlude of recorded music. . .)

Time Out For Creative Thinking!

Right! If we multiply the value of Z by 10 then Z will become a whole number plus a decimal part: 1.45159. We can then take its INTeger value and strip off the decimal part, leaving the left-hand digit standing alone. Let's label the left-hand digit L and see what happens. Enter:

```
9∅ M = Z * 1∅
1∅∅ L = INT (M)
11∅ PRINT " L = ";L
```

. . .and RUN.

Now, that's more like it. It reads:

```
X = 3.14159

Y = 3

Z = .14159

L = 1
```

We peeled off the leftmost digit in the decimal. Can you think of any way we might use a FOR-NEXT loop in order to strip off some more?

After all, these digits might not be just a more accurate value of pi, but a coded message from a cereal box. If we don't have the decoder ring, it's tough luck Charlie — unless we have a computer!

(. . .More recorded music. . .)

Enough thinking there on company time! Enter these lines:

```
95 FOR A = 1 TO 5
```

```
120 M = M - L
130 M = M * 10
140 NEXT A
```

. . .and RUN.

VOILA! (Never did figure out what that means, but I think it's positive.) The PRINTout reads:

```
X = 3.14159
Y = 6
Z = .14159
L = 1
L = 4
L = 1
L = 5
L = 8
```

They are all there, but what's with the last value of L. L = 8? It's supposed to be 9!

Well, let's analyze the program first, then worry about that little detail.

Line 95 began a FOR-NEXT loop with 5 passes, one for each of the 5 digits right of the decimal.

Line 120 creates a new decimal value of M (just a temporary storage location) by stripping off the INTeger part. (Plugging in the values, M = 1.4159 − 1 = .4159).

Line 130 does the same as line 90 did, multiplying the new decimal value times 10 so as to make the left-hand digit an INTeger and vulnerable to being snatched away by the INT function (M = .4159 * 10 = 4.159).

Line 140 moves the control back to line 95 for another pass through the clipping program. . .and the rest is history.

Now about that little detail. . .the wrong value in the last digit. So what gives? You have discovered the computer's limit of accuracy. Just like a calculator (or a person), a computer can never be perfectly accurate all the time. For short arithmetic expressions, the TRS-80 is accurate to the fifth or sixth decimal place. In longer, more complex expressions, a minute error in the sixth place can be magnified to where it becomes significant. All programmers have to cope with this kind of built-in error.

We now plow head-on into that problem. To understand it better change line 95 to read:

```
95 FOR A = 1 TO 10
```

. . .and RUN.

Where did all those other numbers come from? (Beats me.) Again the last digit or 1 at the end of a number is not to be trusted.

But there is a solution. Change line 95 back as it was, then change line 3Ø to read:

```
30 X = 3.1415900
```

. . .and RUN.

Whew! Had us a little nervous there for a while. By our declaring that the accuracy of X is to be a few decimal places greater than we really need, we are assured that those digits we do need are reliable, even though the last couple may still be off. There are other ways to do this and we will learn them in later chapters.

But let's not get diverted from the main theme of *this* chapter.

Is This Too Hard To Follow?

No — it isn't hard to follow, and you could go through and indicate every value just like I did and it would be perfectly clear (to coin a phrase). Let's instead learn a way to let the computer help us understand what it is doing.

We can insert temporary PRINT lines anywhere in any program to make it tell us what it's doing at every step in its execution. The computer can actually overwhelm us with data, but by carefully indicating what we want to know, we can observe the inner details of the calculation. Start by adding this line:

```
92 PRINT " #92 M = " ;M
```

. . .and RUN.

The essentials of this "test" or "debugging" or "flag" line are:

1. It PRINTs something.

2. The PRINT tells the *line number*, for analysis and easy location for later erasure.

3. It tells the *name* of the variable we are watching at that point in the program.

4. It gives the *value* of that variable at *that point*.

This "flagging" is such a wonderful tool in troubleshooting stubborn programs that we will want to make a habit of never forgetting to use it when the going gets tough.

It is extremely helpful when inserted in FOR-NEXT loops — so:

```
97 PRINT " #97 A = ";A
```

. . . and RUN.

Wow! The data really comes thick and fast! Hard to keep track of so much information, and we've barely begun. This tells what is happening during each pass of the loop. Is there some way to make it more readable? Sure. Can you think of a way?

Yes, there are lots of ways. Indenting is just one simple way to keep the answers separated from the troubleshooting data. Change lines 92 and 97 as follows:

```
92 PRINT ,"#92 M = " ;M
97 PRINT ,"#97 A = " ;A
```

. . .and RUN.

Ahh. How sweet it is. That is so easy to read, let's monitor some more points in the program. Type in:

```
125 PRINT , ,"#125 M = " ;M

135 PRINT , ,"#135 M = " ;M
```

. . .and RUN.

Egad, Igor! We've created a monster!

There it is. All the data we can handle (and then some). By using the SHIFT and @ Keys to temporarily halt execution, we can study the data at every step to understand how the program works (or doesn't work). Do it. Understand this program and all its little lessons completely. When you are satisfied, go back and erase out the "flags". You have learned quite enough for this chapter.

(Use the HOLD Key for Model II.)

EXERCISE 16-1: Enter this straightforward little program for finding the area of a circle.

(First type NEW.)

```
10 P=3.14159

20 PRINT "RADIUS", "AREA"

30 PRINT

40 FOR R=1 TO 10

50  A = P * R * R

60  PRINT R,A

70 NEXT R
```

Area equals π times the radius squared (that is, the radius times itself). RUN it to make sure it works.

Pretty routine stuff — huh? Problem is, who needs all those little numbers to the far right of the decimal point? *Oh, you do?*   Well, there's one in every crowd. The rest of us can do without them. Without giving any big hints, modify the resident program to suppress all the numbers to the right of the decimal point.

EXERCISE 16-2: Now, knowing just enough to be dangerous, and in need of a lot of humility, change line 55 so that each value of *area* is rounded (down) to be accurate to one decimal place. For example:

```
RADIUS                    AREA

 1                        3.1
```

etc.

Ummm — yaas. Hang in there. It's super simple.

EXERCISE 16-3:   Carrying the above assignment one step further, modify the program line 55 to round (down) the value of area to be accurate to two decimal places.

Learned in Chapter 16

Functions

INT(X)

Miscellaneous

Flags

More Branching Statements

It Went That-A-Way

Enter this NEW program:

```
10 INPUT "TYPE A NUMBER BETWEEN 1 AND 5";N
20 IF N = 1 GOTO 110
30 IF N = 2 GOTO 130
40 IF N = 3 GOTO 150
50 IF N = 4 GOTO 170
60 IF N = 5 GOTO 190
70 PRINT " THE NUMBER YOU TYPED WAS NOT BETWEEN 1 AND 5 ---
DUMMY!"
```

Notice anything funny about line 70? It takes up two lines on the display! (Not on Model II, of course.) That's because it contains more than 64 characters (including line number and blank spaces). This is perfectly all right, as you may already have discovered in your own programming efforts. In fact, a program line can contain up to 256 characters (including line number and spaces). To enter or LIST such a long line takes up four display lines; but it's still just one numbered program line!

```
99 END
110 PRINT "N = 1"
120 END
130 PRINT "N = 2"
140 END
150 PRINT "N = 3"
160 END
170 PRINT "N = 4"
180 END
190 PRINT "N = 5"
```

RUN it a few times to feel comfortable with it and be sure it is "debugged".

"Debugged" is an old Latin word which, freely translated, means "getting all the errors out of your computer program".

Anyway, this program works fine for examining the value of a variable, N, and sending the computer off to a certain line number to do what it says there. If there are lots of possible directions in which to branch, however, we will want to use a greatly improved test called **ON-GOTO** which cuts out lots of lines of programming. Let's examine an **ON-GOTO** after we do the following:

DELETE lines 2Ø, 3Ø, 4Ø, 5Ø and 6Ø. Remember how? (DELETE 2Ø-6Ø).

Enter this new line:

```
20 ON N GOTO 110,130,150,170,190
```

. . .and RUN the program a few times, as before.

Works just the same, doesn't it?

The **ON-GOTO** statement is really pretty simple, though it looks hard. Line 2Ø says:

IF the INTeger value of N is 1 THEN GOTO line 11Ø.

IF the INTeger value of N is 2 THEN GOTO line 13Ø.

IF the INTeger value of N is 3 THEN GOTO line 15Ø.

IF the INTeger value of N is 4 THEN GOTO line 17Ø.

IF the INTeger value of N is 5 THEN GOTO line 19Ø.

IF the INTeger value of N is not one of the numbers LISTed above, THEN move on to the next line.

Remember, an INTeger is just a whole number.

The ON-GOTO statement has its own built-in INT statement. It really acts like this:

```
2Ø ON INT(N)GOTO...ETC.
```

RUN again and type in the following values of N to prove the point:

```
1.5
3.9999
Ø.999
5.999
6.ØØØ1
```

Get the picture?

Variations On A Theme

There are lots of tricks that can be played to milk the most from ON-GOTO. For example, if we want to branch out to 15 different locations but don't want to type that many different numbers on an ON-GOTO line, we can use several lines, like this:

```
2Ø ON N GOTO 11Ø,13Ø,15Ø,17Ø,19Ø
25 ON N-5 GOTO 21Ø,23Ø,25Ø,27Ø,29Ø
3Ø ON N-1Ø GOTO 31Ø,33Ø,35Ø,37Ø,39Ø
```

and fill in the proper responses at those line numbers.

In line 25 it was necessary to subtract 5 from the number being INPUT as N, since each new **ON-GOTO** line starts counting again from the number 1. In line 3∅, since we had already provided for inputs between 1 and 10, we subtract 10 from the **INPUT N** to cover the range from 11 through 15. By using the **ON-GOTO** statement, we have programmed into three lines what would otherwise have taken 15 lines. By packing more branching options into each **ON-GOTO** line, we could have done it in two lines or less, depending on the number of digits in the line numbers of the branch locations.

As in most of our examples, we could have used any letter after "ON", not just N. As we just saw, N can be the value of a letter variable, or a complete expression, either calculated in place (as here) or in a previous line.

Trade Secret

Due to the vagaries of rounding error and the chance the error might just round a number like "N" a tad below the **INTeger** value expected, it is common to see something like this:

```
5∅ ON N+.2 GOTO 1∅∅,2∅∅,3∅∅ ETC.
```

The effect of this shifty move is to add just a "pinch" to the incoming value of N, knowing full well that the **ON-GOTO** statement contains its own **INT** function. If N happens to have been rounded down to say 1.98 (instead of the 2.000 expected), 0.2 will be added to it making N $1.98 + .2 = 2.18$ which the built-in **INT** will round down to the desired 2. Pretty sneaky. Values between .1 and .5 are often added to the N for this purpose in well-written programs.

Give Me A SGN(X)

Using the **ON-GOTO** along with a new function called **SGN** (it's pronounced "sign"), plus a modest amount of imagination, produces a most useful little routine. But first, let's learn about SGN.

The SGN function examines any number to see whether it is negative, zero, or positive. It tells us the number is negative by giving us a (-1). (In computer language, "it returns a -1".) If the number is zero it returns a $(∅)$. If positive, we get a $(+1)$. It's a very simple function.

In order to sneak easily into the next concept, we will simulate the built-in SGN function with a **SUBROUTINE**.

So What Is A Subroutine?

Funny you should ask. A subroutine is a short but very specialized program (or routine) which we build into a large program to meet a specialized need. BASIC stores many of them in a special place in memory and they can be called up by a simple set of letters.

As an example of how to create functions that are not included in our BASIC, we are going to use a five-line subroutine instead of the "SGN" function to accomplish the same thing. Even though TRS-80 BASIC has its own "SGN" function, you must complete this chapter to be sure you learn about subroutines. We don't want to turn out dummies, ya know.

"Scratch" the program now in the computer by typing NEW, *then,* very carefully so you don't make any mistakes, type in the SGN subroutine:

```
30000 END
30800 REM * SGN(X) * INPUT X, OUTPUT T = -1,0, OR +1
30810 IF X < 0 THEN T = -1
30820 IF X = 0 THEN T = 0
30830 IF X > 0 THEN T = +1
30840 RETURN
```

"CALLING" A Subroutine — (Sort of like calling hogs)

To use a subroutine, use the GOSUB ##### statement.

"#####" represents the line number.

This statement directs the computer to go to that line number, execute what it says there and in the lines following, and when done RETURN back to the line containing that GOSUB statement. We will use line 20 here.

```
20 GOSUB 30800
```

A RETURN statement is a vital part of every subroutine, and you'll find ours at line 30840. We have reserved line number 30000 to hold a protective END block for all of our subroutines, so the computer doesn't come crashing into them when it is done with the main program.

Getting Down To Business

Okay, now let's combine GOSUB with SGN (in a subroutine) to see what all this fuss is about. Add:

```
10  INPUT "TYPE ANY NUMBER";X

20  GOSUB 30800

30  ON T+2 GOTO 50,60,70

45  END

50  PRINT "THE NUMBER IS NEGATIVE."

55  END

60  PRINT "THE NUMBER IS ZERO."

65  END

70  PRINT "THE NUMBER IS POSITIVE."
```

. . .etc. (the subroutine is already typed in).

Try this same program again using ON-GOSUB instead of ON-GOTO.
Remember, change lines 55 and 65 to RETURN and add line 75 RETURN.

Try entering negative, zero and positive numbers to be sure it works. Most of the program workings are obvious, but here is an analysis:

Line 1Ø inputs any number.

Line 2Ø sends the computer to Line 3Ø8ØØ by a GOSUB statement. This is different from an ordinary GOTO, since a GOSUB will return control to the originating line like a boomerang when execution hits a RETURN. The call to GOSUB is not complete and will not move on to the next program line until a RETURN is found.

Lines 3Ø8ØØ through 3Ø84Ø contain this rather simple subroutine.

Line 3Ø84Ø contains the RETURN which sends control back to Line 2Ø, which silently acknowledges the return and allows movement to the next line.

Line 3Ø is an ordinary ON-GOTO statement, but adds 2 to the

value of its variable, in this case "T". It is really saying,

If T is −1 THEN GOTO line 5∅.

If it is ∅ THEN GOTO line 6∅, and

If it is +1 GOTO line 7∅.

By adding 2 to each of those values we have "matched" them up with the 1, 2, and 3 which are built into the ON-GOTO.

Lines 45, 55, and 65 are routine protective blocks.

By the way, many subroutines are not this simple — as a matter of fact, they can contain rather hairy mathematical messes.

Preview Of Coming Attractions?

Like so much of what we are learning, this is just the tip of the iceberg. The ON-GOTO and SGN functions have many more clever applications, and they will evolve as we need them. As a hint for restless minds, note that the VALUE of X (which we INPUT) was not used, but it didn't go away. All we did was find its SGN. Hmmm. . .

Routines VS subroutines

We just studied a special-purpose routine used as a subroutine. All routines can be built right into any program instead of being set aside and "called" as a subroutine. The main value as subroutines is that they can be "called" repeatedly from different parts of a program. This is often desirable. An ordinary routine is usually only used once.

One value of using special routines as subroutines is that some are exceedingly complex to type without error. If one is typed once and SAVEd on tape or disk, it can be quickly and accurately LOADed back into the computer as a first step in creating a new program.

We'll have more to say in a later chapter. When you see just how powerful subroutines are, you'll feel like your TRS-80 is even smarter than it thinks it is.

Now it's your turn.

> *EXERCISE 17-1:* Remove all traces of the subroutine from the resident program. Use the SGN function that is already built into TRS-80 BASIC to accomplish the same thing we have been doing with a subroutine. Hints: T = SGN(X)

Learned in Chapter 17

Functions	Statements	Miscellaneous
SGN (X)	ON-GOTO	Debugging
	GOSUB	Routines
	ON-GOSUB	
	RETURN	

RaNDom Numbers

At RaNDom

A true RaNDom number is one with a value that is unpredictable. A "Random Number Generator" is a device which pulls RaNDom numbers "out of a hat". Our computer can act as such a device, and we set it up this way:

```
N = RND(X)
```

Where N is the random *number*,

RND is the abbreviation and symbol for *random*,

X is a dummy variable which can be either typed between the parentheses or brought in as a variable from elsewhere in the program.

Type this NEW program:

```
40 FOR N = 1 TO 10
50 PRINT RND(0)
60 NEXT N
```

. . .and RUN.

Did you observe:

1. A different number appeared each time?

2. All numbers were between 0 and 1?

3. Very small numbers were expressed in exponential notation?

Let's put a semicolon behind our PRINT statement so we can get more numbers on the screen at one time, and increase our FOR-NEXT loop to 90 passes. Change the program accordingly:

```
40 FOR N = 1 TO 90
50 PRINT RND(0);
60 NEXT N
```
        . . .and RUN.

You get the idea.

This Is Fairly Exciting!

Well, maybe so, but we ain't seen nothing yet! Virtually all computer games are based on the RND(X) function, and we'll soon be playing some and designing our own.

RND(X) With Racing Stripes

The RND(0) we just experimented with is the traditional Random Number Generator. In other BASIC dialects you may see it written as just plain RND. TRS-80 BASIC also has a non-traditional version of RND which permits us to generate numbers larger than 1 without having to resort to mathematical chicanery. We just insert a number larger than 0 between the parentheses.

Change line 50 to read:

```
50 PRINT RND(15)
```

        . . .and RUN.

Wow! That's more like it — real live RaNDom INTegers. And they all are values that fall between 1 and 15. Figured it out already? Pretty simple, isn't it?

1. If the number in parentheses (or its INT value) is Ø, the numbers generated are between Ø and 1.

2. If the number in parentheses is 1 or larger, the numbers generated are from 1 to the INT value of that number (inclusive).

3. The largest permissible value of Ø is 32767.

Skeptical? You don't believe the numbers are really random? You want proof? A natural reaction. OK — how about pretending to repeatedly flip a coin and see how many heads come up compared to the number of tails?

The Old Coin Toss Gambit

Remember now, we could toss a thousand heads in a row and the odds on the next toss are *exactly* 50/50 that a head will come up again. Every toss is totally independent of what happened before it. *It is too!*

In the long RUN, however, the number of heads and tails should be exactly the same. (Casinos live off people who go broke waiting for their particular scheme to pay off. . ."in the long run".) This computer will give us a complete education in "odds" and various games of chance, and allow us to prove or disprove many ideas involving probability. This is known as computer "modeling" or "simulation".

Type in this coin toss simulation carefully, to avoid errors:

```
10 INPUT "HOW MANY TIMES SHALL WE FLIP THE COIN";F
20 CLS
30 PRINT "YOU STAND BY WHILE I DO THE FLIPPING — — — — —"
40 FOR N=1 TO F
50 X = RND(2)
60 ON X GOTO 90,110
70 PRINT "IT BOMBED! WAS NEITHER A 1 NOR A 2."
```

```
80 END
90 H = H + 1
100 GOTO 120
110 T = T + 1
120 NEXT N
130 PRINT "HEADS","TAILS","TOTAL FLIPS"
140 PRINT H,T,F
150 PRINT 100*H/F;"%",100*T/F;"%"
```

. . .and RUN.

"Flip the coin" 100 times on the first RUN to get a feel for the program and the RUN time. RUN as many times as it takes to convince you that the random number generator produces really random numbers. When it's time for lunch or you can wait quite awhile for the answer, try 25,000 flips or more.

Program Analysis:

Line 10 INPUTs the number of flips desired.

Line 20 CLearS the screen to start the next PRINT line at the top.

Line 30 Prints a "Standby" statement.

Line 40 begins a FOR-NEXT loop that RUNs "F" times.

Line 50 is the RND(X) generator. We have told it to generate INTegers between 1 and 2, and of course that restricts it to just the numbers 1 and 2. Heads is "1" and Tails is "2".

Line 60 has an ON-GOTO test sending $X=1$ to line 90 where the "Heads" are counted, and $X=2$ to line 110 where the "Tails" are counted.

Lines 70 and 80 are used as default lines. If $X=$ other than 1 or 2, the error message will be PRINTed and execution will END. It will never happen, but we are insisting on proof.

Line 9Ø sets up H as a counter. Each time the ON-GOTO test sends control to this line because X=1, H is incremented by one and keeps count of the "Heads".

Line 1ØØ sends control to line 12Ø where only the first statement, NEXT N, is executed. When the N Loop has gone through all "F" number of passes, control moves on to line 13Ø. Until then, the NEXT N sends it back to line 4Ø.

Line 5Ø generates another RaNDom number (1 or 2). If the next X = 2. . .

Line 6Ø sends control to line 11Ø.

Line 11Ø keeps track of the "Tails".

Line 12Ø passes control to line 13Ø when the last "N" is "used up".

Line 13Ø PRINTs the Headings.

Line 14Ø PRINTs the values of H, T and F.

Line 15Ø calculates and PRINTs the percentage of heads, and percentage of tails.

SAVE this program as COINTOSS.

More Than One Generator At A Time

It is possible to generate more than one random number by using more than one generator in a program. This has special value when the ranges of the generators are different, but is helpful even if their ranges are the same.

It could also be done with a single generator, but that wouldn't make our point — would it!?

To make the point, we will create a computer game of "Craps" — where two dice are "rolled". Each "die" has six sides, each side having 1,2,3,4,5 or 6 dots, respectively. When the two dice are rolled, the number of dots showing on their top sides are added. That sum is important to the game. Obviously, the lowest number that can be rolled is 2, and the highest number is 12. We will set up a separate Random Number Generator for each die, give each a range from 1 to 6, and call them die "A" and die "B".

Type NEW, then the following:

```
50  A=RND(6)
60  B=RND(6)
70  N=A+B
80  PRINT N
```

. . .RUN a few times to get the idea.

As we see, each number PRINTed falls between 2 and 12. We only need to PRINT N since the dice are always both thrown at the same time, and only the *sum* of the two is of interest here.

Why would the following be wrong?

```
50  PRINT RND(11) + 1
```

Answer: Adding random numbers created by two generators, each picking numbers between 1 and 6 will create many more sums which equal 3,4,5,6,7,8,9,10 and 11 than a single generator which picks an equal amount of numbers 1 through 11 (to which we add 1, to make the range 2 through 12).

Rules Of The Game

In its simplest form, the game goes like this:

1. The player rolls the two dice. If he rolls a sum of 2 (called "snake eyes"), a 3 ("cock-eyes"), or a 12 ("boxcars") on the first roll, he loses and the game is over. That's "craps".

2. If the player rolls 7 or 11 on the first throw (called "a natural"), he wins and the game is over.

3. If any other number is rolled, it becomes the player's "point". He must keep rolling until he either "makes his point" by getting the same number again to win, or rolls a 7, and loses.

> *EXERCISE 18-1:* You already know far more than enough to complete this program. Do it. Put in all the tests, PRINT lines, etc. to meet the rules of the game and tell the player what is going on. It will take you awhile to finish, but give it your best before you turn over to Section C (User's Programs) under CRAPS for a sample solution. Gook luck!

RaNDom numbers are unpredictable; properly functioning computers are not. So how do we get RaNDom numbers out of our computer? We don't. We get *pseudo-RaNDom* numbers. Each time we use the RND function, the computer uses an internal "seed number" to produce the desired RaNDom number.

This is neither the time nor the place to get technical, so we'll give the following tip without further explanation:

When you're running game programs using RND, it's a good idea to set the seed to an unpredictable value. This will ensure that you don't get the same pseudo-RaNDom number sequence each time you turn on the computer and play the game. Put the following line at the beginning of your program where it will be executed only *once*:

```
1 RANDOM
```

Learned in Chapter 18

Statements	Functions	Miscellaneous
RANDOM	RND($\emptyset$) for RANDOM numbers greater than $\emptyset$ and less than 1	RANDOM vs Pseudo-RANDOM
	RND(X) for RANDOM numbers from 1 to X	Seed Numbers

READing Data

So far, we have learned how to enter numbers into our programs by two different methods. The first is by building the values right into the program:

```
10 A = 5
```

The second is by using an INPUT statement to enter a number through the keyboard:

```
10 INPUT A
```

The third principal way is through the DATA statement.

Enter this NEW program:

```
10 DATA 1,2,3,4,5
20 READ A,B,C,D,E
30 PRINT A;B;C;D;E
```

. . .and RUN.

The DATA statement is in some ways similar to the first method in that a DATA line is part of the program. It's different, however, since each DATA line can contain many numbers, or pieces of data, each separated by a comma. Each piece of DATA must be read by a READ statement. Each READ statement can READ a number of pieces of DATA if each variable letter is separated by a comma.

The display shows that all five pieces of DATA in line 1Ø, the numbers 1,2,3,4 and 5 were READ by line 2Ø, assigned the letters A through E, and PRINTed by line 3Ø.

Keep in mind this important distinction: DATA lines can be read *only* by READ statements. If more than one piece of DATA is placed on a DATA line, they must be separated by commas. INPUT statements are used to enter data from the keyboard.

DATA lines are always read from left to right by READ statements; the first DATA line first (when there is more than one), and *it does not matter where they are in the program.* This may seem startling, but do the following and you will see:

1. Move the DATA line from line 1Ø to line 25 and RUN. No change in the PRINTout, right?

2. Move the DATA line from line 25 to line 1ØØØØ. Same thing — no change in the PRINTout.

Data lines can be placed anywhere in the program.

This fact leads different programmers to use different styles. Some place all DATA lines at the beginning of a program so they can be read first in a LIST and found quickly so data may be changed.

Others place all DATA lines at a program's END where they are out of the way and there are more line numbers available to keep adding DATA lines as the need arises. Still others scatter the DATA lines throughout the program next to the READ lines which bring that DATA into use. The style we use is of little consequence — *but consistency is comfortable.*

The Plot Thickens

Since we now know all about FOR-NEXT loops, let us see what happens when a DATA line is placed in the middle of a loop. Erase the old program with NEW and type in this program:

```
10  DATA 1,2,3,4,5
20   FOR N = 1 TO 5
30     READ A
40     PRINT A;
50   NEXT N
```

. . .and RUN.

That DATA line started outside the loop. Now move it to line 25 and RUN. What happened?

Nothing different! It is important to absorb this fact or we wouldn't have gone to the trouble to do it. Note that as we went through the N loop five times, we READ the letter A, and the PRINT statement only PRINTed A, but A's value was different each time. Its value was the same as the value it last READ from the DATA line.

The reason — each piece of DATA in a DATA line can only be READ *once* each time the program is RUN. The next time a READ statement requests a piece of DATA, it will read the NEXT piece of data in the DATA line, or, if that line is all used up, move on to the next DATA line.

Change line 2Ø in the program to read:

```
20 FOR N = 1 TO 6
```

. . .and RUN.

We, of course, told the READ statement to READ a total of six pieces of DATA but there were only five. An error statement caught us, as the screen shows:

```
1 2 3 4 5
```

```
?OD Error In 30     (OD = Out of Data.)
```

Now change line 2Ø so the number of READs is *less* than the DATA available.

```
20 FOR N = 1 TO 4
```

. . .and RUN.

The program ran just fine as long as we didn't try to use more than the available DATA. The point is, each piece of DATA in a DATA statement can only be READ once during each RUN.

Exceptions, Exceptions!

Because it is sometimes necessary to READ the same DATA more than once without having to RUN the complete program over, a statement called RESTORE is available. Whenever the program comes across a RESTORE, all DATA lines are RESTOREd to their original "unread" condition, both those that have been READ and those that have not, and all are available for READing again, starting with the first piece in the first DATA line.

Change line 2∅ back to:

```
20 FOR N = A TO 5
```

and insert:

```
35 RESTORE
```

. . .and RUN.

Oh-oh! The screen PRINTs five l's instead of 12345. Can you figure out why?

Line 3∅ READ A as 1, but line 35 immediately RESTOREd the DATA line to its *original unREAD condition*. When the FOR-NEXT loop brought the READ line around for the next pass it again read the first piece of data, which was that same 1. Same thing with all successive passes.

READ and DATA statements are extremely common. The RESTORE statement is used less often.

String Variables

Who knows where some of these seemingly unrelated words come from? If they weren't so important we could ignore them. We have been using the letters A through Z to indicate numbers. They are called *numeric variables*. We can use the same 26 letters to indicate *string variables* by just adding a "$".

A$, for example, is called "A String". String variables can be assigned to indicate *letters, words* and/or *combinations* of letters, numbers and spaces. Type NEW, then type in:

```
10 INPUT "WHAT IS YOUR NAME";A$
20 PRINT "HELLO THERE, ";A$
```

   . . .and RUN.

Hey-hey! How's that for a grabber? If that, along with what we have learned in earlier chapters doesn't make the creative juices flow, nothing will.

That's Two. . .

We now know two ways to PRINT words. The first, learned long ago, is to imbed words in PRINT statements (and is called "PRINTing a string"). The second is to bring word(s) through an INPUT statement (called "INPUT ing a string"). If you can't think of the third way, go back and check the title heading at the top of this chapter.

Ah yes, brilliant student! Ahem . . .*(Reading a string)*.

Change the program to read:

```
10 READ A$
20 DATA RADIO SHACK TRS-80
30 PRINT "SEE MY FOXY";A$
```

   . . .and RUN.

```
SEE MY FOXY RADIO SHACK TRS-80.
```

Let's use two string variables to accomplish the same thing, seeing how they work with each other. Reword the program to:

```
10 READ A$
```

```
15 READ B$
2Ø DATA RADIO SHACK, TRS-8Ø
3Ø PRINT "SEE MY FOXY ";A$;" ";B$
```

Analyzing the program:

Line 2Ø contains two data items, separated by a comma.

Line 1Ø READs the first one.

Line 15 READs the second one.

Line 3Ø contains four PRINT expressions.

The first one PRINTs "SEE MY FOXY", leaving a space behind the "Y" since string variables always RUN letters together, which allows us the option of inserting our own spaces.

The second PRINT is A$, RADIO SHACK.

The third PRINT inserts the space which is enclosed in quotes.

The fourth PRINT is TRS-80.

Together, they PRINT the entire message.

In other words, a semicolon between STRING variables does *not* cause a space to be PRINTed between them. We have to insert a space using " " marks.

Learned in Chapter 19

Statements

READ
DATA
RESTORE

Miscellaneous

String Variables A$, B$, etc.
Numeric Variables

Part III

Strings

"THIS NEXT PART IS VERY IMPORTANT IT CAN CHANGE YOUR COMPUTER INTO AN OBEDIENT GIANT OR A MALEVOLENT MONSTER..."
"DO YOU SUPPOSE I COULD HAVE A COPY OF THE MALEVOLENT MONSTER PROGRAM?"
Rich Berner

Intermediate BASIC

Intermediate Features Of *TRS-80 BASIC*

Now that we've learned "Elementary" BASIC we can get serious about "Intermediate" BASIC. The next chapter is sort of a "catch up" and "catch all", showing a lot of little features that didn't find a convenient home in the previous chapters. Study each of them, do the sample programs and think about them. Each one is brief, but important.

Multiple Statement Lines: (Now he tells us!)

BASIC allows us to put more than one statement on each numbered line, separating them by a colon (:). For example, a timer loop such as:

```
100 FOR N = 1 TO 500
110 NEXT N
```

becomes . . .

```
100 FOR N = 1 TO 500 : NEXT N
```

Caveat Emptor (Don't buy a used computer from a stranger.)

Control yourself! It's easy to get carried away. While we will be using multiple statement lines often, from here on, we will quickly see that it's possible to pack the information so tightly it becomes hard to read, and also very hard to modify.

More Caveat (or is it more Emptor?)

Multiple statement lines require careful understanding. Especially critical are statements of the IF-THEN variety.

Enter the following program:

```
10  INPUT "TYPE IN A NUMBER";X
20  IF X = 3 THEN 50 : GOTO 70
30  PRINT "HOW DID YOU GET HERE?"
40   END
50   PRINT "X = 3"
60 END
70 PRINT "CAN'T GET FROM THERE TO HERE."
```

. . .and RUN it a number of times with different INPUT values.

Line 20 has an error in logic. If the test in the first statement in the line passes, control branches off to line 50. That's OK. If the test fails, however, control drops to the next line in the program — line 30. There is no way the second statement in line 20 (GOTO 70) can ever be executed.

The Message: *If* we put an IF-THEN (or ON-GOTO) type test in a multiple statement line, it must be the *last* statement in that line.

Next Message: We cannot send control to any point in a multiple statement line except to its first statement. Look at line 20. There is no way to address the GOTO 70 portion. It shares the same line number as the first statement in the same line. Only the first statement is addressable by a GOTO or IF-THEN. Others in the line are accessed in sequence, IF the prior tests are passed.

Variable Names

We know we can use the 26 letters of the alphabet as names for variables. We can also use the numbers 0 through 9 in conjunction with these letters:

```
A3 = 65

F9 = 37

        etc.
```

Although the 26 letter variables are usually enough, addition of the numbers give us an additional 26 * 10 = 260. They can be very handy, particularly if we want to label a number of "sub" variables (D1,D2,D3,etc.) which combine to make a grand total which we can just call D.

In addition, we can use *almost* any two-letter combination for a name. For example:

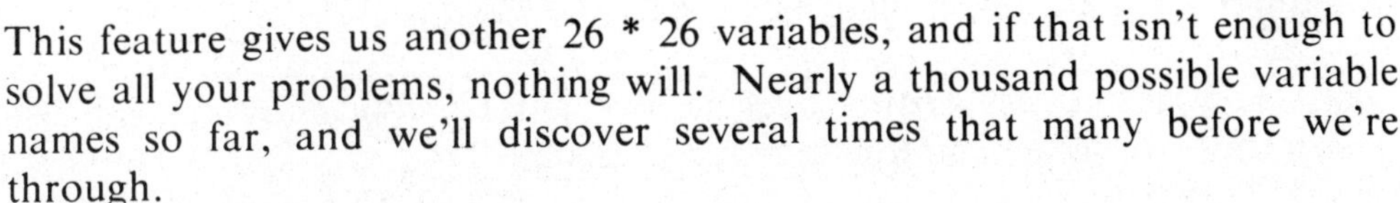


```
PI = 3.14159

C = PI*D   Circumference = 3.14159 * Diameter
```

(Now that really looks valuable.)

This feature gives us another 26 * 26 variables, and if that isn't enough to solve all your problems, nothing will. Nearly a thousand possible variable names so far, and we'll discover several times that many before we're through.

Enter this program and RUN, watching for an error message:

```
1 CLS : PRINT
10 RATE = 55
20 TIME = 3
30 DISTANCE = RATE * TIME
40 PRINT RATE, TIME, DISTANCE
90 PRINT : LIST
```

Did you see how cleverly we can use LIST in the program so after the RUN it LISTs itself?

?SN got us in line 3Ø. Is the word DISTANCE too long? Let's cut it back to DISTA and RUN again.

OK, that got us past line 3Ø, but the same problem exists in 4Ø. Cut DISTANCE back to DISTA and try again.

That's more like it. Looks pretty good doesn't it? We can actually use words to name our variables. Add this line and RUN:

```
35 DIME = 10
```

Another SN error? What's wrong with DIME?

It just so happens that the word DIM (dimension) is only one of a mess of "reserved" words, and we can't use them in variable names for obvious reasons. DIM is the first 3 letters of DIME. The problem with DISTANCE in line 3Ø wasn't length, as we suspected (words can be hundreds of characters long). It contained TAN, another reserved word. Ah, so!

Many of the reserved words in Appendix F are not reserved for regular TRS-80 BASIC, but for "Advanced" BASIC as used with the DISK system. The result is the same — we can't use them. (Better take a look now at Appendix F. . .there's big trouble ahead if you don't.)

Okay, how about just cutting back to two letters. We know we can use *almost* any two-letter combination for a name. Try: ON TO IF and OR (won't work).

Now try:

```
35 DI = 10
```

. . .and RUN.

It ran, but look at the answer! Our variable DISTA was printed with a value of 1Ø instead of 165. What happened? DISTA surely can't be the same as DI. Well, it might look different but the computer only sees the first two letters of any variable, and they *are* the same. The DI in line 35 gave the DI in DISTA a new value.

The lesson here should be pretty clear. It's very easy to get all carried away with fancy variable names and, in the process, find lots of trouble. Remember KISS? (Keep It Simple, Stupid!)

New String Variables

So far we've used only A$ and B$ as string variables. We actually have *all* the letters of the alphabet available for strings. And the numbers 0 through 9 too, plus any two-letter combination. These are valid string names:

```
X$

D8$

Pi$

WHATAGREATBOOK$
```

    etc.

Almost another thousand variable names.

Shorthand

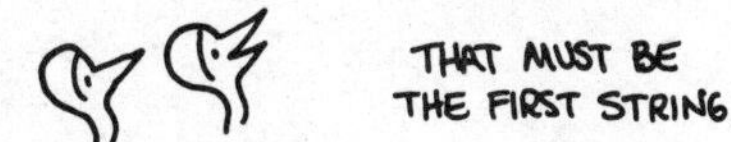

There are several little "shorthand" tricks we can use.

The first is the use of ? in place of the very common word PRINT. Type NEW, then this line:

```
10 ?"QUESTION MARK"
```

    . . .and LIST it.

Awwk! The pumpkin turned into a coach. The computer rewrote it as:

```
10 PRINT"QUESTION MARK"
```

It also works at the command level. Try:

```
?3*4.
```

    and we get

12

If you have the numeric keypad you'll especially appreciate this feature since the same upper-case characters are available above the pad numbers as above the keyboard ones. They just aren't marked. Try it.

The value of this is that a touch typist can type ? (for PRINT) and " with the right hand by hitting the number 2, while the left hand holds down the left SHIFT .key, considerably speeding up the typing of PRINT lines.

The ' is shorthand for REM, and is especially nice when documenting the purpose of a line. It makes program lines into multiple statement lines. ' is the same as :REM.

```
50 X = Z*C/4 + 33   ' THE SECRET EQUATION
```

The only place ' can't be used unaided is in a DATA line, and that problem can be overcome by actually adding a : to the DATA line. See lines 1000 and 1010 in this program.

```
10 REM   * SEVERE WEATHER ALERT SYMBOL AS SEEN ON KTIV-TV *
20               ' H = HORIZONTAL STARTING POSITION
30               ' V = VERTICAL STARTING POSITION
40 CLS           ' N = NUMBER OF VERTICAL BLOCKS TO BE SET
50 READ H,V,N  :   V1 = V ' READ DATA & STORE V FOR RECALL
60 IF N = 0 GOTO 60       ' LOCKING LOOP WHEN OUT OF DATA
70   FOR H = H TO H+2     ' 3 PASSES FOR TRIPLE BLOCK WIDTH
80     FOR V = V TO V+N-1 ' COUNTS PRINTING OF N BLOCKS
90       SET(H,V): NEXT V ' SETS LIGHT BLOCKS AND CLOSES LOOP
100 V=V1 : NEXT H : GOTO 50 'RESETS V TO DATA LINE VALUE
1000 DATA 102,3,9,105,10,1,108,7,3,111,6,1:'DATA IS IN
1010 DATA 114,7,3,117,10,1,120,3,9,0,0,0:'H,V,N  ORDER
```

The Period . is of minimal value as a BASIC shorthand feature, but *if* you've just typed a new line, LISTed one, or edited one, you can repeat it without typing its number:

```
90 REM TEST LINE      ENTER
```

then type:

```
LIST.
```

and line 9Ø will be LISTed. This works even *if* the program has been RUN, which can be an aid in troubleshooting a line without writing down its number. It also works with a line that keeps popping up due to an error message.

The [ENTER] Key

If you're the very observant type, you will have noticed that program execution begins when the [ENTER] key is *pressed*, not when it's released.

Special Keys

The keyboard is pretty self-explanatory, but there are several keys:

[→] is used as a preset TAB. Go ahead and press it a few times. It TABs over in increments of 8 spaces, starting with Ø, following a Ø, 8, 16, etc. sequence. It is helpful when typing a program containing nested FOR-NEXT loops.

A [SHIFT] [→] converts the screen display from 64 characters to 32 characters. Try it. The [CLEAR] Key clears the screen and returns it to 64 characters per line.

[←] is for people who change their mind a lot. You've already used it for correcting errors, one at a time. By pressing the [SHIFT] key at the same time, you can wipe out the entire line just typed.

[BACKSPACE] on Model II.

[↑] is used with [SHIFT] in EDITing to end the INSert mode.

[ESC] on Model II.

[↓] is also called the "Linefeed". It moves the cursor down to the next line.

Use Of Quotes and Semicolons

Technically, it is not necessary to use quotes to close off many PRINT statements.

```
10 PRINT"WHERE IS THE END QUOTE?
```

RUNs just fine. Leave it off at your own peril.

Also, semicolons are not absolutely necessary to separate a TAB number and the opening quote marks:

```
10 PRINTTAB(10) "OOPS, WE MISSED A SEMICOLON"
```

RUNs just fine. Leave it off at your own peril.

A BASIC interpreter that is "too forgiving" is like an airplane that is "too forgiving". It allows us to become sloppy, and when we really need all the skill we can muster, it is gone from the lack of practice imposed by its discipline. You are strongly encouraged *not* to take these and other "cheap" short-cuts.

INPUT

When INPUTing several variables in a single INPUT line, if we fail to input them all separated by commas, the special prompt ?? alerts us to the fact that more DATA must be INPUT. Type this program and enter only one number at a time, followed by `ENTER`. Watch for the ??:

```
10 INPUT A,B,C
```

    . . .and RUN.

RUN again, this time typing all three numbers separated by commas. It should "swallow"them all in one gulp.

RUN again and try to INPUT a letter instead of a number. It responds with:

```
?REDO
```

There is extensive information in Appendix H dealing with Error Messages. *Redo* reminds us that we can't INPUT a string variable into a request for a numeric one.

Optional NEXT

FOR-NEXT loops don't always have to specify which FOR we are NEXT-ing. This can be useful when the loops are nested.

Type this NEW program:

```
10 FOR N = 1 TO 5 : PRINT N
20   FOR Q = 1 TO 3 : PRINT ,Q
30      FOR R = 1 TO 4 : PRINT ,,R
40 NEXT : NEXT : NEXT
```

RUN it several times to get the flavor. Note how commas were used to place PRINTing in the zones we want.

This method of NEXTing should not be used *if* the program contains tests which might allow a loop to be broken out of. Better, then, to be specific, as we've already learned, or use this little short-cut:

```
40 NEXT R,Q,N
```

IF-THEN-ELSE

ELSE is an interesting addition to our stable of conditional branching state-ments. It allows us an option other than dropping to the next line *if* a test fails. Try this one:

```
1  CLS : PRINT
10 INPUT "ENTER A NUMBER";N
20 IF N=0 PRINT "ZERO" ELSE PRINT "NOT ZERO"
30 PRINT : LIST
```

. . .and RUN.

POS (N)

A new and sometimes useful statement allows the computer to report back the position of the cursor.

This simple program tells all:

```
1 CLS : PRINT
10 INPUT"ENTER A NUMBER BETWEEN -10 AND 53";A
20 PRINT TAB(10 + A)
30 PRINT POS(N)
40 PRINT"WAS THE NUMBER OF THE NEXT PRINT POSITION"
90 PRINT : LIST
```

. . .and RUN.

Line 30 is the key one, containing POS. The N inside brackets is just a "dummy". Most any other variable would work as well — but something has to be placed there. POS reports back any cursor position up through 53. Numbers beyond that start over again with zero, as you will see if you INPUT a number larger than 53.

255 Characters per line

TRS-80 BASIC permits up to 255 characters in a single program line — four screen widths of 634 characters each. (Don't ask me to degug such a line!)

Learned in Chapter 20

Statements	Functions	Miscellaneous
IF-THEN-ELSE	POS (N)	Multiple Statement Lines
		Variable Names
		Some Shorthand
		Special Keys
		TABbing
		Quotes and Semicolons
		Multiple INPUTing
		Optional NEXT

The EDITor — Second Semester

You could probably live happily ever after thinking you were in fat city with what you learned in the previous chapter, but the EDITor has a number of other features which are handy to use when the occasion arises. One which will certainly arise is typified by the following lines. Erase the memory and type:

```
10 PRIMT "THAT ISN'T HOW YOU SPELL PRINT"
```

NOTE: PRIMT is deliberately misspelled.

. . .and RUN.

```
?SN Error in 10
READY
10
```

This means there is a syntax error in line 1Ø. The computer is telling us *"what? — I don't understand what you are saying"*. It *automatically* puts us in the EDITor mode at the line which contains the error. This always happens when there is a syntax error. (More on Syntax and other errors in later chapters.) Meanwhile, proceed normally by typing:

L   to LIST the line

SM   to find the first M

CN   to CHANGE it to an N

L   to LIST for final look

`ENTER`   to return to BASIC

While we're at it, let's examine another simple but sometimes troublesome point. Let's go back into EDIT and find the first P in the program.

EDIT 1Ø `ENTER`

1Ø ▪

SP

what happened . . .?

Isn't the first P in the word PRINT? Yes, but when the computer starts out in the EDIT mode, the cursor positions itself in place of the *first letter* of the *first word*, so it was *already* at the first P. Our SP searched out the NEXT P, which was in SPELL. Now you know. Hit `ENTER` to get out of the EDITor.

There is a third and often convenient way to enter the EDIT mode, particularly when experimenting. . .switching back and forth from BASIC to EDIT, then back to BASIC again to test some programming change.

For example, we just EDITed line 1Ø. To enter EDIT1Ø again, simply type:

EDIT.   (note the period)

Try it.

EDIT followed by a period is just an abbreviation for EDIT followed by the line number *of the line last EDITed*. Obviously, if we didn't recently EDIT a line, this feature has no meaning.

On some early TRS-80's the EDIT (.) feature is a bit squirrelly.

Q   Is For Quit (Without Changes)

We know that whenever we type RUN, all values are initialized to zero, but hold their last value *after* the RUN. It turns out that whenever we do an EDIT, the values are also reset to zero. This can be a disadvantage if we are in the process of troubleshooting and are automatically thrown into EDIT by a syntax error. Let's enter this short program to demonstrate the point:

```
10 T = T + 1
20 PRIMT T
```

RUN the program and let it crash.

```
?SN Error in 20
```

Don't make any changes in line 20 at this time, but just exit the EDITor by hitting ENTER .

Check the value of T in memory by typing:

```
PRINT T
```

at the command level. $\emptyset$ is the value indicating T has been reset to $\emptyset$.

RUN the program again, crashing it again, but this time exit the EDITor by typing a simple:

Q   which stands for "quit without changes".

Then

```
PRINT T
```
shows its value to be

```
1
```

This may not really be all that profound, but if you're chasing a real ornery bug and want to check the values of the variables before doing any EDITing, Q is the way to do it. A fast

EDIT.

will bring back the EDITor at the offending line without our even having to write down its number or having to remember it.

Q also lets us escape from EDIT if we change our mind and don't really want to make those changes we already did.

E   Is For END and EXIT

E is the opposite of Q. When we are satisfied with the changes, type E and we're back in BASIC. E does the same thing as hitting⟨ENTER⟩, but without printing the remainder of the line.

A   Is For ABORT

If after making some changes via the EDITor and looking at them with an L you decide you don't want to make them, type an A. The changes, regardless of how drastic, are not final until we exit the EDITor, and A will kick them all out and let us start over again. Type L, following the A, to see what the original line looks like again. Now type:

EDIT 20

and change the M to an N. Type A and then L to get the feel for it. If you enter INSert as part of an EDIT, be sure to exit it first with a ⟨SHIFT⟩ ⟨↑⟩ or the AL won't work.

K   Is For KILL

K is a combination of SEARCH and DELETE, starting with the *beginning* of the line. Type:

EDIT 20

then

KT

then

LL

to see what happened.

It KILLED everything up to (but not including) the first T. "Take it all back" by typing an A, then L, then try:

2KT

then

LL

and see that everything up to the second T was KILLED.

AL

takes it all back.

H   Is For HACK

HACK is sort of the mirror image of KILL in that it DELETEs everything from the cursor *to the end* of the line. It just "hacks" off the end of the line, without showing it on the screen, *and* goes into the INSert mode. Nice if you need it, and great for "hackers".

If you don't need to go into the INSert mode, the old traditional "99D", meaning DELETE the next 99 characters (which is usually more than enough to erase the rest of the line), is the best approach.

To implement HACK, SEARCH for the starting point, then H off the end of the line, and type the new ending in its place.

X   Is To EXTEND

Suppose we wanted to go to the end of a line and add some more to it — to extend it. We can type X which also throws the EDITor into INSert. X is a one-step replacement for:

S   which searches for the carriage return.

I   puts EDITor into INSert

Give it a try on one of the program lines . . .

THAT'S — 3$\emptyset$ —

With steady but persistent practice, you will become very skillful at using the EDITor. It will in turn reward you handsomely with great savings in time and frustration.

Model II users can use the EDITing features in the immediate mode when entering a command or new line. While entering any line, press:

F1

The screen will show:

!

indicating that we are now in EDIT mode. Modify the line using any of the previously covered EDITing commands.

EXERCISE 21-1: Use the editor to change:

```
1Ø PRINT I : FOR I = 1 TO 1Ø : PRINT
```

to:

```
1Ø FOR I = 1 TO 1Ø : PRINT I * I : NEXT I
```

Learned in Chapter 21

Commands	Miscellaneous
EDIT	More EDITing features

The ASCII Set

The purpose of this chapter is to learn how to use ASC and CHR$. Before doing so, however, we must learn about something called "the ASCII set". (No, they're not like the "horsey set".)

ASCII is pronounced *ASK'-EE* and it stands for American Standard Code for Information Interchange. Since a computer stores and processes only numbers, not letters or punctuation, it's important that there be some sort of uniform system to specify which numbers represent which letters and symbols. The ASCII Chart in Appendix B shows the relationship between the number system and symbols as used in your TRS-80.

Type this program into your computer:

```
10 FOR N = 32 TO 255
20 PRINT "ASCII NUMBER";N;
30 PRINT "STANDS FOR ",CHR$(N)
40 FOR T = 1 TO 500 : NEXT T
50 NEXT N
```

As you RUN it, observe that the characters between ASCII code numbers 32 and 191 are printed on the screen. Those numbers from 97 to 122 are just lower case duplicates of numbers 65 to 90, but the unmodified Model I TRS-80 prints only upper case. Numbers 128 to 191 are special graphic characters.

If you end up in the Big House serving time for computer fraud, the following little program will make up your license plate combinations, putting CHR$ to good use.

Enter:

```
1 CLS
10 REM * LICENSE PLATE NUMBER GENERATOR *
20 FOR N=1 TO 3 : PRINT RND(10)-1;
30 NEXT N : PRINT " ";
40 FOR N=1 TO 3 : PRINT CHR$(RND(26)+64);
50 PRINT " "; : NEXT N : PRINT, : GOTO 20
```

. . .and RUN.

The RND generator in line 40 spits out numbers between 1 and 26. We add 64 to each number to make the sum fall in the range between 65 and 90. What do we see on the ASCII conversion chart between 65 and 90. Hmm???

ASCII code numbers between 0 and 31 are used for special control purposes in the TRS-80:

Models I & III

Code	Function
0-7	None
8	Backspaces and erases current character
9	TAB(0,8,16,24,. . .)
10-13	Carriage return
14	Turns on cursor
15	Turns off cursor
16-20	None
21	Swap space compression/Special characters
22	Swap special/alternate characters
23	Converts to 32 character mode
24	Backspace cursor
25	Advance cursor
26	Downward linefeed
27	Upward linefeed
28	Home, return cursor to display position (0,0)
29	Move cursor to beginning of line
30	Erases to the end of the line
31	Clear to the end of the frame

Model II/16

00	
01	Turns on blinking cursor
02	Turns off cursor
03	
04	Turns on steady cursor
05	
06	
07	
08	
09	Backspaces cursor and erases character
10	Advances cursor to next 8-character boundary
11	Line feed
12	
13	Carriage return
14	
15	
16	
17	
18	
19	
20	
21	
22	
23	Erases to end of line
24	Erases to end of screen
25	Sets white-on-black mode
26	Sets black-on-white mode
27	Clears screen, homes cursor
28	Moves cursor back
29	Moves cursor forward
30	Sets 80-character mode and clears Display
31	Sets 40-character mode and clears Display

Note: Model II users skip to "So What Is CHR$(N)?"

The Code numbers between 128 and 191 are for graphic characters, nearly all of which are irrelevant for the ordinary computer user. SET, RESET and POINT serve most everyday graphic needs, and will be learned in Part V.

The ASCII numbers between 192 and 255 are so-called "Space Compression Codes". We can use them to insert from 0 to 63 blank spaces in a printed line. Code 192 stands for 0 spaces and 255 stands for 63 spaces. The in-between numbers correspond. Erase the memory and RUN this program:

```
10 PRINT"HELLO OUT";CHR$(222);"THERE"
```

    . . .and RUN.

CHR$(222) inserted 30 blanks, or "TABbed over" 30 spaces between OUT and THERE. To see the difference between using these ASCII code numbers and using TAB, add this line:

```
20 PRINT"HELLO OUT";TAB(30);"THERE"
```

    . . .and RUN.

TAB spaces from the *beginning* of the line, while this series of ASCII numbers inserts spaces from the *last PRINT* position in the line.

There is, in practice, little international uniformity (or even inside the U.S.) in the use of ASCII code numbers other than those used for just letters and numbers. Fortunately, that is sufficient for most of our everyday needs. If you contemplate the problems faced by the Japanese, Europeans and others who need special letters and characters, you will get some idea of how these numbers between 127 and 255 can be put to good use.

EXERCISE 22-1: Write a program using a FOR-NEXT loop that will print the words "SPACE" and "COMPRESSION" 64 times. Each time the words are printed, insert an additional space between the two.

Yup. We are in full control of these higher order ASCII codes. *Today the TRS-80, tomorrow the world!*

So What Is CHR$(N)?

We have used CHR$ freely so far without describing it, but you undoubtedly figured it out anyway. CHR$(N) produces the ASCII character (or control action) specified by the code *number* N. It is a one-way converter from the ASCII CODE to the ASCII *character*, and allows us to throw characters around with the ease of throwing around numbers.

Enter this simple program:

```
10  INPUT "TYPE ANY NUMBER BETWEEN 33 AND 127";N
20  PRINT CHR$(N)
30  RUN
```

. . .and RUN.

Almost all of our activity with ASCII numbers will be confined to this range. However, these "quickie" programs show how to use several ASCII numbers that stand for *actions* instead of numbers, letters or characters. Give them a try:

For Model I users *only*:

```
10 REM * CURSOR BLINKER *
20 PRINT CHR$(14)
30 FOR N=1 TO 500 : NEXT N
40 PRINT CHR$(15) ;
50 FOR N=1 TO 500 : NEXT N
60 GOTO 20
```

For Everyone:

```
1 REM * DOUBLE WIDTH DEMO *
10 CLS
20 PRINT CHR$(23)
```

Model II use CHR$(31)

```
30  PRINT "HELLO OUT THERE"
40  FOR X=1 TO 500 : NEXT X
50  PRINT CHR$(28)
60  FOR X=1 TO 500 : NEXT X
70  GOTO 20
```

Model II use CHR$(30)

> *EXERCISE 22-2:* Use the ASCII chart (Appendix B) and the CHR$ function to print TRS-80.

What Then Is ASC($)?

ASC is the exact opposite of CHR$(N). ASC is a one-way converter from the ASCII *character* to its corresponding ASCII *number*.

Type:

```
10  INPUT "TYPE ALMOST ANY LETTER, NUMBER, OR CHARACTER";A$
20  PRINT"ITS ASCII NUMBER IS";ASC(A$)
30  PRINT
40  GOTO 10
```

It will print the ASCII number of almost all characters. (I don't have any idea why some TRS-80's don't work with ,": but then, strings can be a real mystery at times, as we will see.)

The second way to use ASC is to imbed the character within quotes, thus:

```
10  PRINT ASC("A")
```

This latter method isn't always convenient.

Before we can really understand what we are doing, we must learn a lot more about strings. Before we could learn about strings we had to learn something about ASCII. It's like "Catch Chapter 22".

Model III Special Character Sets

Both the Model I and Model III computers use ASCII codes 192 — 255 as Space Compression Codes. Since these characters are used rather infrequently, Tandy incorporated two alternate sets of characters that can be used in place of the space compression characters. This can be a bit confusing since the ASCII number 255, for example, can represent any of three different characters.

Note: Model I and II users should skip to the next chapter.

The controls can be mastered if we keep a level head.

When the computer is first turned on, ASCII codes 192 - 255 give us space compression codes. By printing ASCII code 21, we change the space compression codes into a set of special characters.

Enter this program:

```
10 PRINT CHR$(21)
20 FOR N=192 TO 255
30 PRINT "ASCII NUMBER ";N;
40 PRINT "STANDS FOR",CHR$(N)
50 FOR T = 1 TO 500 : NEXT T
60 NEXT N
```

    . . .and RUN.

Reduce 5ØØ in the FOR-NEXT loop if you want to speed things up.

How 'bout that? The last time we looked at ASCII codes 192 to 255 we saw space. (Can one really see space?)

RUN the program again and notice we are switched back in the space compression mode again. The computer stays in the last mode until it receives another CHR$(21).

RUN the program a few times until you are convinced, then stop with the special character set displayed on the screen. Pay attention, we don't want anyone getting lost.

Now, try this program:

```
NEW
10 CLS : PRINT CHR$(23)
30 FOR I=192 TO 255
40 PRINT I; CHR$(I)
50 NEXT I
```

Look out PAC-MAN! Just imagine all the special applications for these characters. We have playing card suits, Greek letters, a few math symbols, faces, and even a rocket ship.

CHR$(23) in line 10 set the screen to double-width so that we can get a better look at them.

Add this line:

```
20 PRINT CHR$(22)
```

. . .and RUN.

Does this madness ever end? Not only does the computer have special characters, it also has an alternate set of special characters. This time we're looking at Japanese Kana characters.

What do you suppose would happen if we ran the program again? Try it.

Oh, each time it sees CHR$(22), it switches between these special characters. CHR$(22) can also switch characters in the immediate mode.

Type:

```
PRINT CHR$(22)   ENTER
```

As long as the characters are displayed on the screen, CHR$(22) will change character modes. "Toggle" back and forth until you have the special characters displayed.

Let's finish with this last message:

```
NEW
10 CLS : PRINT CHR$(23)
20 PRINT "TIME TO MOVE ON"
30 PRINT CHR$(196);" ";CHR$(244);CHR$(245);CHR$(246)
```

. . .and RUN.

If the message didn't make sense, type:

```
PRINT CHR$(22)    [ENTER]
```

> *EXERCISE 22-3:* Input a single character from the keyboard and test its ASCII value to determine if it is a number. If not, return program control to the INPUT statement. Hint: Use two IF statements and ASC.

Learned in Chapter 22

Functions

CHR$

ASC

Miscellaneous

ASCII Codes

Model III Special
Characters and Kana
Characters

Strings In General

It was not our intention to "string you along" in the previous chapter, but we really can't understand how strings work without first understanding the ASCII concept of numbers standing for letters, numbers and other characters and controls.

Comparing Strings

One of the most powerful string handling capabilities is the ability to *compare* them. We compare the numbers between *numeric* variables all the time. How can we compare *strings* of letters or words? Well, why do you suppose we put the ASCII Chapter just before this one? *Right!* The computer can compare the ASCII *code numbers* of letters and other characters. The effective result is a comparison of what's in the corresponding strings.

Type in this NEW program:

```
1 CLS
10 INPUT"WHAT IS YOUR NAME";A$
20 IF A$ = "ISHKIBIBBLE" THEN 50
30 PRINT"SORRY. YOUR NAME ISN'T ISHKIBIBBLE!"
40 END
50 PRINT"IT'S ABOUT TIME. FORGET HOW TO SPELL YOUR NAME?"
```

. . .and RUN, using your name, then ISHKIBIBBLE.

If the computer can compare *that* name it should be able to compare anything!

During the process of comparing what we enter as A$ in line 1∅ to what's already in quotes in line 2∅, the ASCII code numbers of each letter found in one string are compared, letter for letter, from left to right with those in the other. Every one must match, or the test fails.

Strings and "quotes" go together like beer and chocolate cake. (Beer and chocolate cake. . .?) You know this from *earlier* chapters where every PRINT "XXX" has its string enclosed in quotes. (PRINT "XXX" is called a string *constant*, compared with A$, a string *variable*.) RUN the above program again, this time answering the question with "ISHKIBIBBLE", but enclosed in quotes.

Sure — it ran OK. Worked either with or without quotes. BASIC has become increasingly lenient about this matter, but every once in awhile the rules come up from behind and bite us if we play fast and loose with them.

If we READ a string from a DATA line and it has no commas, semicolons, leading or trailing spaces in it, we don't need to enclose it in quotes. We will never go wrong by *always* enclosing strings in quotes, but that can be a nuisance.

> *EXERCISE 23-1:* Write a program that will compare two strings entered from the keyboard. Print them in alphabetical order.

READing Strings from DATA Lines

Erase the resident program and type in this next one, which READs string data from a DATA line.

```
1 CLS
1∅ READ A$,B$,C$
2∅ PRINT A$
3∅ PRINT B$
```

```
40 PRINT C$
100 DATA COMPUSOFT PUBLISHING, SAN DIEGO, CA 92119
998 PRINT : LIST
```

. . .and RUN.

Look carefully at the results. The screen shows:

```
COMPUSOFT PUBLISHING

SAN DIEGO

CA
```

That's fine, but where is the ZIP Code? And why weren't SAN DIEGO and CA PRINTed on the same line? The answer, my friend, is blowing in the . . .er, in the commas. Ahem.

Because of the commas in the DATA line, the READ statement sees four pieces of DATA, but only READs three of them. What do we have to do in order to PRINT a comma as part of a string? Right — enclose it, or the string containing it, in quotes.

```
EDIT100
```

and change line 100 to read:

```
100 DATA COMPUSOFT PUBLISHING, "SAN DIEGO, CA", 92119
```

. . .and RUN.

Aaaah! That's more like it. Notice that we didn't have to enclose every piece of string DATA in separate quotes, but we could have.

What would happen if we enclosed the *entire* DATA line in quotes, leaving the existing quotes in there? (Think about it, then try it. Every question raised has a specific purpose.)

Our EDITor is so easy to use, let's make it read:

```
100 DATA"COMPUSOFT PUBLISHING,"SAN DIEGO, CA", 92119"
```

. . .and RUN.

Awwk! Disaster. A Syntax error in line 100?

Yes, there is no straight-forward way to PRINT quotes as part of a string constant, not even by enclosing them inside another pair of quotes. The computer just isn't smart enough to figure out which quote mark is which. The usual way to overcome this BASIC language deficiency is to substitute ' for ", inside other quotes. Let's try it.

```
100 DATA"COMPUSOFT PUBLISHING,'SAN DIEGO, CA', 92119"
```

. . .and RUN.

Ooops, Out of DATA in 10? Of course. With quotes surrounding the whole works there is now just one piece of DATA and we are trying to read three pieces. Let's change line 10 to just read one piece:

```
10 READ A$
```

. . .and RUN.

There we go, might look a little strange, but it proves the point and warns us a little about the "touchiness" of strings.

When it comes to strings, that classic old ballad from the hills is so appropriate:

"Ah — cigareets, and whuisky, and wild computers, they'll drive you crazy, they'll drive you insane!"

But, undaunted by this high class philosophy, we steer our vessel towards the next chapter.

And as the sun sinks slowly in the west, tropical breezes fill the sails and water laps against the bow. Stars appear and from the beach fires, plaintive native chants are heard calling . . .

Learned in Chapter 23

Miscellaneous

String comparison

INPUTing Strings

READing Strings

Measuring Strings

LEN and DEFSTR

One of the most frequently needed pieces of string information is its length.
Fortunately, the LEN function makes it easy to find. Type:

```
1 CLS : PRINT
10 INPUT"ENTER A STRING OF CHARACTERS";A$
20 L = LEN(A$)
30 PRINT A$;" HAS";L;"CHARACTERS"
90 PRINT : LIST
```

RUN several times, entering your name and other combinations of letters
and numbers. Try entering your name, last name first, with a comma after
your last name.

Aha! Can't INPUT a comma. How about if we put it all in quotes? Try
again.

Yep. Just like it said in the last chapter.

LEN has only one significant variation, and it's not all that useful — unless we really need it. Change lines 1∅-3∅ to read:

```
1∅  INPUT "ENTER A NUMBER";A
2∅  L = LEN(A)
3∅  PRINT A;" HAS";L;"CHARACTERS"
```

. . .and RUN.

Crash time again! "TM ERROR" (type mismatch) means we tried to INPUT a *number* into LEN — but it requires a STRING. OK, let's change LEN to make it a string:

```
2∅  L = LEN("A")
```

. . .and RUN, entering a Number.

Hmmm. Doesn't seem to matter what number we INPUT; it always comes back saying that we have only one character.

The answer is, LEN evaluates the LENgth of what is actually between its parentheses (or quotes). At first we brought in a string from the "outside" and measured its length. That worked fine. We are now measuring the length of what's between the quotes, and that *length* doesn't change with the *value* of A. We are using A as a "literal string constant", not a variable string.

Like we said, this second way to use LEN has its limitations, but does tell us the length of what's there. (Change the resident program back to the way it appears at the beginning of the chapter.)

DEFSTR — For Thrill Seekers Only

Those among us who attract trouble will love this next one. As if handling strings isn't complex enough, this very powerful statement looks nice and clean but can be the greatest source of heartburn since the horseradish pizza.

DEFSTR (pronounced "DEFine STRing") allows us to define which variables are to be string variables, so we don't have to use the $ any more. (Hmm. . .Uncle Sam could put some of this DEFSTR business to good use.)

Add this line:

```
5 DEFSTR A
```

and use the Editor to remove the $ in lines 1Ø, 2Ø, and 3Ø. Then RUN.

Works great, doesn't it. A was declared by line 5 to be a string variable. So what's all the fuss about?

Well, this is a very simple program, but let's change 5 to read:

```
5 DEFSTR A-Z
```

which makes *all* letters string variables

. . .and RUN.

Crasho again! The L in line 2Ø is now *also* a string. Since LEN gives us the length of a string as a number, it doesn't set at all well with L (really L string). Imagine the fun this can create in a long program.

Good thing we can learn by our errors!

DEFSTR can be used to define individual variables. For example:

```
DEFSTR A,N,Z
```

defines only A, N and Z as string variables.

It Came Upon A Midnight Clear
(Is that like a midnight requisition?)

When the computer is first turned on, 50 bytes of memory space are

---

100 Bytes on Model II.

---

automatically set aside for use by strings — *all* strings combined. Not very much space if we're into a biggie. At the command level, type NEW, then:

```
PRINT FRE(A$)
```

The computer should respond with :

```
5Ø
```

100 on Model II.

FRE asks the computer, "How much space is left for strings?", not only A$, but *all* strings. The "A$" is just a "dummy" we have to use with FRE. B$, C$, or anything similar would work as well. PRINT FRE(X) (using most any character, but without the $ sign) tells us the same thing as PRINT MEM — how much *total* memory space is available.

The CLEAR command/statement allows us to change the amount of reserved string space to anything we want, up to almost the total available memory. Going the other way, we can eliminate all reserved space, leaving all memory for non-string use. Let's play around with some combinations and see what happens:

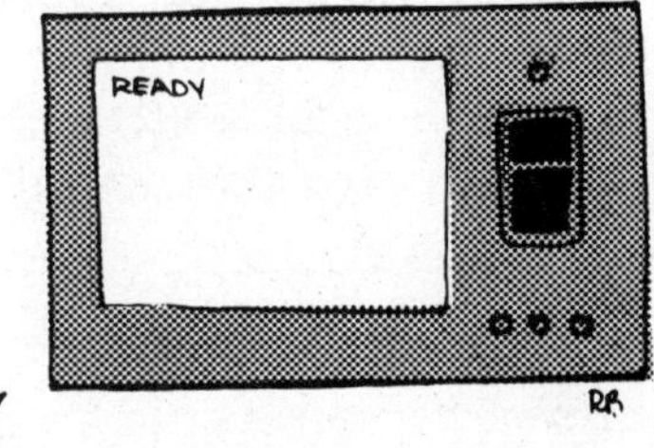


```
CLEAR Ø

PRINT FRE(A$)
Ø
```

Is that what you got? CLEARed zero and got zero? Good.

Type NEW and measure again.

```
NEW
PRINT FRE(A$)
Ø
```

What? Still zero? That's right. The CLEAR command is a high level one and is not affected by NEW. "Power-up" automatically sets aside 50 bytes, and wherever we reset it, there it stays until it's reset again.

Try:

```
PRINT MEM
15364
```

33708 on Model II.

You might get a little different number — but it should be in the ballpark. Model I users should get about 15570.

```
CLEAR MEM/4
PRINT FRE(A$)
3840
```

8426 — Model II.

We just arbitrarily said, "Let's set aside a fourth of the memory for use by strings." CLEAR MEM/4 did it. If it turns out to be too much (wasteful) or too little (computer will say ?OS *Out of string Space*), it's easily changed. A very adept programmer could even come up with an error-trapping routine that would CLEAR additional memory as needed if an ?OS message came through, and the operator wouldn't even know that something happened.

Be careful with CLEAR. It erases all program variables.

PRINT FRE(A$) can also be used as a program statement. Try it in any program using strings to watch what happens.

Type:

```
CLEAR 50
```

CLEAR 100 — Model II.

---

and get us back to "normal".

Concatenation

Concatenation? Concatenation??? Now what is that supposed to mean? Isn't even in the dictionary. Did you ever wonder who pays whom to sit around and think up such non-descriptive words? It must have been done on a government grant. Wait till Senator Proxmire hears about this.

Concatenation (pronounced *con-cat-uh-na'tion*) is a national debt-sized word which means "add". In our case it means "add strings together". It's easier to do than to pronounce.

Type this NEW program:

```
1 CLS : PRINT
10 FOR N = 1 TO 16
20 READ A$
25 B$ = B$ + A$
30 PRINT B$
40 NEXT N
90 PRINT : LIST
100 DATA ALPHA,BRAVO,CHARLIE,DELTA,ECHO,FOXTROT,GOLF,HOTEL
110 DATA INDIA,JULIETE,KILO,LIMA,MIKE,NOVEMBER,OSCAR,PAPA
```

Check it carefully but don't RUN it yet. The key line is 25, which simply says B$ (a new variable) equals the old B$ (which starts out as nothing) plus whatever is in A$. It then cycles around and keeps adding what is in B$ to what is READ from DATA as A$. Now RUN.

Gotcha! We ran out of string space, says the ?OS. B$ just keeps growing and growing until the 50-byte set-aside isn't enough.

---

100 bytes on Model II.

How much is enough? Easy question, tough answer. The VARPTR statement will give us the answer, but its use requires a PhD from the funny farm where they only talk in ones and zeros.

The easiest way is to stay within the noblest engineering tradition — add some more string space and see what happens. It's "cut and try" time.

```
5 CLEAR 100
```

   . . .and RUN.

Getting closer. Let's try again. (This warms the cockles of any true experimenter's heart — and drives any true theoretical scientist right up the wall.) *(Chuckle.)*

```
5 CLEAR 150
```

   . . .and RUN.

Still not enough. Looks close though, doesn't it?

```
5 CLEAR 175
```

   . . .and RUN.

Sweet success. All due to our extensive planning, no doubt.

Better do a quick

```
PRINT MEM
```

to see that there's plenty of space left — and there is.

The purist will keep experimenting and find out that we need exactly. . .*message garbled in transmission*. . .bytes of string space to make the program RUN, yet not waste any. (Hint: If you add the number of characters in the last line printed to those in the next-to-last line, you'll be so close to the answer it may bite you. We could even figure that one out in advance.)

Anyhoo, the point of all this is *concatenation*. Line 25 just did it, and that's about all there is to it. We added strings together.

Not done playing you say? OK, you non-believers, have some fun with this simple program:

```
1 CLEAR 35
10 REM * CLEAR DEMO *
20 A$="0" : B$="/"
```

```
30 PRINT A$;LEN(A$)

40 A$ = A$ + B$

50 GOTO 30
```

We'll soon learn how to tear strings into little pieces. We've just learned how to put them back together. (Somebody got something backwards here. . .)

EXERCISE 24-1: Use the LEN function to check the length of a string INPUT from the keyboard. Print a message telling us if the string exceeded ten characters.

EXERCISE 24-2: INPUT a word from the keyboard and compare it to a secret password.

If there is a match, PRINT "CORRECT PASSWORD, YOU MAY ENTER".

If not, PRINT "WRONG PASSWORD. GET LOST MAX-WELL SMART!"

Store the ASCII number for each letter of the password in a DATA line. READ each value and use CHR$ to build (concatenate) the password string.

Learned in Chapter 24

Statements	Functions	Miscellaneous
DEFSTR	LEN	Concatenation (+)
CLEAR	FRE	
	MEM	

VAL($) and STR$(N)

The "hassle factor" is unusually high when converting back and forth between strings and numerics.

By definition, if we change a string variable to a numeric variable, we can't change any letters or other characters to numbers. Only the *numbers* in a string can be converted to a numeric variable. (Don't get this confused with ASCII conversions.)

Conversely, if we convert a numeric variable (can hold only a number) to a string variable (can hold most anything), the *content* of that new string is still the original number. No letters or other characters were converted (except for a leading space) since they weren't in the numeric variable to start with.

If you'll keep the two previous paragraphs in mind, it'll save an awful lot of grief in dealing with strings.

VAL

Let's give string-to-numeric conversion a shot. The VAL function converts a *string* variable which holds a *number* into a *number*, if the number is at the beginning of the string. Try this VAL program:

```
1 CLS : PRINT
10 INPUT"WHAT STRING SHOULD I CONVERT TO A NUMBER ";A$
20 A = VAL(A$)
30 PRINT"THE NUMERIC VALUE OF ";A$;" IS ";A
90 PRINT : GOTO10
```

. . .and RUN.

Try lots of different INPUTs, such as:

```
12345
ASDF
123ASD
ASD123
1,2,3
A,B,C
```

and the same ones over again, but enclosed in quotes.

The tube tells all.

Using the EDITor, take the $ out of Lines 1Ø, 2Ø, and 3Ø and RUN, IN-PUTing both numbers and letters.

What you're seeing is typical of the frustrations that bedevil string users who don't follow the rules. VAL only evaluates STRINGs, and we've put A, a numeric value, in where a string belongs.

Trying to mix numbers with strings is called a *type mismatch.*

Let's put that A in quotes and see what happens.

```
20 A = VAL("A")
```

. . .and RUN.

No help at all! The rule remains unchanged. VAL converts a STRING which holds a *number* into that *number*. Looking at the screen, we see it's just not in the cards. Remember this frustration when we get in the thick of debugging a nasty string-loaded program.

STR$

Now let's try the opposite: Converting a numeric variable to a string variable. Change the program to read:

```
1 CLS : PRINT
10 INPUT"WHAT NUMERIC SHOULD I CONVERT TO A STRING";A
20 A$ = STR$(A)
30 PRINT"THE STRING VALUE OF";A;"IS";A$
90 PRINT : GOTO 10
```

...and RUN, using the same INPUTs we used when wringing out VAL.

There it is. A short but very important chapter. You should spend as much time on this one as any other chapter. If you really learn the pitfalls in using these two powerful functions, the time spent will come back manyfold in future debugging time.

> *EXERCISE 25-1:* INPUT your street address (e.g., 2433 LA PALMA). Use VAL to extract the street number. Add the number 4 to the street number and report this new number as your neighbor's street number.

> *EXERCISE 25-2:* Write a program using STR$ to PRINT the 20 following Store Item Stock Numbers: 101WT, 102WT, 103WT,.. 120WT. Hint: Looks like a natural for a FOR-NEXT loop.

Learned in Chapter 25

Functions

VAL

STR$

Having A Ball
With String

LEFT$, RIGHT$, MID$

Three different, yet very similar, functions are used for playing powerful
games with strings. They are LEFT$, RIGHT$ and MID$. Let's start our
exercise of them with this program:

```
1 CLS : PRINT

30 S$ = "KILROY WAS HERE"

60 PRINT LEFT$(S$,6),

70 PRINT MID$(S$,8,3),

80 PRINT RIGHT$(S$,4)

90 PRINT : LIST
```

. . .and RUN.

The screen shows:

```
KILROY          WAS          HERE
```

(How about that one, nostalgia buffs?)

Learning to use these functions is exceedingly simple. Study the program slowly and carefully as we explain what happened.

LEFT$ PRINTed the LEFT-most 6 characters in the string named S$.

MID$ PRINTed 3 characters in the string named S$, starting with the 8th character from the left. (Count 'em.)

RIGHT$ PRINTed the 4 RIGHT-most characters in the string named S$.

We added commas after lines 6Ø and 7Ø in order to PRINT everything on one line.

Let's move some lines around to exercise our new-found power. Move line 7Ø to line 5Ø:

```
5Ø PRINT MID$(S$,8,3)
```

RUN . . . and we get:

```
WAS                 KILROY              HERE
```

Now move line 8Ø to line 4Ø and add a trailing comma.

```
4Ø PRINT RIGHT$(S$,4),
```

RUN. . . and we get:

```
HERE                WAS                 KILROY
```

These 3 functions can really do wonders with strings. Let's type in a NEW program and examine each in more detail:

```
1 CLS : PRINT
10 FOR N - 1 TO 15
20 PRINT "N = ";N,
30 S$ = "KILROY WAS HERE"
40 PRINT LEFT$(S$,N)
```

```
50 FOR T=1 TO 500 : NEXT T
60 NEXT N
90 PRINT : LIST
```

    . . .and RUN.

The "slow motion" picture tells it faster than we can in words. LEFT$ picks off "N" letters from the *left* side of S string, and we PRINT them. See how this could be used to strip off only the first three digits of a phone number, or the first letter of a name, when searching and sorting?

Change line 1Ø to read:

```
10 FOR N = 1 TO 20
```

    . . .and RUN.

As you see, even though there are only 15 characters in the string, the over-RUN is ignored. (Change line 1Ø back to N = 1 TO 15.)

RIGHT$ works the same way, but from the RIGHT:

Change line 4Ø to read:

```
40 PRINT RIGHT$(S$,N)
```

    . . .and RUN.

It's the mirror image of LEFT$.

Time to exercise MID$ and see where it goes. Change line 4Ø to:

```
40 PRINT MID$(S$,N,1)
```

    . . .and RUN.

It very methodically scanned the string from left to right, picking out one let-ter at a time. We again slowed it down with the delay loop in line 5Ø to better study what's happening.

With only a slight change we can make MID$ act like LEFT$. Change line

4Ø to:

```
40 PRINT MID$(S$,1,N)
```

. . .and RUN.

It PRINTed N characters, counting from number 1 on the left.

MID$ can also simulate RIGHT$. Change line 4Ø:

```
40 PRINT MID$(S$,16-N,N)
```

. . .and RUN.

Would you believe RIGHT$ backwards, one at a time?

```
40 PRINT MID$(S$,16-N,1)
```

. . .and RUN.

How about a sort of "histogram-" type graph:

```
40 PRINT MID$(S$,N,N)
```

. . .and RUN.

Make your notes in the right-hand column for future reference. If all these examples don't spark some ideas for your future use, I give up.

Let's select a specific position in the string and PRINT its character. Make the program read:

```
1 CLS : PRINT
10 INPUT"WHICH CHARACTER # DO YOU WANT TO PRINT";N
30 S$ = "KILROY WAS HERE"
40 PRINT MID$(S$,N,1)
50 FOR T = 1 TO 500 : NEXT T
90 PRINT : LIST
```

. . .and RUN.

Just to make the point, we can assign any of these statements to a variable.

That variable can, in turn, be used in tests against other variables. Change:

```
40 V$ = MID$(S$,N,1)
45 PRINT V$
```

        . . .and RUN.

A short book could be written about these three functions, but I think we've made the point. They are used *very* frequently in complex *sort* and *select* routines. If we remember to dissect them into their simple components, they *can* be understood. The next section is a good example.

EXERCISE 26-1: Write a program that asks the question "ISN'T THIS A SMART COMPUTER". Input a *yes* or *no* answer. If the first character in the answer is a Y, PRINT "AFFIRMATIVE". If the first character is an N, PRINT "NEGATIVE". Otherwise PRINT "THIS IS A YES OR NO QUESTION" and send control back to the INPUT statement.

EXERCISE 26-2: READ in the following part numbers: N106WT, A208FM, and Z154DX. Use MID$ to find the numbers. PRINT the number with the largest numeric value.

INSTRING Routine

INSTRING is a built-in (or *intrinsic*) function. It can be of great value when searching for a needle in a haystack since it compares one string (or *every-string*) against another (or *all*) strings to see if they have anything in common. We're going to build our own routine made up of LEN and MID$ in order to learn them better.

Suppose we have a LIST of names and want to see if another certain name (or part of that name) is included in our LIST. It's the "part of" which makes this operation very different from a straight comparison of name-against-name, which we already know how to do with ordinary string-against-string comparisons. Here we learn how to locate a name (and similar names) by asking for just a small part of it.

Start our NEW program by entering this LIST of Names:

```
10000 DATA SMITH, JONES, FAHRQUART, BROWN, JOHNSON
10010 DATA SCHWARTZ, FINKELSTEIN, BAILEY, SNOOPY,
JOE BFTSPLK,*
```

That was the easy part. We have to provide a means of READing these names, one at a time and comparing them, or parts of them, with the name or part of a name which we INPUT. Add these lines:

```
10 CLEAR 100 : CLS
20 INPUT"ENTER THE NAME YOU ARE SEEKING ";N$ : PRINT
30 READ D$
40 IF D$ = "*" THEN PRINT "END OF SEARCH" : END
50 GOSUB 1000
60 IF T = 0 GOTO 30
70 PRINT N$;" IS PART OF ";D$
80 GOTO 30
```

Now this takes a bit of explaining:

Line 10 CLEARS 100 bytes for strings, and CLEARS the screen.

Line 20 INPUTs the name or part of the name we are trying to locate, and PRINTs a blank space for easier reading to give this book some class.

Line 30 READs a single name from our DATA file.

Line 40 checks to see if we're at the end of the DATA file. If so, it says so and ENDs execution.

Line 50 shoots us to the INSTRING subroutine (covered next) which does all the sorting.

Line 6Ø checks the value of T, a number sent back from the sub-routine. If its value is Ø it means no such name (or part) was found, and we should READ the next one. If it was found, we drop to:

Line 7Ø which PRINTs both what we're looking for and what we found.

Line 8Ø sends us back to READ another name from DATA.

That last part of the program isn't nearly as shaggy as the sort routine itself. Enter these final three lines:

```
1ØØØ FOR T = 1 TO LEN(D$) - LEN(N$) + 1
1Ø1Ø IF N$ = MID$(D$,T,LEN(N$)) THEN RETURN
1Ø2Ø NEXT T : T=Ø : RETURN
```

RUN it a few times to get the hang of what's going on, then we'll take it apart.

Line 1ØØØ starts off by setting up a FOR-NEXT loop. How far that loop continues depends on what number comes out of the difference between the length of D$ (from the DATA line) and the length of N$ (the name or part we entered). Even if that number comes out zero or negative, we'll still go through the next two lines at least once.

Line 1Ø1Ø is of the IF-THEN variety. If the characters we INPUT in N$ are the same as the characters taken from D$, we RETURN to line 6Ø. LEN(N$) *counts* the number of characters we INPUT, so MID$ can take the same quantity from D$. T gives MID$ the starting point to count from.

At line 6Ø, we know T will *not* equal Ø since we just said it equalled 1 in line 1ØØØ. Execution will therefore fall through to line 7Ø which PRINTs the good news that we have a "match". Line 3Ø starts the search process over again in another DATA name, looking for other possible matches.

If, on the other hand, we did *not* get a match in line 1Ø1Ø (by far the most frequent event), execution falls through to line 1Ø2Ø.

Line 1020 increments T by one digit, and execution returns to line 10000, dropping to line 1010; 1010 again tests our INPUT against the same name READ from DATA, but this time the starting point T, moves over by one place and a different set of characters is selected. The same scenario as before repeats.

Eventually the FOR-NEXT loop RUNs out of T's, and line 1020 moves to its next statement, T=0. T=0 sets up a signal for line 60 that the FOR-NEXT loop has RUN its course and it's time to READ a new name from DATA. The RETURN in 1020 returns execution back to line 50, then 60.

Now that wasn't too bad, was it? ('Twarn't nothin', really.) A little time beside the pool reflecting on the logic will do wonders.

For those with only a silver fingerbowl, but no pool, this extra line will show the inner machinations of line 1000.

```
1005 PRINT"T=";T,"LEN(D$)=";LEN(D$),"LEN(N$)="
;LEN(N$),"DIFF=";LEN(D$) - LEN(N$)
```

RUN it through a number of times, halting execution as necessary. It really does make sense!

When we've got that one under control, DELETE line 1005 to cut down the clutter. Better yet, go into EDITor and place a single ' at the beginning of 1005, making it a REM line which can be converted back to a working program line without having to retype it.

Now add line 1007 to show what 1010 is doing.

```
1007 PRINT"T";T,"N$=";N$,"THE MID$=";
MID$(D$,T,LEN(N$)9,"D$=";D$
```

. . .and RUN.

This one really tells a story! Step right up and see for yourself!

Does the string we INPUT really match up with what MID$ is pulling out?

It doesn't matter how hard a program seems, when broken down to its individual parts it isn't very hard. Like we've pointed out before, "The BASICs are everything".

EXERCISE 26-3: Change the DATA in lines 10000 and 10010 of the INSTRING program to:

```
10000 DATA P-RUTH, C-CAMPANELLA, SS-LEOTHELIP, P-KOUFAX
10010 DATA SB-MORGAN, OF-MANTLE, P-FELLER, *
```

What string would we enter to LIST the pitchers only?
  A. P

  B. PITCHER

  C. P—

  D. None of the above

Snarled STRING

In the last chapter we learned about STR$, which lets us convert a numeric variable to a string variable. For the purpose of confusion (no doubt), there is another "string-string" that does something completely different. Fortunately, it is written differently.

STRING$(N,A) is a specialized PRINT *modifier* which allows us to PRINT a single ASCII character, represented by A, a total of N times. Quite simple, really.

Type NEW, then:

```
5 CLEAR 50
10 PRINT STRING$(23,42);
20 PRINT"STRING$ FUNCTION";
```

```
30 PRINT STRING$(23,42);
```

   . . .and RUN.

Model II use strings 32, 42.

Wow! That really moves. It PRINTed ASCII character number 42, which is a *, 23 times, then PRINTed the phrase STRING$ FUNCTION, then PRINTed * 23 more times. This just has to have some good applications.

Suppose we need to type a "header" across the top of a report — let's say the first line of it is to be solid dashes. What is the ASCII code for a dash? Forgot? *Me too.* Everybody back to Appendix B to find the code number.

45 it is. We want to PRINT 64 times, the character represented by ASCII code 45. That's the full width of a line on our screen. The NEW program should look something like:

```
10 PRINT STRING$(64,45)
```

Model II change 64 to 80.

   . . .RUN it and see what happens.

```
OUT OF STRING SPACE IN 10
```

Suckered in again! Though STRING$ is really a sort of PRINT statement, it's also a STRING function, so is subject to the string space restriction. Now what do we do?

Change:

```
5 CLEAR 64
```

An even easier way to use STRING$ is by replacing the ASCII code of the character we wish to PRINT with the actual character itself. (It must be enclosed in quotes.) This works fine with characters that really PRINT, such as letters, numbers and punctuation marks. Change line 1Ø so the program reads:

```
5 CLEAR 64
10 PRINT STRING$(64,"-")
```

. . .and RUN.

Works nice, doesn't it? And we didn't have to look up the ASCII code.

As with most string functions, we can bring in the string via a string variable. This simple NEW program shows a variation on the theme, and may trigger some ideas:

```
10 INPUT"ENTER ANY LETTER, NUMBER OR SYMBOL";A$
20 PRINT STRING$(40,A$)
30 PRINT : GOTO 10
```

Play around with STRING$ a while. It's really very helpful when we need it, particularly for giving our PRINTouts some class. An obvious advantage is its ability to do a lot of PRINTing with very little programming.

> *EXERCISE 26-4:* Print a string of 30 asterisks centered at the top of the screen.

On The Lighter Side

The specialized string functions allow us to do all sorts of exotic things. Here is the beginning of a simple, but fun, NEW program which uses LEN and MID$. You can easily figure it out, especially after you've seen it RUN.

Enter:

```
1 REM * TIMES SQUARE BILLBOARD :
10 CLEAR 400
20 CLS:N=0:PRINT:READ A$
30 L=LEN(A$) : F=1
80 IF L>N THEN L=N+2
90 B$ = MID$(A$,F,L)
```

```
100  PRINT  TAB(62-N);B$
110  FOR  T=1  TO  20 : NEXT  T
190  IF  N=55  GOTO  220
100  N=N+1 :  IF  N<55  GOTO  290
220  L=L-1 :  F=F+1 :  IF  L<0  THEN  L=0
230  IF  L=15  GOTO  20
290  CLS :  PRINT  CHR$(2):  GOTO  80
```

Model II users: 290 CLS : PRINT CHR$(2):GOTO 80.

. . .and RUN.

Your assignment, if you choose to accept it, is to complete the program so it repeats, ends, or otherwise does not crash.

Good luck!

..............Fsssss!

Learned in Chapter 26

Functions

LEFT$
MID$
RIGHT$
STRING$

Miscellaneous

INSTRING Routine

Part IV

Variable Precision
And Math

"IN SINGLE OR DOUBLE PRECISION?"

What Price Precision?

Unless told otherwise, TRS-80 BASIC stores variables to an accuracy of seven digits, and *PRINTs them out accurate to six digits. This is called "SiNGle precision" and is more than adequate for most applications.*

The old slide rule was accurate to only three digits.

For large businesses or special scientific applications, however, greater accuracy is needed and we have a capability called "DouBLe precision". By telling the computer to go "DouBLe precision", it will store numbers accurate to 17 digits, and PRINT them out accurate to 16. We pay a price for this precision, however, both in the additional memory it takes to store and process big numbers, and the extra time required to do so.

Type in this NEW program:

```
1 CLS : PRINT
20 X = 1234567890987654321          (check 'em)
30 Y = .00000000000123456789        (check 'em)
40 Z = X * Y
50 PRINT X;"TIMES";Y,"EQUALS";Z
90 PRINT : LIST
```

   . . .and RUN.

`1.234568E`

Ummm-hmmm. A very large number times a very small number, and the answer − all expressed in exponential notation. Accuracy clipped to six places.

LIST the program, and find that the numbers in Lines 2Ø and 3Ø have also been converted to exponential notation. We'll explain the "D" in those lines in a minute.

DouBLe Precision

We can easily convert storage, processing and PRINTing of X, Y and Z to DouBLe precision. This is almost too easy:

`1Ø  DEFDBL A-Z`

DEFDBL stands for "DEFine as DouBLe precision", and A-Z means "make every variable starting with A through Z DouBLe precision".

Add the line and RUN.

Quite a difference, eh? Those lost digits came back from the hinterland, and expanded our PRINTout from 6 places to 16. (The D stands for DouBLe precision exponential.)

Such a line is terribly wasteful of memory space and time, except in short programs; but fortunately only a few variables really need to be so precise.

Since the letters X, Y and Z are in sequence, we could tell the computer to handle only those three variables in DouBLe precision, and leave all other variables (of which there are none, right now) as SiNGle precision. Change line 1Ø to:

`1Ø  DEFDBL X-Z`

        . . .and RUN.

Same results.

There is a way to override the DEFDBL declaration. Suppose we wanted Z to be PRINTed as just SiNGle precision. We can override line 1Ø by changing those lines which contain Z, as follows:

```
4Ø  Z! = X * Y

5Ø  PRINT X;"TIMES";Y;"EQUALS";Z!
```

     . . .and RUN.

Our "raw" data and the calculating was held at high precision, but our final answer is PRINTed out with single-precision accuracy — just what we asked for. A very specific declaration (like the !, which stands for "SiNGle precision") always takes precedence over a global declaration like in line 1Ø. (Global means "valid for the entire program", not just one character or one line.)

Double Precision — Simplified

There is another way to calculate with high precision but PRINT the answer in SiNGle precision. Since single precision is the "default" mode, we can simply not include Z in line 1Ø.

```
1Ø  DEFDBL X,Y            (or  DEFDBL X-Y)

4Ø  Z = X * Y

5Ø  PRINT X;"TIMES";Y;"EQUALS";Z
```

Global Override

It is possible to override the "global" DEFDBL declaration with a global single precision declaration. Single is more powerful than double! DEFSNG will change everything back to SiNGle precision. Let's try it by adding:

```
6Ø  DEFSNG X-Y

7Ø  PRINT X;"TIMES";Y;"EQUALS";Z
```

     . . .and RUN.

Good Grief — our "redeclared" DEFSNG numbers turned to zeros but the Z answer is correct!

Well, it turns out that X *DouBLe precision* is a completely separate variable from X *SiNGle precision*. It's as different from X as is Y, or any other variable. If we want to use X and Y again as SiNGle precision numbers, we have to go back and assign them values *after* declaring them to be *SiNGle precision*. Hmmmm. This is getting complicated.

A cheap and dirty way to show the point is to change line 7Ø to:

```
7Ø GOTO 2Ø
```

. . .and RUN — hitting the `BREAK` key after both DouBLe and SiNGle precision versions are PRINTed in line 5Ø.

Line 6Ø reDEFines X and Y as single precision, then control goes back to line 2Ø and the calculations are performed again. (Fortunately, there is rarely reason to *reDEFine* a variable within a program. If necessary, we can do so with conventional string techniques.)

DouBLe Precision, Another Way

Instead of a "global" declaration of accuracy, we can do it one variable at a time. Change the resident program (carefully!) to read:

```
1 CLS : PRINT
2Ø X# = 1234567890987654321
3Ø Y# = .00000000001234567889
4Ø Z# = L# * Y#
5Ø PRINT X#;"TIMES";Y#,"EQUALS";Z#
9Ø PRINT : LIST
```

. . .and RUN.

Same results as before. The # sign declares that the variable letter preceding it is to be handled as DouBLe precision, overriding the normal presumption that it is SiNGle precision.

Remember, X# is not the same as X − it is an entirely different variable. Same with Y# and Z#. To nail this point down, add:

```
10 X = 4.321
60 PRINT "X =";X
```

     . . .and RUN.

The values of X# and X stayed completely separate, didn't they?

INTeger Precision

In a few cases, where the numbers at issue are INTegers (and in the range between −32768 and +32767), execution can be speeded up by declaring them to be INTegers using the % sign or the DEFINT statement. Enter this NEW program:

```
20 FOR N = 1 TO 4000
30 NEXT N
80 PRINT : LIST
```

Using a stopwatch or clock with a second hand, measure the time it takes for the 4000 passes through the FOR-NEXT LOOP. Should be around ten seconds.

Now, let's declare N to be an INTeger (which is all the accuracy we need), and time it again. Add:

```
10 DEFINT N
```

     . . .and RUN.

Aha! It took only about seven seconds. That's an increase from about 400 passes per second to about 570, a very significant difference.

We can accomplish the same thing using specific declarations. Delete line 10 and change the program to read:

```
20 FOR N% = 1 TO 4000
30 NEXT N%
```

```
90 PRINT : LIST
```

. . .and RUN.

One More Way

The conversion functions CSNG(#), CDBL(#) and CINT(#) provide three additional ways to declare numbers as SiNGle, DouBLe or INTeger precision. Enter this NEW test program:

```
1 CLS : PRINT
20 X = 12345.67890
30 PRINT X
40 PRINT CSNG(X)
50 PRINT CDBL(X)
60 PRINT CINT(X)
90 PRINT : LIST
```

. . .and RUN.

We get:

```
12345.7
12345.7
12345.6787109375
12345
```

Line 30 PRINTed the value of X, the same as we specified in line 20, to six digits.

Line 40 PRINTed the *SiNGle precision* value of X — same as line 30.

Line 50 PRINTed the *DouBLe precision* value of X, but it sure isn't a duplicate of what we said X was to be in line 20! Same old precision problem — don't try to be more accurate than what we begin with. (It's the programmer who's supposed to be creative, not the computer!)

Line 6Ø PRINTed the INTeger value of X. No surprises here. It behaved in the same manner as the INT statement itself.

Let's make the value of X negative and see what happens. Change line 2Ø to:

```
2Ø  X  =  -12345.67890
```

. . .and RUN.

Again, no big surprises. CINT acted just like INT does for this case, rounding downward to get the -12346.

DouBLe the Trouble — DouBLe The Fun

Now let's go back and declare the value of X to be DouBLe precision, change it to a positive number, and do all our PRINTing in DouBLe precision. The new program should read:

```
1  CLS  :  PRINT
2Ø  X#  =  12345.67890
3Ø  PRINT  X#
4Ø  PRINT  SCNG(X#)
5Ø  PRINT  CDBL(X#)
6Ø  PRINT  CINT(X#)
9Ø  PRINT  :  LIST
```

. . .then RUN.

and the display reads:

```
12345.6789
12345.7
12345.6789
12345
```

All makes sense, and all is quite predictable, isn't it?

What do you think will happen if we again change the value of X to a negative number? Think it through; then change and RUN it.

Some Caveats

The computer makes assumptions. If a constant is written with eight or more digits, or written in exponential notation with a "D", it is automatically stored as DouBLe precision. When that or any other DouBLe precision number is used in a calculation, the entire calculation will be performed as though *all* numbers involved are DouBLe precision. This isn't necessarily bad, but an answer with lots of digits is no more precise than its least accurate ancestors.

Division follows suit. If we declare the numerator or the denominator (or both) to be DouBLe precision, the division is done with DouBLe precision. All other division is done in SiNGle precision. If an INTeger answer is needed, massage the answer with INT or CINT, or name it with a plain old INTeger variable.

If a plain old number falls outside the range of -32768 to +32767 or if it contains a decimal point or if it is written in exponential with an "E", it will be stored in SiNGle precision. Otherwise, it is stored as an INTeger.

Finally, *logical* operations can be performed only after the numbers involved are converted to INTegers by the computer.

In Memorium

This is really a very important chapter. Most readers find it necessary to study it more than just once. Degrees of precision may not be the most inspiring subject, nor seem to be the most consistent, but if we have command of this chapter we'll not be caught off-guard nor be deceived by numbers that never were.

Learned in Chapter 27

Statements	Functions	Miscellaneous
DEFDBL	CDBL	DouBLe Precision (#)
DEFSNG	CSNG	SiNGle Precision (!)
DEFINT	CINT	INTeger Precision (%)

Intrinsic Math Functions

BASIC includes a number of mathematical functions, sometimes referred to as "Library Functions". These math functions are all very straightforward and easy to use, but if our math skills are a bit rusty, we will want to refresh them to fully understand what we're doing. We'll keep everything here at the 9th-grade Algebra level so there's no need to panic (unless maybe you're in the 6th grade. . .but even so, just hang on and you'll be OK).

INT(N)

We studied the INTeger function in some detail in an earlier chapter so we won't cover that ground again. INT stores and executes numbers as single precision.

FIX(N)

FIX is just like INT, but instead of rounding negative numbers downward, it simply chops off everything to the right of the decimal point.

Try this simple test at the command level:

```
PRINT INT(-12345.67)
```

produces −12346

```
PRINT FIX(-12345.67)
```

produces —12345

Which one we use depends on what we want.

SQR(N)

The SQuare Root function is simple to use.

Type in this NEW program:

```
10 INPUT"THE SQUARE ROOT OF";N
20 PRINT "IS ";SQR(N)
30 PRINT
40 GOTO 10
```

. . .and RUN.

Another way to take the square (or any) root of a number is by using the ⬆ (up arrow).

Model II PRINTS ^ and Model III PRINTS [instead of ⬆.

It of course means "raised to the power". Finding the square root of a number is the same as raising it to the 1/2 power. Change line 20 to:

```
20 PRINT "IS ";N[(1/2)
```

. . .and RUN some familiar numbers.

The same logic which allows us to find the square root with the ⬆ will let us find any other root. (Even the thought of doing that in pre-computer days drove men mad.) Out of the sheer arrogance of power, let's find the 21st root of any number. Change the first two lines:

```
10 INPUT"THE TWENTY-FIRST ROOT OF";N
20 PRINT "IS ";N[(1/21)
```

. . .and RUN.

Now there is real horsepower! Problem is, how are we sure that the answers are right? Well, it's easy enough to add a few lines that take the root back to its 21st power to find out. Let's clean up the program a bit and make it read:

```
10  INPUT"THE TWENTY-FIRST ROOT OF";N

15  R=N[(1/21)

20  PRINT"IS ";R

30  PRINT

33  PRINT R;"TO THE 21ST POWER = ";R[21

36  PRINT

40  GOTO 10
```

   . . .and RUN.

They come out pretty close, don't they? This "proof" process might not stand up under rigorous scrutiny, but the answers are correct.

EXERCISE 28-1: Pythagoras discovered that the sides of a right triangle always obey the rule:

$$C^2 = A^2 + B^2$$

where C is the longest side (hypotenuse). Another way to state this relationship is "The length of side C equals the square root of the sum of the squares of sides A and B ($C = \sqrt{A^2 + B^2}$). " If side A = 5 and side B = 12, write a program to calculate the length of side C.

ABS(N)

ABSolute value has a lot to do with signs, or without them. The ABSolute value of any number is that number *without* a sign. If you've forgotten, this program will quickly refresh the memory:

```
10  INPUT"ENTER ANY NUMBER ";N

20  A = ABS(N)
```

```
30 PRINT A
40 PRINT
50 GOTO 10
```

 . . .and RUN.

Try various large and small numbers, positive and negative, and zero.

They all came out as they went in, didn't they, except the sign is missing?

LOG(N)

No, a LOG isn't what we build cabins out of. But even the swiftest among us have to refresh their memories from time to time to keep all the details straight.

A LOG (logarithm) is an *exponent. Exponent of what? The exponent of a base.* What's a *base*? A *base* is the number that a given number *system* is built on. Aren't all number systems built on 10? 'Fraid not.

$10^3 = 1000$

1Ø is the BASE.

3 is the LOG(exponent), and

1ØØØ is the answer.

(Think it has something to do with "new math", but I was too old to take it, too young to teach it, and grateful for having missed learning it from those who didn't understand it.)

As if life isn't complicated enough, the LOG system is centered around what are called *natural* logs. What that means is the subject of another discussion, but we're stuck with it anyway. Natural logs use the number 2.718282 as their base. (Really makes your day, doesn't it!) Some BASICs provide a second LOG option using 10 as the base, as in our decimal system, but making the conversion isn't too bad — and we still do have to live with it.

Enter this program:

```
10 INPUT"ENTER ANY POSITIVE NUMBER";N
```

```
20 L = LOG(N)
30 PRINT"THE LOG OF";N;"TO THE NATURAL BASE =";L
40 PRINT
50 GOTO 10
```

> The LOG function is not valid for negative numbers or zero.

. . .and RUN.

Ummm Hmmm. Can't relate to the answers?

Enter the number 100 and get the answer 4.60517. What that means is, 2.718282 to the 4.60517 power = 100. Lay that one on them at the next meeting of the Audubon Society and they'll think you're weird for sure.

Let's jack this thing around to where the vast majority of us, who have to work with LOGs, can use it. . .into the decimal system.

Decimal-based Logs are called "common" logs. Add this line:

```
35 PRINT"THE LOG OF";N;"TO THE BASE 10 = ";L*.4342945
```

. . .and RUN, using 100 as the number.

Ahhh! That's more like it. We can all see that 10 to the 2nd power equals 100. It's good to be back on *relatively* solid ground.

The magic conversion rules are:

> *To convert a natural log to a common log, multiply the natural log by .4342945.*

> *To convert a common log to a natural log, multiply the common log by 2.3026.*

And that's the name of that tune.

This final program clears it up and lays it out:

```
1 REM * LOGARITHM DEMO *
```

```
10 CLS : PRINT
20 INPUT "ENTER A POSITIVE NUMBER";N
30 PRINT
40 PRINT "THE NUMBER","NATURAL LOG","COMMON LOG"
50 PRINT N,LOG(N),LOG(N)*.4342945
60 PRINT
70 GOTO 20
```

Wring it out until you're comfortable with the concept.

EXP(N)

EXP is sort of the opposite of LOG. EXP computes the value of the answer, given the EXPonent of a *natural* log. (Another winner.)

2.718282 raised to the EXP power = the answer.

Type in this NEW program:

```
10 INPUT"ENTER A NUMBER";N
20 A = EXP(N)
30 PRINT"2.718282 RAISED TO THE";N;"POWER = ";A
40 PRINT
50 GOTO 10
```

. . .and RUN.

You're entering the EXPonent now, so it's easy to get answers that are too big for the computer and cause it to *overflow*.

As a benchmark against which to test our program, enter this number:

```
4.60517
```

The BASE of the natural log system raised to this power should equal 100 (or very close).

Being this far into logs, we can create our own advanced test programs,

214

checking the results against a LOG table. *And if you're not too comfortable with all this. . .try making a log cabin with the remainders!*

EXERCISE 28-2: (**For math fans only.**) Convince yourself that the LOG and EXP Functions are inverses of each other (hint: LOG(EXP(N) = N). Try putting the two functions together in the opposite order using both positive and negative values for N. Why do the negative values create havoc?

Learned in Chapter 28

Functions	**Miscellaneous**
INT	Natural Logs
FIX	Common Logs
SQR	
ABS	
LOG	
EXP	

The Trigonometric Functions

Since this is about as deep as we'll get into mathematics, we'll have to assume you know something about elementary trig.

Trigonometry, of course, deals with triangles, their angles, and the ratios between the lengths of their sides. In the triangle below, the Sine (abbreviated SIN) of angle A is defined as the *ratio* (what we get after dividing) of the *length* of side **a** to the *length* of side **c**. COSine and TANgent are defined similarly:

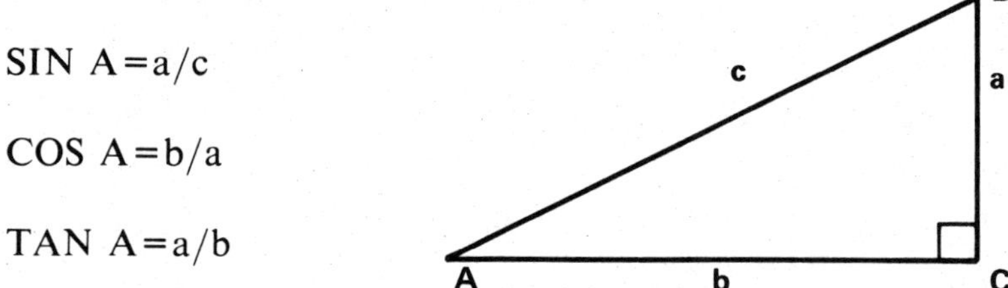

SIN A = a/c

COS A = b/a

TAN A = a/b

From these relationships, we can find any ratio if we know the corresponding angle. Let's try this simple NEW program:

```
10 INPUT"ENTER AN ANGLE BETWEEN 0 AND 90 DEGREES";A
```

```
20 S = SIN(A*.0174533)
30 PRINT"THE SIN OF A";A;"DEGREE ANGLE IS";S
40 PRINT : GOTO 10
```

. . and RUN.

It really works! Try the old "standard" angles like 45°,30°,60°,90°,0°, etc.

Unless you're right up to snuff on trig, line 20 undoubtedly looks strange. Well, it turns out that most computers think in radians, not degrees (always has to be some nasty twist, doesn't there. . .!) A radian is a unit of measurement equal to approximately 57° (heard some cringe at that one). In order to convert to degrees — which most of us use, we changed the degrees we INPUT to radians. The SIN function will not work correctly without this conversion.

To convert angles from degrees to radians, multiply the degrees by 0.0174533.

To convert angles from radians to degrees, multiply the radians by 57.29578.

Failure to make these conversions correctly is *by far* the greatest source of computer users' problems with the trig functions.

COSine and TANgent work the same way. Change the resident program to:

```
10 INPUT"ENTER AN ANGLE BETWEEN 0 AND 90 DEGREES";A
20 C = COS(A*.0174533)
30 PRINT"THE COS OF A";A;"DEGREE ANGLE IS";C
40 PRINT : GOTO 10
```

. . .and RUN.

We know that the COS of 90° should be 0. Unfortunately, the computer is slightly off because it calculates these functions by approximation. It's doing the best that it can. . .Honest!

For TANgent, RUN this program:

```
10  INPUT"ENTER AN ANGLE BETWEEN 0 AND 90 DEGREES";A
20  T = TAN(A*.0174533)
30  PRINT "THE TAN OF A";A;"DEGREE ANGLE IS";T
40  PRINT : GOTO 10
```

> The TAN function is not even defined for 90°, though the TRS-80 will *try* to calculate it for us.

This next NEW simple program displays all three major trig functions at the same time. Note in line 30 we *divide* our incoming angle by 57.29578 instead of multiplying it by 0.0174533. The results are the same.

```
10  CLS
20  INPUT"ENTER AN ANGLE BETWEEN 0 AND 90 DEGREES";A
30  A = A/57.29578
40  PRINT
50  PRINT"ANGLE","SIN","COS","TAN"
60  PRINT A*57.29578,SIN(A),COS(A),TAN(A)
```

When we try to find the TANgent of 90 degrees, a "division by zero" error occurs because the computer first finds the SIN of 90, which is 1, then divides into that the COS of 90, which is 9. 1/0 is a no-no as far as the computer is concerned.

Inverse Trig Functions

The opposite of finding a ratio between two sides of a triangle, when an *angle* is known, is finding an angle when the *ratio* of two sides is known. There are three functions commonly used in trig to do this, but most computers only make provision for one, called ATN (Arc of the TaNgent).

This simple NEW program takes the angle we INPUT, computes and PRINTs its TANgent, then takes that tangent and computes its arc (angle) as a proof check. The letter "I" is used in the program since the arctangent is also known as the "Inverse" (sort of the "opposite") of the tangent.

```
1 CLS
10 REM * ATN DEMO *
20 INPUT"ENTER ANY ANGLE BETWEEN 0 AND 90 DEGREES";A
30 T = TAN(A/57.29578)
40 PRINT "TANGENT =";T,
50 I = ATN(T) * 57.29578
60 PRINT"ARC OF THE TANGENT = ";I
```

If you're one of those rare types who is very familiar with trig, you can probably throw numbers around in such a fashion that the other two "inverse" trig functions, ARCSIN and ARCCOS, are not needed. But for those of us who still get confused when we run out of fingers and toes, the following conversions are all built into one simple program. The accuracy is close enough for "government" work. Give it a try:

```
10 CLS : REM * INVERSE FUNCTION DEMO PROGRAM *
20 INPUT "ENTER A NUMBER-THE RATIO OF 2 SIDES OF A TRIANGLE"
;R
30 AS = 2 * ATN(R/(1+SQR(ABS(1-R*R)))) * 57.29578
40 AC = 90-AS: PRINT
50 PRINT "RATIO", "ARCSIN", "ARCCOS", "ARCTAN"
60 PRINT "(NUMBER)","(DEGREES)","(DEGREES)","(DEGREES)"
70 IF ABS(R)>1 THEN 100
80 PRINT R, AS, AC, ATN(R)*57.29578
90 PRINT : GOTO 20
100 PRINT R, "U", ATN(R)*57.29578
110 PRINT : GOTO 20
```

Remember, while a TANgent can be any number, SIN and COS are both mathematically "undefined" when our ratio moves outside the range -1 to 1. Also, ARCTAN and ARCSIN produce angle measures between -90 and 90 degrees, but ARCCOS has a range between 0 and 180 degrees.

Learned in Chapter 29

Functions

SIN

COS

TAN

ATN

Miscellaneous

Degrees

Radians

Part V

Graphics And Display Formatting

"HONEST, MISS HUDSON. I DREW
THE PICTURE USING THE RANDOM NUMBER
GENERATOR. I DIDN'T KNOW IT WOULD
DRAW A PICTURE THAT WAS OBSCENE!"

Video
Display Graphics

And It Draws Pictures Too!

**Model II users skip the next two chapters since SET and RESET are not in-
cluded in Model II's BASIC.**

Our TRS-80 can draw an endless variety of pictures on the Video Display
screen. We will learn some of the basic procedures and capabilities in this
chapter. After that, what you create is limited only by your own imagination. Who knows. . .you may write a graphics program artistically
equivalent to the Mona Lisa.

Now, the two most basic of the four graphic commands:

SET turns on (or lights up, if you will) a particular section, block
or "light" on the screen.

RESET turns off (or blackens) a particular "light".

For graphics, the screen is divided into a large number of sections. See the
Video Display Worksheet on the next page. Each "light" is a rectangular
block three dots wide by four dots high, and each has its own "address".

TRS-80 Video Display Worksheet

TITLE _______________ PROGRAMMER _______________ COMMENTS _______________ PAGE _____ OF _____

For example:

```
SET(55,32)
```

means "turn on the light" at the junction of 55th "X" Street and 32nd "Y" Avenue.

X is the horizontal address, counting across from the left-hand side of the screen. Y is the vertical address, counting down from the top of the screen. So everything starts from the upper left-hand corner.

Type in:

```
50  SET(55,32)
```

Clear the screen and RUN.

There it is! The light came on. Check the Video Display Worksheet carefully to find the address of that light. Did it show up in about the right place?

Careful now, don't mess up the screen. Type:

```
50  RESET(55,32)
```

   . . .and RUN.

How about that. You found the ON-OFF switch!

Want to really press your luck? Try turning the light back on. That's right, type:

```
50  SET(55,32)
```

   . . .and RUN 5 times in a row. Then:

```
50  RESET(55,32)
```

   . . .and RUN.

Oh well, can't win 'em all. Why didn't it work? It has to work. It *did* work! Then why didn't the fool lights go *off?*

Answer: The Line Feed keeps moving it up away from its original address, and only what's at a specific address gets turned *on* and *off*. The lights may move, but the screen addresses never move.

The point of all this, obviously, is that we can control whether each block on the screen is light or dark (on or off) by "talking" to it at its individual address with SET and RESET statements.

Blinking Lights In the Sky — Flying Saucers or Lightning Bugs?

If one has an ON-OFF switch, what does one do with it? With a little imagination one could create blocks that don't just go *on* and *off*, but do so to attract attention...*by blinking*. This simple program illustrates how to set up a "blinker".

Simple FOR-NEXT loops at 45 and 55 could control the blinking rate.

```
10 CLS
20 X = 60
30 Y = 25
40 SET(X,Y)
50 RESET(X,Y)
60 GOTO 40
```

Back For More. . .

In the horizontal direction, there are 128 light-block addresses, numbered from 0 to 127. 0 is at the far left, 64 is near the middle and 127 is at the far right.

In the vertical direction, there are 48 light-block addresses numbered from 0 to 47. 0 is at the top and 47 is at the bottom.

The statement "SET (X,Y)" whitens the block which is the Xth block from the left in the horizontal direction and the Yth one down from the top in the vertical direction. And, you've figured out that RESET works in the same way except that it "turns the light off".

Let's try it out. This program will lighten any one block of your choosing.

Type:

```
NEW
10 INPUT "HORIZONTAL ADDRESS (0 TO 127) IS";X
20 INPUT "VERTICAL ADDRESS (0 TO 47) IS";Y
30 CLS
40 SET(X,Y)
```

. . . .and RUN many times using various values of X and Y.

You may have noticed that if a block is lit in the upper left-hand corner, the READY and the ■ destroy it. Try X=6 and Y=6. Then X=5 and Y=5. We can avoid this problem by not returning control to the prompt by adding:

```
99 GOTO 99
```

at the end of the program. After running the program, this line locks the computer in an endless loop. To break the loop, press BREAK key. You should put an endless loop at the end of every graphics program. Do it here, then try X=5 and Y=5. Now try X=0 and Y=0. Remember the BREAK key to stop a properly "locked out" graphics program, before starting another.

While we have a key that RESETs every block on the screen to *off* in one operation (the CLEAR key), we don't have a similar key to turn them all *on*.

However, we can easily write a program that "lights", "whitens" or "paints" the entire screen. It uses one CLS (not really a *must*, but always a good habit to use in graphics programs), two FOR-NEXT loops and one endless "locking loop". Type this:

```
10 CLS
20 FOR X = 0 TO 127
30  FOR Y = 0 TO 47
40   SET(X,Y)
50  NEXT Y
60 NEXT X
99 GOTO 99
```

. . .and RUN.

NOTE: When running graphics, you may want to turn up both the contrast and brightness slightly. Don't forget. . .first we have to use the `BREAK` key to stop the endless loop.

The program fills the screen from left to right. Redesign it so it starts at the top and fills to the bottom.

Answer:

```
10 CLS
20 FOR Y = 0 TO 47
30  FOR X = 0 TO 127
40   SET(X,Y)
50  NEXT X
60 NEXT Y
99 GOTO 99
```

Next, rewrite it so it starts painting at the bottom and fills to the top.

Answer:

```
10 CLS
20 FOR Y = 47 TO 0 STEP-1
30  FOR X = 0 TO 127
40   SET(X,Y)
50  NEXT X
60 NEXT Y
99 GOTO 99
```

Forgot you could STEP it backwards, eh? Try a few of those and see how it works. Try different increments ($-2, -8$, etc.).

OK, now rewrite it so it starts painting at the right-hand side and fills to the left-hand side.

Answer:

```
10 CLS
20 FOR X = 127 TO 0 STEP-1
30  FOR Y = 0 TO 47
40   SET(X,Y)
50  NEXT Y
60 NEXT X
99 GOTO 99
```

Try some other step increments too. . .

Fantastic — now we can paint the old barn at least four ways!

EXERCISE 30-1: Write a program which will allow painting only a small part of the screen (you determine which part). Allow keyboard **INPUT** of the starting and ending block numbers in both the horizontal and vertical directions.

Getting the hang of it?? Great. Enough playing with blocks. . .let's draw some lines. Erase the resident program.

Of course you haven't forgotten how to do that, have you! Type ERASE. . .no, no, no! Type NEW.

We'll start with a straight line. This program gives us a straight horizontal line across the entire screen. Type:

```
10 INPUT "VERTICAL ADDRESS (0 TO 47)"; Y
20 CLS
30 FOR X = 0 TO 127
40  SET(X,Y)
50 NEXT X
99 GOTO 99
```

. . .and **RUN** several times.

We can just as easily create a straight vertical line. Try this.

```
10  INPUT "HORIZONTAL ADDRESS (0 TO 127)"; X
20  CLS
30  FOR Y = 0 TO 47
40   SET(X,Y)
50  NEXT Y
99  GOTO 99
```

. . .and **RUN** a number of times.

Now, let's see if we can modify this last program so we can **INPUT** both the starting vertical address and the length (in blocks) of the line.

```
12  INPUT "THE STARTING VERTICAL  ADDRESS #(0 TO 47) IS"; V
14  INPUT "HOW MANY VERTICAL BLOCKS DO YOU WISH TO FILL"; A
16  IF V + A < 48 GOTO 20
18  PRINT "TOO MANY VERTICAL BLOCKS. NOT ENOUGH ROOM!"
19  END
30  FOR Y = V TO V + A
```

. . .and **RUN.**

Now that we can draw straight lines, we can form figures — like squares and rectangles. This program forms a rectangle. After NEW, type:

```
10  INPUT "HORIZONTAL STARTING POINT (0 TO 127)"; X
20  INPUT "VERTICAL STARTING POINT (0 TO 27); Y
30  INPUT "LENGTH OF EACH SIDE (IN BLOCKS) --- (0 TO 47)"; K
40  CLS
50  FOR L = X TO X + K
60   SET(L,Y)
```

```
70    SET(L,Y+K)
80   NEXT L
90   FOR M = Y TO Y+K
100  SET(X,M)
110   SET(X+K,M)
120  NEXT M
999  GOTO 999
```

. . .and RUN.

Since our building blocks are not square, but 3 by 4 rectangles, we always get a rectangle. How can we change the program to always form a square?

> Remember, we can't draw pictures off the screen. If you get an error message like: ?FC ERROR IN 70, that means you tried to do it.

Exercise 30-2: Modify the resident program so it always draws a square (on the inside).

You may want to come back later for some heavier study.

Press on. . .

A Little Diversion

All our graphics work up to this time has been done by drawing white lines on a darkened screen. We can do just the reverse by painting the screen white first, then darkening the desired areas with RESET. This program, for example, draws a black horizontal line on a white background.

> Whew! That's not really very easy, but with some careful study (remembering that we have to account for the width of the blocks) it falls into line. Try your own approach a few times before going back to Section B to look at our suggestion. Don't cheat now!

Type:

```
10 INPUT "VERTICAL POSITION (Ø TO 47)"; Y
20 CLS
30 FOR X = Ø TO 127
40   FOR J = Ø TO 47
50     SET(X,J)
60   NEXT J
70 NEXT X
80 FOR X = Ø TO 127
90   RESET(X,Y)
100 NEXT X
999 GOTO 999
```

. . .and RUN.

If you're interested, go back and try similar easy modifications to other demonstration programs and have some fun with these reverse (or "negative") displays.

Learned in Chapter 30

Statements

SET
RESET

Intermediate Graphics

Model II users GOTO next chapter.

We can draw other straight (more or less) lines by just changing X and Y addresses of SET in the FOR-NEXT loop. Try this next program to draw a diagonal line:

```
10 INPUT "HORIZONTAL STARTING POINT (Ø TO 127)"; X

20 INPUT "VERTICAL STARTING POINT (Ø TO 47)"; Y

30 INPUT "DIAGONAL LENGTH"; K

40 CLS

50 FOR L = Ø TO K

60   SET(X+L,Y+L)

70 NEXT L

99 GOTO 99
```

Once we have the diagonal line, we can form a right triangle by adding:

```
70 SET(X,Y+L)

80 SET(X+L,Y+K)

90 NEXT L
```

or

```
70  SET(X+K,Y+L)
80  SET(X+L,Y)
90  NEXT L
```

Try them both. What is the difference in the displays?

Answer: They are inverted, mirror images of each other.

Broken lines

In every graphics program we could have made the lines "broken" by introducing a STEP other than "1" in the FOR-NEXT loops. For example, try drawing a broken horizontal line with:

```
10  INPUT "VERTICAL ADDRESS (1 TO 47)"; Y
20  INPUT "STEP SIZE"; S
30  CLS
40  FOR X = 0 TO 127 STEP S
50    SET(X,Y)
60  NEXT X
99  GOTO 99
```

> Remember, you can't draw pictures off the screen.

RUN this program with various values of S. Note that as you increase S, the line is drawn much faster (since the computer has less work to do). In fact, for S=10 or more, we can hardly see the line being drawn. This is how a TV picture is created — since it too is drawn one unit at a time (but so fast we don't notice the "drawing time").

Change the program as follows:

```
11  REM * Y MUST BE LARGER THAN 0 *
55  RESET(X,Y-1)
70  Y = Y + 1
80  IF Y < 48 GOTO 40
```

234

If S is small, you can see the lines being formed and cleared. But if S is fairly large (try 1∅), the line seems to move in somewhat "old-time movie" fashion. This is the way the illusion of motion is created on a TV set and in some of the popular video games.

Try this NEW program. It paints a dot on the screen and moves it down.

```
1∅  INPUT "HORIZONTAL STARTING POINT (∅ TO 127)"; X
2∅  INPUT "VERTICAL STARTING POINT (1 TO 47)"; Y
3∅  CLS
4∅  RESET(X,Y-1)
5∅  SET(X,Y)
6∅  Y = Y + 1
7∅  IF Y < 48 GOTO 4∅
99  GOTO 99
```

The RESET command simply follows along behind and erases the dot from the last SET. What happens if you omit RESET? When you try it, remember to change line 7∅ to GOTO 5∅.

Details. . .Details

One minor problem. . .RESET and SET don't work with negative coordinates. Take a look at line 4∅:

```
4∅  RESET(X,Y-1)
```

If you INPUT Y equal to ∅, then the Y address really becomes Y-1. . .-1. A no-no!

Back To the Good Stuff

We can just as easily move a point to the right with:

```
1∅  INPUT "HORIZONTAL STARTING POINT (1 TO 127)"; X
2∅  INPUT "VERTICAL STARTING POINT (∅ TO 47)"; Y
3∅  CLS
4∅  RESET(X-1,Y)
```

```
50  SET(X,Y)
60  X = X + 1
70  IF X < 128 GOTO 40
99  GOTO 99
```

> *EXERCISE 31-1:* Change the last two programs so that they move the dot up and to the left, respectively.

Now, let's have the dot move down until it strikes a barrier. The program is:

```
10  INPUT "HORIZONTAL STARTING POINT (0 TO 127)"; X
20  INPUT "VERTICAL STARTING POINT (1 TO 20)"; Y
30  INPUT "LOWER BARRIER (30 TO 47)"; K
40  CLS
50  FOR M = 0 TO 127
60    SET(M,K)
70  NEXT M
80  RESET(X,Y-1)
90  SET(X,Y)
100 Y = Y + 1
110 IF Y < K THEN 80
999 GOTO 999
```

The dot appears to strike the barrier and stick to it.

Now let's have the dot start in the middle and ricochet from both the top and the bottom:

```
10  CLS
20  FOR M = 0 TO 127
30    SET(M,0)
```

```
40    SET(M,47)
50  NEXT M
60  Y = 14
70  D = 1
80  RESET(64,Y-D)
90  SET(64,Y)
100  Y = Y + D
110  IF  Y = 48  THEN  130
120  IF  Y <> -1  THEN  80
130  Y = Y - 2 * D
140  D = -D
150  GOTO 90
999  GOTO 999
```

The change in direction of the moving dot is caused by line 14Ø D = D. Note that we must be careful not to accidentally erase part of the boundary. To do this, we not only move the dot back 2 steps with line 13Ø (after moving it forward 1 in line 1ØØ) but we also return to the SET in 9Ø, rather than to RESET in 8Ø. Tricky, tricky. You can kill the whole day messing around with this silly bouncing ball. Rather good resilience, eh?

Save this program for use in the next chapter.

Real Moving Pictures

We can draw whatever figures we like. Let's try a stick man. First, his legs:

```
10  CLS
20  X = 64
30  FOR K = Ø TO 7
40    SET(X+K,4Ø+K)
50    SET(X-K,4Ø+K)
60  NEXT K
999  GOTO 999
```

. . .and RUN.

Then add his body and arms:

```
70  FOR K = 0 TO 5
80    SET(X+K,34+K)
90    SET(X,34+K)
100 SET(X-K,34+K)
110 NEXT K
```

. . .and RUN.

And finally his head:

```
120 SET(X,32)
130 SET(X+1,33)
140 SET(X-1,33)
```

"OK, so I'm no artist...!!"

. . .and RUN.

Now let's try and move him to the right. Add:

```
45  RESET(X+K-1,40+K)
55  RESET(X-K-1,40+K)
85  RESET(X+K-1,34+K)
95  RESET(X-1,34+K)
105 RESET(X-K-1,34+K)
125 RESET(X-1,32)
135 RESET(X,33)
145 RESET(X-2,33)
150 X = X + 1
160 GOTO 30
```

. . .and RUN.

Sure moves funny, doesn't he? Well, I'm no animator either, but I'm sure you're beginning to get the idea.

This has been one long and active chapter. . .and to think, all this with only the SET and RESET statements. And by simply exchanging RESET for SET, in many cases we could have drawn the same pictures, with dark on a light background instead of light on dark. You might want to give it a try.

Because the ideas come so fast in the area of graphics, we have deliberately chosen to show a lot of examples without getting bogged down in detailed explanations of how each one works. There is no substitute for lots of experimenting with graphics, and you now know the basics. Put in your time, study the examples, and soon you can apply for membership in the artist's guild.

Learned in Chapter 31

Miscellaneous

Diagonal Lines

Broken Lines

Animated Graphics

Display Formatting With PRINT@

Remember the bouncing dot? Wouldn't it be nifty if we could get the screen to say "PING" each time the dot bounced off the barrier? Well, I think it would be nifty, so we're going to do it. But first. . .

We learned all about SET and RESET earlier. Now we will learn about PRINT@ (pronounced *print at*) — a special type of PRINT statement especially useful in graphics.

Caution: Do not use the shift key with @ on Models I and III. @ is shift 2 on Model II.

I Thought You Printed On Not At

Learn something new every day. The PRINT@ statement allows us to *begin* printing at a location number. Example, type:

```
NEW

10 CLS

50 PRINT@ 200, "HELLO THERE 200, WHEREVER YOU ARE."
```

. . .and RUN.

Where is 2ØØ? Back to the Video Display Worksheet from Chapter 30.

With the aid of an ordinary household electron microscope, the words "PRINT AT" are seen on the upper left-hand corner of the sheet. Also, an arrow pointing to a set of numbers. Further scrutiny discloses a tiny "X", obviously referring to the address numbers on the "X" Street, and a tiny "Y" pointing to the "Y" numbers for "Y" Avenue. A truly astute researcher will also see the "TAB" numbers — all 64 of them (starting with 0).

The PRINT@ numbers start at Ø and go through 63 — in the *first line*. They then pick up on the second line with number 64 and continue through number 127.

On Model II, Ø through 79 — first line; 8Ø through 159 — second line, etc.

The third line starts with number 128, etc. The PRINT@ divisions are really the same as those for **TAB**, except PRINT@ does not start over again with zero on the second line. It keeps going right on through PRINT position number 1Ø23.

Position number 1919 on Model II.

This perhaps strange sort of numbering is not so strange when you consider the problems we had very early in the graphics game with the fool carriage return scrolling our light right off the screen.

Remember what scrolling is? An upward line roll.

The PRINT@ statement does not trigger a scroll after it has done its printing, *except in the last line*, between print positions number 96Ø and number 1Ø23.

Position number 1840 — 1919 on Model II.

Further, PRINT@ can *directly* address any of the 1Ø23 printing locations (not light block locations — they are very different). Trailing semicolons are needed only after statements printed on that last or bottom line of the video "page".

We will soon see how valuable all this is.

Oh, It's That Time Already?

> Note: Model II see Appendix E for a formula to translate Model I/III PRINT@ positions to the Model II.

Let's create a 24-hour clock. (Why not. . .sounds like more fun than digging through all this obscure print statement logic?) Type:

```
10 CLS
20 PRINT@407, "H    M    S"
30  FOR H = 0 TO 23
40   FOR M = 0 TO 59
50    FOR S = 0 TO 59
60     PRINT@470,H; ":"; M; ":"; S
70     FOR N = 1 TO 400 : NEXT N
80    NEXT S
90   NEXT M
100 NEXT H
110 GOTO 10
```

. . .and RUN.

Nothing to it. Ahem!

"Hello? Bureau of Standards?"

Of course, the accuracy of this timer depends on how closely we calibrate it. We know that a Model III will execute somewhere around 400 simple FOR-NEXT loops per second when written as shown in line 70, a multiple statement line. If you really get carried away with this program, you will want to calibrate it with a precision-type timepiece (increasing or decreasing the "40-0" figure as needed). Over the short run, this is quite a good timer. Note that we are not triggering this with the power line frequency, but relying solely on the amount of time required to execute FOR-NEXT loops.

Oh, Yes. . .the PRINT@

Anyway, let's not lose sight of the forest for the trees (or something equally trite). The purpose of this little program is to demonstrate the PRINT@ statement. We used it twice. By carefully squinting at the layout chart, you can find address number 407, with number 470 nearly below it.

On Model II, position numbers 748 and 827.

With blazing speed, the HMS (no, no, not Her Majesty's Service — it stands for Hours, Minutes and Seconds) are printed, and the HM and S updated each second.

NOTE: No carriage-return-suppressing semicolons follow the PRINT@ statements since they are not on the bottom print line.

For the real clock nut, see Section C for an operational clock program. It only needs your closer calibration to be an acceptable sundial. . .most expensive clock in the house!

Note: Model II skip to the heading "Merely For Display Purposes" in the next chapter.

That's How the Ball Bounces

Meanwhile, back with the bouncing ball. Let's reload the program from Chapter 31. It reads:

```
10 CLS
20 FOR M = 0 TO 127
30   SET(M,0)
40   SET(M,47)
50 NEXT M
60 Y = 14
70 D = 1
80 RESET(64,Y-D)
90 SET(64,Y)
100 Y = Y + D
```

```
110 IF Y = 48 THEN 130
120 IF Y <> -1 THEN 80
130 Y = Y - 2 * D
140 D = -D
150 GOTO 90
999 GOTO 999
```

Since we did not explain in detail how that fairly simple program worked, take time now to see if you can follow it through. When you have figured it out, tackle this exercise:

Exercise 32-1: Using PRINT@ statement(s), cause the word "PING" to appear near the ball each time it bounces off either the top or bottom boundary.

Isn't it amazing how close we are building towards some of the actual video games that are all the rage? And yet it's really so simple and logical.

Learned in Chapter 32

Statements

PRINT@

Graphing Trig Functions

It is often helpful to graph mathematical functions so we can better understand what's going on. The TRS-80 graphics are adequate for a non-precision examination of many mathematical functions, and the following short demo programs illustrate that capability.

Just imagine there is a coordinate system drawn on the screen (or draw your own, either with the computer or a China Marker). The numbers in these demo programs are not magic, they just allow the graphs to be drawn large, but not so large they try to run off the screen.

These programs are included to show how PRINT@ can be used in a supporting role to the TRS-80 graphics. Experiment to get what you want for your own particular application.

Graphing of Single Sine Wave

```
1 CLS : PRINT@0,"SINE"

10 FOR X = 0 TO 255

20 Y = SIN(X/40)

30 SET(X/2,20-Y*20)
```

```
40 PRINT@50,"X =";  INT(X/2);
50 PRINT@58,"Y =";  INT(20-Y*20);
60 NEXT X
70 GOTO 70
```

Graph of Three Cosine Waves

```
1 CLS : PRINT@7,"COSINE"
10 FOR X = 0 TO 765
20 Y = COS(X/40)
30 SET(X/6,20-Y*20)
40 PRINT@45,"X =";  INT(X/6);
50 PRINT@53,"Y =";  INT(20-Y*20);
60 NEXT X
70 GOTO 70
```

Graph of the Tangent

```
1 CLS : PRINT@7,"TANGENT"
10 FOR X = 0 TO 126
20 Y = TAN(X/90)
30 SET(X,47-Y*8)
40 PRINT@40,"X =";  INT(X);
50 PRINT@48,"Y =";  INT(47-Y*8);
60 NEXT X
70 GOTO 70
```

There is obviously quite an education to be had by careful study of the graphs. Look for such things as relative thickness of the line at different points, the rate at which blocks are lit relative to the other variable, etc. Sure beats the "early days" when we had to try and imagine these things on a blackboard.

NOTE: Model III and some Model I users are able to combine lines 40 and

5Ø of these graphing programs into a single PRINT line. In the Sine Graph
program, for example, try replacing line 4Ø and 5Ø with

```
4Ø  PRINT@5Ø,"X=";INT(X/2);@58,"Y=";INT(2Ø-Y*2Ø);
```

. . .and RUN it.

One noteworthy procedure in this program is the use of trailing semicolons after
PRINT@ statements. The reason, again, is that the printing is taking place in the
last line on the screen so the carriage return would activate a line feed scroll. We
therefore have to suppress the carriage return with the semicolon.

Merely For Display Purposes

A good way to get a feel for PRINT@ (or any feature) is to look at a fairly
simple program which illustrates its use. This program lays out a graph format on the screen. What you do with it beyond that point depends on your
own needs and interests, but it is worth entering, studying and getting a feel
for its use. Type:

```
1Ø  CLS
2Ø  PRINT@2Ø, "G R A P H   H E A D I N G"          Model II 25
3Ø  PRINT@84, "- - - - - - - - - - -"              Model II 105
4Ø  REM * HORIZONTAL MARKERS *
5Ø  FOR X = 1 TO 59
6Ø  PRINT@9ØØ+X,".";                               Model II 1685
7Ø  NEXT X
8Ø  REM * HORIZONTAL NUMBERS *
9Ø  FOR X = Ø TO 5
1ØØ  PRINT@964+1Ø*X,X;                              Model II 1765
11Ø  NEXT X
12Ø  REM * VERTICAL MARKERS *
13Ø  FOR Y = Ø TO 13
14Ø  PRINT@Y*64+68,"-";                            Model II Y*80+84
15Ø  NEXT Y
16Ø  REM * VERTICAL NUMBERS *
```

```
170 FOR Y = 0 TO 13
180 PRINT@Y*64+64,13-Y;                    Model II Y*80+80,20-Y;
190 NEXT Y
999 GOTO 999
```

PRINT@ and Double Width

The use of double-width letters adds considerable impact to visual displays.
There are, however, several rules which must be followed. Type in this
program, then we'll explore them:

```
10 REM     * ON BASE OF STATUE OF LIBERTY *
20 REM     * LARGEST STATUE EVER ERECTED *
30 CLS : PRINT CHR$(23)                     Model II use CHR(30)
40 PRINT@456,"KEEP, ANCIENT LANDS,"         Model II 810
50 PRINT@522,"YOUR STORIED POMP!"           Model II 972
60 FOR T = 1 TO 1700 : NEXT
70 CLS : PRINT CHR$(23)                      Model II use CHR(30)
80 PRINT@128,"GIVE ME YOUR TIRED, YOUR POOR,"   Model II 140
90 FOR T = 1 TO 1500 : NEXT
100 PRINT@256,"YOUR HUDDLED MASSES YEARNING TO"  Model II 480
110 PRINT@324,"BREATHE FREE,"               Model II 565
120 FOR T = 1 TO 1100 : NEXT
130 PRINT@448,"THE WRETCHED REFUSE OF YOUR"  Model II 800
140 PRINT@516,"TEEMING SHORE."              Model II 965
150 FOR T = 1 TO 1900 : NEXT
160 PRINT@640,"SEND THESE, THE HOMELESS,"    Model II 1200
170 PRINT@708,"TEMPEST-TOST TO ME,"          Model II 1285
180 FOR T = 1 TO 2000 : NEXT
190 PRINT@832,"I LIFT MY LAMP BESIDE THE GOLDEN"  Model II 1520
200 PRINT@900,"DOOR!"                        Model II 1685
210 GOTO 210
```

. . .and RUN.

In line 3Ø we used ASCII character 23 to convert the video display to 32 characters per line.

Model II 40 characters

In line 7Ø we needed a CLS, but CLS automatically returns the video to 64 characters per line. This forced us to use another CHR$(23) to get back in the 32-character mode.

Model II 80 characters

Model II CLS doesn't change to regular width.

Look at each PRINT@ statement. See anything at all similar. . .something we haven't discussed? How about it, Sherlock? (Shut up Watson! I know you see it.) Elementary, when you stop and think about it. Every video starting address ends in an even number. Oh, yes. . .(cough). . .of course.

Every letter and number is printed in double width, and the rules state that for double width we must start on an *even* numbered block. Change line 4Ø to PRINT@457 instead of 456 and RUN.

Model II 811 instead of 810

Total wipeout! Can't get much more dramatic than that. Add one more number to make it PRINT@458

Model II 812

. . .and RUN.

Notice anything? Look at the display very carefully. Then change the program line back to PRINT@456

Model II 810

. . .and RUN.

See it?

Right! We have to move over two video print addresses to move the double width display over just one space. Terribly obvious when you think of it. Not very obvious when trying to troubleshoot a program and you aren't aware of it.

This program needs a good graphic display of The Statue, complete with flaming torch. Also, a good paper printout to hang on the wall. How about it, artists?

Learned in Chapter 33

Miscellaneous

Graphing with PRINT@

Double-Width Mode

POINT

Model II users skip this chapter.

What Is the POINT Of All This?

The POINT(X,Y) statement stands pretty much isolated from the other three graphic statements. It needs them, but they don't need it at all.

POINT(X,Y) interrogates (what a great technical word) that graphic point on the screen with the address of (X,Y). If that point is lit, the POINT statement says "-1". If it is dark, the POINT statement says "0". That's really all there is to it. Of such simplicity, great power is derived.

Interrogates just asks a question; but it's in logic form. . .true or yes gives -1 and false or no gives 0.

Let's give POINT a little exercise before looking closer. Since it also works in the calculator mode, type:

```
PRINT POINT(30,30)
```

Since we didn't light 3Ø,3Ø, the answer came back 0.

Let There Be Light

Let's light up a spot on the screen, then interrogate that point and see what happens. Type:

```
10  X=75 - Y=20
20  INPUT "DO YOU WISH TO LIGHT THE BLOCK (Y/N)";Q$
30  CLS
40  IF Q$ = "N" GOTO 80
50  SET(X,Y)
60  GOTO 100
80  RESET(X,Y)
100 IF POINT(X,Y) = -1 PRINT@200,X;Y,"IS LIT"
200 IF POINT(X,Y) = 0 PRINT@200,X;Y,"IS DARK"
999 GOTO 999
```

(Y and N stand for Yes and No.)

And RUN several times. Answer either YES or NO, following the program action to see what is happening. Pretty simple, isn't it? Really sort of a status-reporting system. Think what we could do if we set something like this up in two nested FOR-NEXT loops so we scan the entire screen and get a status report on each point. Hmmm. Almost like a radar scan of the terrain. Hmmm some more.

2001 Here We Come

Snug up your seat belt, type and RUN the following program, then sit back and watch POINT in action. Study the display very carefully as it runs, looking for the many things that occur. This two minute "moving picture" really tells all we need to know about the POINT statement.

```
10 REM * DEMONSTRATION OF GRAPHICS 'POINT' STATEMENT *
20 P = 15 : L = 119
30 CLS
40 PRINT@5,"THIS IS A DEMONSTRATION OF THE POINT STATEMENT---
50 PRINT@56,"X    Y";
```

```
100 FOR I = 1 TO P: SET (RND(113),RND(45+2) : NEXT
110 FOR X = 0 TO 111 : FOR Y = 0 TO 47
120 IF POINT(X,Y) = 0 GOTO 160
130 PRINT@L,X; : PRINT@L+4,Y;
140 L = L+64
150 GOTO 170
160 SET(X,Y) : RESET(X,Y)
170 NEXT Y : NEXT X
180 PRINT @5,"THE COORDINATES OF THE GRAPHICS BLOCKS ARE ";
190 GOTO 190
```

Vectoring In On Darth Vader's Death Star Fleet

If that one didn't blow your mind, let's take the program apart a line at a time:

Line 10 is just the program identification note.

Line 20 sets P at 15, the number of "targets" to be randomly placed on the screen by the FOR-NEXT loop and the random number generator in line 100. L is set at 119, the starting point for printing the coordinates and their headings in lines 130 and 140.

Line 30 clears the screen for action.

Lines 40 and 50 use PRINT@ to print the heading.

Line 100 generates 15 addresses and SETs 15 lights.

Line 110 uses two nested FOR-NEXT loops to establish a "scanner", testing every graphic point on the screen.

Line 120 tests to see if the point being addressed is off. If so, the address printing and related incrementing of the next PRINT@ location in lines 130 and 140 are bypassed. Line 130 prints the values of X and Y if the POINT test in line 120 "fell through", meaning that the point being tested was not off.

Line 14Ø increments the PRINT@ address for the next time line 13Ø prints the coordinates. By adding 64, the next printing will directly line up under the current heading and numbers. (See the layout chart if you can't follow it in your head.)

Line 15Ø is critical, since it jumps over a RESET. Without this jump, the light blocks would be erased when they are interrogated. (Try deleting the line and RUNning to see.)

Line 16Ø is just a foxy display trick. It causes a blinking light to "appear" to be scanning all points. Actually, line 16Ø is just turning blocks ON and OFF as the computer interrogates them. Since we don't want to turn off the blocks that are already supposed to be lit, we hop over this line when a real live block is hit. In reality, then, this "roving eye" never actually "hits" an "ON" block.

Line 17Ø merely closes the FOR-NEXT loops started in line 11Ø.

Line 18Ø replaces the heading that was erased by the POINT scanning process.

Line 19Ø is the locking loop used to keep READY and the prompt from goofing up the display.

Pretty simple when taken a line at a time, isn't it?

Oh yes, did you notice that the "moving dot" turned off the original heading? Did you also notice that it took two passes of the dot to equal the width of one printed character (which of course fits right in with what the layout sheet shows)?

The reason the heading was erased is that we deliberately chose not to protect it (like we protected the blocks) from the RESET in line 16Ø, in order to make the point. You could write a little protective line if you wanted to (or reduce the vertical length of the scan to avoid it).

> *EXERCISE 34-1:* Modify the POINT demo program so that the heading is not erased by the "moving dot".

Alpha Or Omega?

There you have it — a good running start into graphics. Go now to Section C where you will find more ready-to-run programs. Give them careful study. You will see the four graphics statements in use, plus most of the rest you have learned about BASIC programming. The possibilities from here are unlimited.

Learned in Chapter 34

Graphics Functions

POINT(X,Y)

INKEY$

The INKEY$ (pronounced inkey-string) function is a powerful one which enables us to INPUT information from the keyboard without having to use the ENTER key.

Enter this NEW program:

```
1 CLS
10 IF INKEY$="T" THEN 30
20 GOTO 10
30 PRINT"YOU HIT THE LETTER 'T'"
40 GOTO 10
```

. . .and RUN.

The keyboard seems to be dead, until we hit the "T" key. The test in line 1Ø then passes, execution moves to line 3Ø and a message is PRINTed. Then the process starts over.

The way INKEY$ works is clever, if somewhat subtle, so pay close attention. The TRS-80 keyboard is constantly scanned by the computer to detect when any key is pressed. Each time a key is pressed, the character it represents is automatically stored in the INKEY$ "buffer". INKEY$ takes on the value of the current character in the buffer.

This buffer can hold only one character at a time. So, when a new key is pressed, the new character replaces the old one.

Since INKEY$ can only "photograph" one letter or number at a time, if we want to test for more than one character we must write the program to test for each one in sequence. In so doing, however, we must be careful, or INKEY$ can trip us up.

Add these lines to the program:

```
15 IF INKEY$="P" THEN 50
50 PRINT"YOU HIT THE LETTER 'P': GOTO 10
```

     . . .and RUN.

As you can see, we no longer get a response each time the keys are pressed. This distressing situation happens because the INKEY$ buffer is cleared and reset to a null string *each* time the INKEY$ function is used. Aaawk! Just when it was starting to make sense. Type LIST so we can take a good look at the program to see how this clearing of the buffer results in the "loss" of a keystroke.

Suppose that the operator presses the T key just as line 15 begins execution. Where does the T go? Right into the INKEY$ buffer, of course. There it sits until another key is pressed or INKEY$ is called.

Now, as line 15 continues execution, INKEY$ calls. The buffer's current value ("T") is compared to "P". Since the two strings are not equal, control passes to the next line, then back to line 1Ø. In line 1Ø, the INKEY$ function is called again, but when it checks the buffer this time, "T" is not to be found. What happened to the T?

Let's replay that last sequence and zoom in for a close-up on the INKEY$ buffer. As the operator hits the T key, we see the T stored in the buffer. As the INKEY$ function in line 15 is executed, the buffer suddenly goes blank. Ahhhhh! Thank heavens for instant replay. It's now obvious that each time the INKEY$ function is called, the buffer is completely cleared. So if we want to preserve the value of T, we'll need to store it in a temporary string variable.

Change line 1Ø and 15 to get:

```
1  CLS
1Ø  A$=INKEY$ :  IF  A$="T"  THEN  3Ø
15  IF  A$="P"  THEN  5Ø
2Ø  GOTO  1Ø
3Ø  PRINT"YOU  HIT  THE  LETTER'T'"
4Ø  GOTO  1Ø
5Ø  PRINT"YOU  HIT  THE  LETTER  'P'":  GOTO  1Ø
```

. . .and RUN.

Aha!   Now we're getting somewhere. By setting INKEY$ equal to a "regular" string variable, we can store its value for as long as needed and process it much more efficiently and predictably.

Rapid Scanner

If INKEY$ scans the buffer and does not find a pressed key (the usual case), it is said to read a "null string". INKEY$ is a string function, and null means *nothing*. A null string is represented by two quote marks with nothing between them, thus:

" "

The ASCII code for null is Ø.

To see how fast we can scan for INPUT with INKEY$, try this NEW program:

```
1Ø  K$ =  INKEY$ :  IF  K$ = ""  PRINT"NO  KEYBOARD  INPUT"
2Ø  PRINT ,,,K$ :  GOTO  1Ø
```

. . .and RUN.

Type in random characters and see them break the scan.

Get the general idea how to use INKEY\$? So simple, yet the possibilities are enormous. Only a lot of experimenting will make us comfortable with it, but INKEY\$ will keep you awake nights staring at the ceiling, thinking of ways to put it to work.

Out Of The Blue Of The Western Sky . . .

While chasing the solitude needed to write this chapter, your author flew a heavily-loaded light plane, packed with a typewriter, a customized computer with accessories, plus luggage (and, of course, Ham radio) into a medium-sized city airport. Transferring this freight to a car turned out to be a big deal since security wouldn't let a car on the apron to offload the plane. (You're supposed to drop it by parachute?) After some cajoling (and a gratuity) it was agreed that my car could be driven up *near* the apron, and an "officially approved" car would haul the goodies from the plane to my car. It all seemed a bit officious, but election time wasn't close enuf, so. . .

Anyway, to get my car thru the security fence, it was necessary to drive to an electrically-operated gate and punch a secret code into a numeric keypad for some sort of computer to analyze, and automatically open the gate. The secret code number was 1930.

Needless to say, as soon as the computer was set up, I had to write a BASIC program to do everything but actually open the gate. It provides a good example of a real-life application of INKEY\$, and is offered here for your amusement, amazement and study.

```
10 CLS : PRINT@790,"TYPE THE COMBINATION"          On Model II 750

20 PRINT@854,"FOLLOWED BY A PERIOD"                On Model II 830

30 PRINT@147,"THE ELECTRONIC GATE IS CLOSED"       On Model II 105

40 K$ = INKEY$ : IF K$ = "" GOTO 40

50 READ D$ : IF D$ = "." GOTO 100

60 IF D$ = K$ GOTO 40

70 RESTORE : GOTO 40

100 REM * SEE 'CONTROLLING THE WORLD WITH YOUR TRS-80' *

110 REM * BY YOUR FAVORITE AUTHOR FOR DETAILS ON HOW *

120 REM * TO ACTUALLY OPEN AND CLOSE THE ELECTRIC GATE *
```

```
130 CLS : PRINT@133,"YOU MAY ENTER NOW - WAIT FOR THE
ELECTRONIC GATE TO OPEN"                          On Model II 170
140 FOR T = 1 TO 2000 : NEXT T : RESTORE : GOTO 10
1000 DATA 1,9,3,0,.
```

The password (1930 followed by a period) is imbedded, a character at a time, in DATA line 1000. The commas only separate the characters and should not be typed in to open the gate.

Line 40 holds the magic. It checks the INKEY$ buffer looking for something besides a null string. If it finds a key pressed, execution drops to line 50.

Line 50 READs a piece of DATA. If it happens to be a period (which can only be READ from DATA after each of the other code characters have been READ), execution moves to line 100 where the gate will be caused to open and line 140 will tell us to enter the premises.

If, however, the test in line 50 does not find a period, execution defaults to the next test, in line 60.

Line 60 checks to see if the keyboard character matches up with the character READ from DATA. If so, the first hurdle has been passed and execution returns back to line 40 for INKEY$ to await another keyboard character. If the keyboard and DATA characters don't match, the test fails and execution drops to line 70.

Line 70 RESTOREs the DATA pointer back to its beginning, and returns execution to line 40 to start scanning all over again. The keypad puncher sees none of this and has no idea if he is making progress towards cracking the code.

Line 150 merely allows the gate a brief time to open and close (and us to read the screen), then RESTOREs the DATA and starts the program over again from the beginning.

The password can be changed to any combination of characters by changing line 1000.

Chapter 35

If we wanted it to be "TRS-80" for example:

```
1000 DATA T,R,S,-,8,0,.
```

Or, "OPENSESAME"

```
1000 DATA O,P,E,N,S,E,S,A,M,E,.
```

Don't forget that last piece of DATA, the period. By changing line 5Ø, of course, we could change that period to anything we wanted.

Happy gate crashing!

Learned in Chapter 35

Functions	Miscellaneous
INKEY$	INKEY$ buffer

PRINT USING

Of all the ways we have to PRINT, the most powerful (but most confusing) is one called PRINT USING. The name PRINT USING implies that we *print* something *using* something else. That implication is correct.

As originally developed for use on large computers, PRINT USING consists of two parts — PRINT and USING. PRINT prints using the format (called the "image") found in *another* line. The TRS-80 PRINT USING feature is similar, but does not always require a second line for the "image". . .as we will see.

PRINT USING With Numbers

Type in this NEW program:

```
10 A = 123.456789

40 U$ = "###.##"

50 PRINT USING U$;A

90 PRINT : LIST
```

        . . .and RUN.

The answer is PRINTed as:

```
123.46
```

It was rounded UP and PRINTed to an accuracy of two *decimal* places.

Add:

```
20 B = 1.6
60 PRINT USING U$;B
```

    . . .and RUN.

The Display shows

```
123.46
  1.60
```

The first thing to note is that we have called upon line 4Ø, the *image line*, twice — once in line 5Ø and again in line 6Ø. Also, note that two answers appear with their decimal points lined up. Last, see that a Ø has been added to the 1.6 to make it read 1.6Ø. These latter two points are important if you're PRINTing out business reports.

One more addition:

```
30 C =9876.54321
70 PRINT USING U$;C
```

Produces:

```
123.46
  1.60
%9876.54
```

Oh-oh! Vas ist los?

Well, the % sign means we have overrun our *image line's* capacity to PRINT digits *left* of the decimal point, but it PRINTs them anyway. Better to lose our decimal point lineup than important numbers, but it does call our attention to a programming problem.

Let's add another # sign to make room for that extra digit. (We are adding another *element* to the *field* in the *image line*. Got that?)

```
4Ø  U$  =  "####.##"
```

   . . .and RUN.

That's better — but the overrun message would appear again if we tried to PRINT a number with more than four digits on the left.

So far, this PRINT USING business looks like it might have some potential, lining up decimal points like it does. We don't have any other reasonable, straightforward way to accomplish that, and it's essential for PRINTing dollars and cents for business reports. Wonder how we can PRINT a dollar sign?

Let's change our *image line* to:

```
4Ø  U$  =  "$####.##"
```

(count 'em carefully)

   . . .and RUN.

Nice, eh? The dollar signs all line up in a row:

```
$  123.46
$     1.6Ø
$9876.54
```

But suppose we want the dollar signs to snug right up against each dollar amount? Make 4Ø read:

```
4Ø  U$  =  "$$####.##"
```

   . . .and RUN.

and we get:

```
$123.46
  $1.6Ø
$9876.54
```

Not 'specially attractive in this format, but taken singly, as when writing checks, it's almost essential.

The lessons so far are:

1. PRINT USING with # PRINTs the decimal point at the same place for every size number PRINTed.

2. It rounds off the cents (the numbers to the right of the decimal point) to the number of # signs there. It does not round off dollars (left of the decimal point), but sends up an error flag %, PRINTs all dollars, and slips the decimal point to the right if the field isn't large enough.

3. If a single $ is added to the left, dollar signs will be PRINTed and lined up in a column like decimal points. This single $ does not expand the field.

4. If two $'s are placed on the left, one $ will be PRINTed on each line and will be placed immediately in front of the first dollar digit. One $ can replace one # in the field, thereby not expanding it.

We've covered a lot with a very small program, but have a long way to go.

Printing Checks

When using a printer for writing checks, it's usually wise to take extra precautions against "alterations". This is easily accomplished by changing line 4Ø to read:

```
4Ø U$ = "**###.##"
```

(count 'em)

. . .and RUN.

The Display now reads:

```
**123.46
****1.60
****1.60
```

That's swell, it fills up the unused space alright, but we lost the dollar sign. OK, let's replace the first # sign with a dollar sign, like so:

```
40 U$ = "**$##.##"
```

(Aren't you glad you have an Editor for all these changes?)

See it Now:

```
*$123.46
***$1.60
$9876.54
```

just like they do it uptown!

If we want to really impress others with the size numbers we usually deal with at our lemonade stand, we add a lot more # signs to the *image line*, thus:

```
40 U$ = "**$###############.##"
```

and our checks read:

```
***************$123.46
*****************$1.60
***************$9876.54
```

. . .very impressive.

Since we're obviously big-time operators, having now franchised our lemonade stands, it's getting hard to keep track of the big numbers. How about some commas to break them apart? (Knock out those extra #'s first. Too hard to count them.)

```
40 U$ = "**$,##.##"
```

(look closely)

. . .and RUN.

```
**$123.46
****$1.60
$9,876.54
```

Only one of our numbers has more than three digits, but a comma separated its 9 and 8 for easier readability. In the image field, the comma can be placed *anywhere* between the $ and the decimal point, and only *one* comma is required to automatically insert commas to the left of every third digit left of the decimal point. (You really big-time operators who deal in the millions will have to wait 'til the next chapter to see how to go "double precision" to avoid losing the loose change.)

Stringing It Out

Let's rework our resident program to show some other PRINT USING capabilities:

```
1 CLS : PRINT
10 A = 123.456789
20 B = 1.60
30 C = 9876.54321
40 U$ = "#####.##      #####.##      #####.##"
50 PRINT USING U$;A,B,C
90 PRINT : LIST
```

Line 40 could be shortened to:

```
40 U$ = "#####.##"
```

with the same effect. The PRINT USING statement will reuse its image line until all the values are PRINTed.

Anyway, RUN it and see how the same numbers can be displayed horizontally instead of vertically. All depends on what we need at a given time.

```
123.46              1.60              9876.54
```

PRINT USING With Strings

Change the program to read:

```
1 CLS : PRINT
10 A$ = "IT'S"
15 B$ = "HOWDY"
20 C$ = "DOODY"
25 D$ = "TIME"
40 U$ = "%%"
50 PRINT USING U$; A$
90 PRINT : LIST
```

Model II use "/" (CTRL 9) instead of "%".

    . . .and RUN.

The only thing unique about this program is in line 4Ø. As if we didn't already have enough uses for the % sign to worry about, here is another. % is a symbol in TRS-80 PRINT USING which is to strings something like what the # is to numbers.

We used two %'s to reserve two spaces for strings, and only IT was PRINTed. Unlike #, however, to reserve more spaces in the string field, we add blank spaces between the % signs. Change line 4Ø to:

```
40 U$ ="%   %"
```

    . . .and RUN.

Four spaces are set aside and IT'S is PRINTed without clipping.

Let's make room for PRINTing another string on the same line.

```
40 U$ = "%   %%    %"
50 PRINT USING U$,A$,B$
```

    . . .and RUN.

Oops! We ran together.

```
IT'SHOWDY
```

To space them apart we have to put an actual space in the image field just as we did earlier when PRINTing numbers.

```
40 U$ = "%   %  %      %"
```

. . .and RUN.

That's more like it.

Now it's your turn. Complete lines 40 and 50 to print IT'S HOWDY DOODY TIME all on one line.

Answer:

```
40 U$ = "%   %  %      %  %      %  %   %
50 PRINT USING U$;A$,B$,C$,D$
```

(If you have trouble counting the blanks in PRINT USING, add an adjacent "measuring" line like this, to help.)

```
39 PRINT "123456789012345678901234567890"
```

It's time to quit doodling around and get down to business too! Let's change our HOWDY DOODY to some typical report headings.

```
1 CLS : PRINT
10 A$ = "PART NUMBER"
15 B$ = "DATE PURCHASED"
20 C$ = "DESCRIPTION"
25 D$ = "COST"
40    (you figure out this one yourself)
50 PRINT USING U$;A$,B$,C$,D$
90 PRINT :LIST
```

Answer:

```
              (9 spaces)            (12 spaces)              (9 spaces)
4Ø U$ = "%         ↓   %   %           ↓   %   %      ↓        %   ↓
                     (4 spaces)          (4 spaces)           (4 spaces)
%  %"
  ↓
(2 spaces)          (There should be 4 spaces between the %'s where we had to split the line.)
```

Bring On The Money Changers

Here is a straightforward user program which uses PRINT USING in a
practical way. One would be hard-pressed to get the same results in so short
a program without using it.

If you're not in the international currency biz, just type in the program, the
first half-dozen or so DATA lines, plus line 15ØØ, to get a feel for what
PRINT USING can do. See how % and # can be mixed with blank spaces on
the same image line?

Count spaces in line 8Ø *very carefully*. Add a "measuring line", 75, if necessary.

```
1Ø REM  * INTERNATIONAL MONEY CHANGER *
2Ø REM  * RATES AS OF FEBRUARY 1982 *
3Ø CLS
4Ø RESTORE : PRINT
5Ø INPUT "HOW MANY U.S. DOLLARS DO YOU WISH TO
EXCHANGE "; D
6Ø PRINT : PRINT TAB(18); "AT TODAYS RATE YOU WILL
GET" : PRINT
7Ø READ A$,A,B$,B : IF A$ = "END" THEN 4Ø
8Ø P$="%        (14 spaces)        %  ########.##        %  (14 spaces)        %
########.##"
9Ø PRINT USING P$; A$;D/A;B$;D/B
1ØØ  C = C + 1 : IF C<11 GOTO 7Ø
11Ø FOR T=1 TO 5ØØ : NEXT T : C=Ø : PRINT : GOTO 7Ø
```

```
1000 DATA ARGENTINE PESO, .0001
1010 DATA AUSTRALIAN DOLLAR, 1.077
1020 DATA AUSTRIAN SCHILLING, .0601
1030 DATA BELGIAN FRANC, .02128
1040 DATA BRAZILIAN CRUZEIRO, .00733
1050 DATA BRITISH POUND, 1.8365
1060 DATA CANADIAN DOLLAR, .8191
1070 DATA CHINESE YUAN, .5497
1080 DATA COLOMBIAN PESO, .0166
1090 DATA DANISH KRONER, .1259
1100 DATA ECUADORIAN SUCRE, .0404
1110 DATA FINNISH MARKKA, .2210
1120 DATA FRENCH FRANC, .1654
1130 DATA GREEK DRACHMA, .0164
1140 DATA DUTCH GUILLER, .3840
1150 DATA HONG KONG DOLLAR, .1699
1160 DATA INDIAN RUPEE, .1082
1170 DATA INDONESIAN RUPIAH, .00154
1180 DATA IRISH POUND, 1.4925
1190 DATA ISRAELI SHEKEL, .0569
1200 DATA ITALIAN LIRA, .000787
1210 DATA JAPANESE YEN, .004244
1220 DATA LEBANESE POUND, .2041
1230 DATA MALAYSIAN RINGGIT, .4336
1240 DATA MEXICAN PESO, .0267
1250 DATA NEW ZEALAND DOLLAR, .7880
1260 DATA NORWEGIAN KRONE, .1668
1270 DATA PAKISTANI REPEE, .0976
1280 DATA PERUVIAN SOL, .004388
1290 DATA PHILLIPPINE PESO, .1370
```

```
1300 DATA PORTUGUESE ESCUDO, .01445
1310 DATA SAUDI ARABIAN RIYAL, .2925
1320 DATA SINGAPORE DOLLAR, .4751
1330 DATA SOUTH AFRICAN RAND, 1.0285
1340 DATA SPANISH PESETA,.00973
1350 DATA SWEDISH KRONA, .1732
1360 DATA SWISS FRANC, .5318
1370 DATA TAIWANESE DOLLAR, .0270
1380 DATA THAI BAHT, .0435
1390 DATA URUGUAYAN NEW PESO, .0847
1400 DATA VENEZUELAN BOLIVAR, .2329
1410 DATA WEST GERMAN MARK, .4218
1500 DATA END, 0, END, 0
```

EXERCISE 36-1: Duplicate the following statement. Use PRINT USING for all but the column headings.

	CREDITS	TAX	TOTAL
Astral Computer	18.3	.7	19.0
Biofeedback adapter	1.8	.0	1.8
Personality module	7.2	.3	7.5
		DUE:	28.3

Learned in Chapter 36

Statements

PRINT USING

Miscellaneous

Image line

PRINT USING Symbols

. $ * , %

PRINT USING
Round 2

In the previous chapter we learned almost everything really needed to put PRINT USING to work. Here are a few other "tricks" that some of us might find helpful.

When PRINTing big bucks (over 999,999 dollars) it is necessary to use double-precision or we lose the loose change. Type in this NEW program:

```
1 CLS : PRINT

10 A$ = "$$###,#####.##"

20 D = 123456789.01

30 PRINT USING A$;D

90 PRINT : LIST
```

   . . .and RUN.

Sure enough, it rounds to $123,456,800.00. Granted, it's only a few seconds interest on the national debt, but for businesses doing the tax*paying,* the accuracy can be easily improved by simply switching to double-precision.

Change lines 2Ø and 3Ø to:

```
2Ø  D#  =  123456789.Ø1
3Ø  PRINT ;USING A$,D#
```

    . . .and RUN.

There it is — $123,456,789.01 — with enough change left over to tip the porter who hides the public baggage carts. Notice that the *image line* didn't have to change? All we did was use the double-precision techniques learned earlier.

If the 16-place accuracy of double-precision isn't adequate to keep track of the Krugerrands in your mattress, you and Scrooge McDuck can probably afford to spring for a bigger computer.

Profit, Or Loss?

Was that healthy number this quarter's *profit* from the lemonade stand, or was it a *loss*? We can make the *image line* PRINT either. Change it to read:

```
1Ø  A$  =  "+$$###,######.##"
```

    . . .and RUN.

Very nice. Wonder what would happen if D was a negative number?

```
2Ø  D#  =  123456789.Ø1
```

    . . .and RUN.

So far, so good. Suppose we take the + out of the *image line*. Wonder if it will PRINT the negative number anyway? Use the EDITor and remove it from line 1Ø, then RUN.

Pshaw! It goofed it up. Must be the + sign adds an element to the image, and the sign holds that extra place. Well, now we know.

Let's put the + sign back in, this time at the END of the image.

```
10 A$ = "$$####,#####.##+"
```

   . . .and RUN.

Mmmmm. That's nice. Now let's change D back to a positive number and see what happens.

```
20 D# = 123456789.01
```

   . . .and RUN.

Very nice. Looks better to have the signs at the end, not interfering with the dollar sign, don't you think?

Most printers don't PRINT deficits in red. How can we tag them so we don't allow the project manager to slip them by us? (We'll just take all + numbers for granted.) Let's try changing the + to a minus and see what happens.

```
10 A$ = "$$####,######.##-"
```

   . . .and RUN.

Seems normal. How about when it's hit with a negative number?

```
20 D# = -123456789.01
```

   . . .and RUN.

Aha! Sticks out on the printout like a sore thumb. Now about this little deficit here, Smythe. . .

Exercise 37-l: Duplicate this simplified ledger by use of PRINT USING:

REVENUES	EXPENSES	ASSETS
1,203,104.22	0.00	1,203,104.22
0.00	560,143.80	560,143.80

Deviant Forms of PRINT USING

Here's a full-blown weirdo. Even a contradiction in terms. Would you believe a double-precision number, clipped and expressed in double-precision exponential notation, in PRINT USING? Even the technical types among us with mismatched socks and a rope for a belt will cringe at that one. We aren't going to bore the business types with the gory details, except for a quick intro for those who like to explore the morbid (or is it moribund?).

Change or add these lines:

```
10 A$ = "      ###################"           Model II "∧ ∧ ∧ ∧ #·· "
20 D# = 1234567890987654321
22 D = 1234567890987654321
30 PRINT USING A$;D#
40 PRINT USING A$;D
```

      . . .and RUN.

What we see is what we get, both in double- and single-precision. Using the Editor, move the block of four left brackets to the right, one position at a time, filling in with #'s. Have fun!

More On Strings

There is one more PRINT USING character that has real value. Like so many exotic "upgrades" of BASIC, it does nothing that can't be achieved using other BASIC words, but does it easier. ENTER this NEW program:

```
1 CLS : PRINT
20 X$ = "ALEXANDER"
30 Y$ = "GRAHAM"
40 Z$ = "BELL"
50 A$ = "! ! %   %"                          Model II "! ! / /"
60 PRINT USING A$;X$,Y$,Z$
90 PRINT : LIST
```

. . .and RUN.

Who should appear before our very eyes but:

```
A G BELL
```

The ! serves to reserve an element in the field for the *first letter* of the string assigned to it. Very handy when we want the initials and last names of a list of people to line up in a row on a PRINTout.

INPUTing the Image

We move deeper into the woods as we seek to make BASIC's formatting capabilities resemble the superior (and far more complicated) ones of the FORTRAN language from which it was derived. We can even INPUT the *image line*, since it is a string. An easy way to see this is by using our resident program, but change line 5Ø to read:

```
5Ø INPUT A$
```

. . .and RUN.

We now have to respond by typing in the *image line*. (Seems like they're hard enough to create without INPUTing.) The safest one to use is old line 5Ø, so respond to the question mark with:

```
?  "!  ! %  %"                                    Model II "! ! / / "
         ↑
      (2 spaces)
```

and see

```
A G BELL
```

appear again.

RUN again, this time responding with something like:

```
? "%  %   %  %   %  %"
    ↑    ↑   ↑   ↑   ↑
   (2)  (5) (2) (5) (2)
```

and we should see something like:

```
ALEX     GRAH       BELL
```

Try some other INPUTs and see how fast we get into trouble with "Type Mismatch" errors. The down-to-earth value of this particular capability is a little elusive.

Another Short Cut

The final area of PRINT USING worthy of examination is incorporation of the *image line* into the PRINT USING line. It requires some care, and has value primarily when only a few variables are to be PRINTed, or only PRINTed once. In most practical applications, the *image line* is referenced many times during a RUN, frequently by different PRINT USING lines.

Make a few changes in the resident program so it looks like this:

```
1 CLS : PRINT
20 X$ = "ALEXANDER"
30 Y$ = "GRAHAM"
40 Z$ = "BELL"
60 PRINT USING "! ! %   %";X$,Y$,Z$
90 PRINT : LIST
```

  . . .and RUN.

We simply did away with A$ and incorporated its elements into a built-in *image line*, separated from the variables by a semicolon. It does save space, and for short and uncomplicated PRINT USING applications, has its value. For the long and complicated ones, it's better to keep the *image* and PRINT USING lines separate.

PRINT@ USING . . .

Combine the PRINT@ feature from Chapter 32 with the PRINT USING statement and you get total control over the application. Change these lines:

```
50 A$-"!!%   %"
60 PRINT@543, USING A$;X$,Y$,Z$
```

. . .and RUN.

That's the best of both features. Try moving it around on the screen and see what mastery you can achieve.

Fini

As you've seen, PRINT USING is the most complex of our PRINT statements, but by far the most powerful. If you're a serious programmer you should master PRINT USING completely. Then you can take our many simple learning examples and expand them into large, useful, business routines.

Learned in Chapter 37

Miscellaneous

PRINT USING symbols + − ↑ !
Double-Precision PRINT USING
PRINT@ USING

Part VI

Arrays

"WARDEN, I THINK I'VE FOUND A COMPUTER PROGRAM THAT CAN HELP US IN THE LICENSE PLATE SHOP!"
"I THINK THERE'S A RAY OF HOPE"

Arrays

Array?. . .must be some kind of new math weapon?

We know that we can use combinations of the 26 letters of the alphabet and digits 0-9 to create variable names. We've also discovered that very few of our programs have required anywhere near that many variables. There are times, however, when we need more variables — sometimes *hundreds* or even *thousands* of them, to use as names for the many different pieces of data we are storing and want to "retrieve" easily.

The way out of this little dilemma is with an *array*. Array is just another word for "lineup", "arrangement" or "series of things".

Let's talk about a collection, arrangement or lineup (array) of autos, all of which have different license plates (address numbers).

We have ten cars lined up, as in an array. They are all the same except for their engine size — and each has a different license plate number. Let's say the license plate numbers are from 1 to 10, and we want to use the computer to quickly spit out the engine size when we identify a specific car by license number. This might not seem like a real heavyweight problem, but as before, we discover the full potential of these things by learning them little steps at a time.

Assume the license number and engine sizes are as follows:

LICENSE#	ENGINE (cubic inches)
1	300
2	200
3	500
4	300
5	200
6	300
7	400
8	400
9	300
10	500

Now, we could give each of these cars a different letter name, using the variables A through J, but what a waste — and what will we do when we have a thousand cars, not just ten?

TRS-80 BASIC allows any valid variable name to be used as an array name. An array named "A" is not the same as the ordinary variable "A", and it is not the same as string variable A$. It is a third and totally separate "A". We call it A-sub(something).   We will name the cars A(1) through A(10) (pronounced A sub 1 through A sub 10).   Get the idea?

What's that — you don't believe there can be three separate and different storage places for these "A" items? OK, try it. Type:

```
A = 12
A$ = "(YOUR NAME)"
A(1) = 999
```

then:

```
PRINT A, A$, A(1)
```

Makes you a believer, eh?

Next, let's store the car engine sizes in a line or two of DATA statements.

Type in:

```
100 DATA 300,200,500,300,200
110 DATA 300,400,400,300,500
```

Notice how carefully we kept the DATA elements in order from 1 to 10, so the first car's engine size is found in the first DATA location, and the tenth one is in the tenth location.

Now we have to "generate" an array inside the computer's memory to make these data elements *immediately addressable* (big words meaning "so we can find a car fast!"). Think how difficult it would be to try to address the seventh engine (or the seven thousandth!), for example, using only what we've learned so far. It *can* be done using only DATA, READ and RESTORE statements, but it's very messy and slow.

The easy way to create the array is to type in:

```
50 FOR L = 1 TO 10
55  READ A(L)
60 NEXT L
```

. . .and RUN.

Nothing happen? Yes, it did. *Something* happened because it took a little time for READY to return. We simply didn't display what happened.

The program used a FOR-NEXT loop to READ ten pieces of DATA, and named the elements (or "cells") in which they're stored, A(1) through A(10). Let's see if we can PRINT the values in those array elements.

Type:

```
200 FOR N = 1 TO 10
210  PRINT A(N)
220 NEXT N
```

. . .and RUN.

Aha! It works, but how? We READ the DATA elements into an array called A(L), but PRINTed them out of an array called A(N). Again, it's the A that counts, not the (L) or (N). They are only "variables of convenience".

The array's *name* is "A". The location of each data element within that array is identified by the number which we place inside the parentheses. We can "load" that number inside the parentheses by using any of our numeric variables, and can even do some simple arithmetic inside the parentheses if we wish.

Remember, the array we are using is named "A". Its elements are numbered, and called A-sub(number).

Some pure mathematicians might insist on calling A(X)   A "OF" X.

Let's work some more on the program.

Type:

```
170 PRINT
180 PRINT "LICENSE#","ENGINE SIZE"
210 PRINT N,A(N)
```

> . . .and RUN.

Now that's more like it. We have every license number, every engine size, and are not "using up" any of the alphabetic variables. Having demonstrated that point, let's find an engine size by specifying the license plate number. Erase lines 200, 210 and 220, and type:

```
10 INPUT "WHICH CAR'S ENGINE SIZE DO YOU WANT TO KNOW";W
210 PRINT W,A(W)
```

> . . .and RUN.

Get the idea? Can you see the beginning of a simple inventory system for a small business?

Let's go one small step (for mankind) further. Suppose we know the color of each of the ten cars and, for simplicity, suppose the colors are coded 1, 2, 3 and 4. We might then have a master chart that looks like this:

LICENSE#	ENGINE (cubic inches)	COLOR CODE
1	300	3
2	200	1
3	500	4
4	300	3
5	200	2
6	300	4
7	400	3
8	400	2
9	300	1
10	500	3

In the language of professional computer types, this is called a *matrix*. A matrix is just an array that has more than one dimension (our first array had the dimension of 1 by 10. . .1 *column* by 10 *rows*.) This new array has a horizontal dimension of 2 and a vertical dimension of 10. If we wanted to be terribly inefficient about the matter, we *could* say that this is a 3 by 10 array, counting the license number. If so, our first one would be a 2 by 10 array — but who needs it? As long as we keep our license numbers in a simple 1 to 10 FOR-NEXT loop, and our DATA in proper sequence, we can keep our arrays simpler and easier to handle.

> You might want to think of a matrix as a chart with a certain number of columns of information. First we set up the chart, then how many columns of info can we get in. . .?

How then can we handle this 2 by 10 matrix? We have already used up our A array elements numbered 1 through 10. Oh, you want to know how many elements we have to work with? Very good!

> Since we do not store the license number in the computer, it is only a "pointer" or an "index". That's why we don't consider it as another "DIMension" to our matrix.

Let's just arbitrarily assign array locations 101 through 110 to hold the color code. We also have to put the color code info in the program using a DATA statement. From the table, type:

```
300 DATA 3,1,4,3,2,4,3,2,1,3
```

and

```
80 FOR S = 101 TO 110
85 READ A(S)
90 NEXT S
```

. . .to load the color code DATA into the array. The array element numbers 11 through 100 are not used, nor are those from 111 to the end of memory, since they have not been formally assigned any values.

. . .RUN it.

Awwk!! What is this ?BS business? (Stands for "subscript out of range".) Well, since arrays take up a lot of memory space, the TRS-80 automatically allows us to use up to only 11 array elements without question. (They can be numbered from 0 to 10.) Then our credit runs out. We earlier used elements numbered from 1 to 10 without any problem.

To use array elements numbered beyond ten in the array called "A", we have to "reDIMension" the array space available. Our highest number in Array "A" needs to be 110, so we'll add a program DIMension line:

```
5 DIM A(110)
```

. . .and RUN again. That's better.

Now we need to find some way to display all this good information. Change these lines:

```
10 INPUT "WHICH CAR'S ENGINE & COLOR DO YOU WANT TO KNOW";W
180 PRINT "LICENSE#","ENGINE SIZE","COLOR CODE"
210 PRINT W,A(W),A(W+100)
```

. . . then RUN.

Check your answers against the earlier two-dimensional matrix chart.

Let your imagination go. Can you envision entire charts and tables stored in this manner? Entire inventory lists? How about trying to *find* the car which has a certain size engine *and* a certain color? Hmmm. We will come back to the Logic needed for that last one.

EXERCISE 38-1: Assume that your inventory of 10 cars includes three different body styles, coded 10, 20 and 30, as follows:

LICENSE#	BODY STYLE
1	20
2	20
3	10
4	20
5	30
6	20
7	30
8	10
9	20
10	20

Modify the resident program to PRINT the body style information along with the rest when the car is identified by license number.

A Smith & Wesson Beats Four Aces

If we want to create a computerized card game (they make good examples to show so many things), how can we set it up so we draw the 52 or so cards (watch the dealer at all times) in a totally random way? Answer: Spin up the deck into a single-dimension array, pick array elements using a random number generator and as each card is "drawn", set its array element value equal to zero, then test each card drawn to be sure it isn't zero. Now that is *really* simple!

We will now, a step at a time, write a program which will draw at random, all 52 cards numbered from 1 through 52, and PRINT the card numbers on the screen as they are drawn. No card will be drawn more than once. When all cards have been drawn, it will PRINT "END OF DECK".

You do a step first, then check against my example. Then change yours to match mine — otherwise we might not end up at the same place at the same time.

STEP 1: Spin up all 52 cards into an array.

```
30  DIM A(52) : FOR C=1 TO 52 : A(C) = C : NEXT C
50  DATA 1,2,3,4,5,6,7,8,9,10,11,12,13,14,15,16,17,18,19,20
55  DATA 21,22,23,24,25,26,27,28,29,30,31,32,33,34,35
60  DATA 36,37,38,39,40,41,42,43,44,45,46,47,48,49,50,51,52
```

At this point, all we can tell when RUNning is that processing time is required since the READY doesn't come back right away.

Shhhh! I know there's a shorter way to program this special case, but it doesn't teach what's needed.

STEP 2: Draw 52 cards at random, PRINTing their values.

```
90  FOR N = 1 TO 52
100 V = RND(52)
110 PRINT A(V);
120 NEXT N
```

. . .and RUN.

True, 52 card values are PRINTed on the screen, but if you look carefully, the same number appears more than once. This means that some "cells" are not being READ and some READ more than once.

STEP 3: When a card is drawn, set its array address equal to zero. Test each card drawn to be sure it is not 0. When 52 cards have been drawn and PRINTed, type END OF DECK.

```
90  P = 52
105 IF A(V) = 0 GOTO 100
120 A(V) = 0
```

```
130 P = P - 1
140 IF P<> 0 GOTO 100
150 PRINT "END OF DECK!"
```

Line 120 sets the value in cell A(V) equal to zero only if line 105 finds it *not* already equal to 0, letting the program pointer fall through.

When a "fall through" occurs:

1. The card's value is PRINTed (line 110).

2. The number stored in that cell is set to zero (line 120).

3. Line 130 counts down the number of cards PRINTed. Line 90 initialized the number of PRINTs at 52.

4. The number of PRINTs is tested (line 140). When there are no more PRINTs to go, END OF DECK! is PRINTed (line 150).

Pretty slick — and we don't have to watch the dealer (just the programmer).

But how do we really know that every card has been dealt? Write a quick addition to the program to "interrogate" each array cell and PRINT its contents.

```
200 FOR T = 1 TO 52
210 PRINT A(T);
220 NEXT T
```

. . .and RUN.

Every cell comes up zero. If you don't really trust all this, change line 90 to read:

```
90 P = 50
```

. . .and RUN and see what happens.

Aha! It flushed out those two cards up the sleeve, didn't it?

Change P back to 52, eliminate test program lines 2ØØ, 21Ø, and 22Ø, and we end up with a good card-drawing routine. You might want to clean it up to your satisfaction and save it on tape for future projects.

Question: Why does the PRINTing of card numbers slow down to a near halt as those last few cards are being drawn? Is the dealer reluctant?

Answer: The random number generator has to keep drawing numbers until it hits one that is the array address of an element which has not been set to zero. Near the end of the deck, almost all elements have been set to zero. The random number generator has to keep drawing numbers as fast as it can to find a "live" one.

Look again at the card numbers PRINTed. There will not be any duplication. No stray aces.

> *EXERCISE 38-2:* Change the program so the original array can be loaded with the card numbers without having to READ them in from DATA lines.

New DIMensions

DIM is to arrays what CLEAR is to strings. We have done some DIMensioning with single-dimension *numeric* arrays. When we have a string array, we must do the same thing.

Suppose we have a program like this: (Type it in.)

```
1 CLS : PRINT
1Ø FOR N = 1 TO 16
2Ø READ A$(N)
3Ø PRINT A$(N),
4Ø NEXT N
9Ø PRINT : LIST
1ØØ DATA ALPHA,BRAVO,CHARLIE,DELTA,ECHO,FOXTROT
```

```
110 DATA GOLF,HOTEL,INDIA,JULIETTE,KILO,LIMA,MIKE
120 DATA NOVEMBER, OSCAR, PAPA
```

. . .and RUN.

Oops. There's that same problem. "Subscript out of range in 2∅" means "not enough space set aside for an array". You'll recall that only 11 elements *per array* (from 0-10) are set aside on power-up. We are trying to read in 16 of them, starting with 1. The solution:

```
5 DIM A$(16)
```

. . .and RUN.

That's better. DIMensioning a string array is just like dimensioning a numeric one — just call it by its name. In this case, its name is A$. You "high speed" types will want to know that to do "dynamic reDIMensioning" (that's doing it while a program is running), the program must encounter a CLEAR first. Oh.

Array Names

A(N)

BC(N)

D3(N)

E4$(N)

XY$(N)

are all legal forms of array names. The last two are for "string arrays".

EXERCISE 38-3: Study the user programs in Section C to better understand the use of arrays for storage and access purposes. Time spent studying programs written by others is wisely invested.

Learned in Chapter 38

Statements

DIM

Miscellaneous

Arrays

SEARCH and SORT

One of the computer's most powerful features is its ability to *search* through a pile of DATA and *sort* the findings into some order. Alphabetical, reverse alphabetical, numerical from smallest to largest, or the reverse — all are common. The search/sort feature is so important we are going to spend an entire chapter learning how to use it.

Typical applications of search and sort include:

1. Arranging a list of customers' or prospects' names in *alphabetical* order.

2. Sorting names in *ZIP-code* order for lower-cost mailing.

3. Sorting the names of clients in phone Area Code order.

While not really all that complicated, the sorting process is sufficiently rigorous that we are going to take it *very slowly* and examine each step. Once we get the hang of it, the computer can blaze away without our considering the staggering number of steps it's going through.

Let's start with a problem. We have the names of 10 customers (if that doesn't grab you, make it 10 million — the search/sort process is identical). We wish to arrange them in alphabetical order.

Start by storing their names in a DATA line. Type in:

```
1000 DATA BRAVO, XRAY, ALPHA, ZULU, FOXTROT, TANGO, HOTEL,
SIERRA
```

Since we are sorting by *name* rather than by number, we have to use STRING variables, STRING arrays, etc. They work equally well with numbers such as zip codes, while numeric variables and arrays work *only* with numbers.

The backbone of a sort routine is the array. Each name is to be READ from DATA into an array. So add:

```
10 REM * ALPHA SORT OF STRINGS FROM DATA *
20 CLS : FOR D = 1 TO 8 : READ A$(D) : N=N+1 : NEXT D
```

Line 1Ø is, of course, just the title.

Line 2Ø clears the screen, then "loads the array" by READing the 10 names into storage slots A\$(1) to A\$(8). N is simply a counter which will follow through the rest of the program. In this simple program we could have made N=8, since we know how many names we have. In the next sample program we won't know how many names there are, so let's leave N the way it's usually used.

Important to the sort routine are two nested FOR-NEXT loops.

 1. The first one, F, controls the first name.

 2. The second one, S, controls the name to be compared against the first one.

Names and words are compared as we learned in the chapter on the ASCII set, remember?

Let's establish our loops first, then fill in the guts later:

```
30  FOR F = 1 TO N-1      'F=FIRST WORD TO BE COMPARED
40    FOR S = F+1 TO N    'S=SECOND WORD TO BE COMPARED
90    NEXT S              '  MAKES 7 PASSES
100 NEXT F               '  MAKES 7 PASSES
```

It may seem puzzling that F and S only have to make seven passes when there are eight names. Think of it this way: Whichever word *isn't* smaller (ASCII #) than the rest, just ends up last. No need to test again to prove that.

The F loop READs array elements 1 through 7 (N-1 = 7). The S loop READs array elements 2 through 8. This always provides us with *different* array elements to compare against each other.

Now let's jump to the end of our program and prepare it to PRINT out what we are about to do. Type:

```
110 FOR D = 1 TO N : PRINT A$(D), : NEXT D
```

When the sorting is done, the contents of A$(1) to A$(10) will be the same as what is READ from DATA, but will be in alphabetical order. We'll PRINT the array contents on the screen.

```
50    IF A$(F) <= A$(S)  THEN 90   'TEST FOR SMALLER ASCII#
60    T$ = A$(F)          '  TEMPORARY STORAGE FOR FIRST WORD
70    A$(F)J = A$(S)      '  COPY SECOND WORD TO FIRST PLACE
80    A$(S) = T$          '  SWITCH FIRST WORD TO SECOND PLACE
```

And there is the biggie! If you can understand the last four lines, the rest is duck soup.

Line 50 says, "If the first word is smaller than (or equal to) the second word, leave well enough alone and bail out of this routine by going to line 90, which will end this pass and READ another word to compare against F. If not, drop to the next line."

Line 60 says, "Oh, they weren't in the right order, eh? We'll just store the first word in a temporary storage location called T$ and hold it there for future use. I'm sure we'll need it again."

Line 7Ø copies the name held in the second cell into the first array cell. If the second one had an earlier starting letter than the first one, we do want to do this, don't we?

Line 8Ø completes the switch by copying the name temporarily held in T$ into the second array cell. A$(1) and A$(2) contents have now been exchanged with the aid of the temporary holding pen, T$.

Us simple country boys find this one easy: *There are two brahma bulls in separate pens, A$(1) and A$(2), and we want to switch them around. Ain't no way we're going to put them in the same pen at the same time. (Not with me in there anyway. Already broken too many 2 by 4's between their horns, and have some scars in the wrong end from escapes that were a hair too slow.) That's why we have a temporary holding pen called T$.* Got it?

   . . .and RUN.

If we did everything right, in a flash, the names appear on the screen in alphabetical order:

```
ALPHA           BRAVO           FOXTROT         HOTEL
SIERRA          TANGO           XRAY            ZULU
```

Printing will be in standard 16-space tab zone format.

RUN it to your heart's delight. It's one of the most powerful things your computer can do, and can do it so well. Exactly the same thing takes place with a very long list of names (or zip codes, or whatever), but we would of course have to reDIMension for a larger array, and CLEAR more string space.

Aw c'mon Horse − Whoa!

To get a really good look at what's happening, it's necessary to slow the beast *way* down, and insert a few extra PRINT lines. This lets us examine what's going on inside by watching the tube.

Add these temporaries:

```
45      PRINT F;A$(F),,S;A$(S)

47      FOR Z = 1 TO 1ØØØ : NEXT Z
```

```
55        PRINT "                    <<--<<          SWITCHEROO"
85        PRINT F;A$(F),,S;A$(S)
```

> Allow four spaces after the arrow — that way it will look nice on the screen when you RUN it.

. . . and RUN.

If that wasn't slow enough, change line 47 so there is time to completely think it through. Pretend you're the computer and make the decision that line 5Ø has to make. Take it from the top — very slowly!

. . .and RUN.

```
1   BRAVO                                    2   XRAY
```

Means "in cell #1 is the word BRAVO. In cell #2 is the word XRAY". (Just like they came from the DATA line.) Of those two words, BRAVO is the "smallest" (ASCII#), so let's leave it in the number 1 place. On to the next pass of S.

```
1   BRAVO                                    3   ALPHA
```

Oops. BRAVO is in #1 and ALPHA is in #3, but ALPHA s smaller than BRAVO. We better switch them around So:

```
        <<--<<          SWITCHEROO
```
```
1   ALPHA                                    3   BRAVO
```

Don't worry too much about what is happening in the second column. S is scanning through the array and its contents are always changing (testing against what's in the first column). It's what *ends up* in the *first* column that counts — and they should be in increasing alphabetical order.

As the program keeps RUNning, watch the new words appear in S, the second loop and column, and compare them against what's in F, the first one.

Try to guess what the computer's going to do. Also keep an eye on the increasing numbers on the left. It's the *final word* with a given number in the first column, which will appear in the final PRINTout.

RUN the program as many times as it takes (and in as many sessions as it takes) to really follow what's happening. It's awfully clever, awfully important, and awfully fundamental. We can carry this principle over to many useful programs in the future, but only if we *really* understand it.

When you feel it's under control, let's add one more little display to the screen. What is T$ holding while all this sorting is going on? Add to these lines so they read:

```
45 PRINT F;A$(F),,S;A$(S),"T$=";T$
85 PRINT F;A$(F),,S;A$(S),"T$=";T$
```

    . . .and RUN.

"T$=" starts off with nothing since there is nothing in the holding pen. As F gets replaced in the switching process, however, T$ holds it. On a clear head it's not hard to follow what's happening. You'll probably want to save this program and review it several times for a deep understanding of the process.

Sorting From The Outside

We don't really have to keep all our names, numbers or other information in DATA lines. It can be INPUT from the keyboard, from disk, or from cassette. The following program is quite similar to the first, and the logic is identical. Change these resident program lines:

```
5 D=1 : REM * ALPHA SORT OF NAMES VIA INPUT *
10 INPUT"NEXT NAME";A$(D) : IF A$(D)="END" GOTO 30
20 D=D+1 : N=N+1 : GOTO 10
```

Delete lines 1000 and 1010.

    . . .and RUN.

Enter several random names and, when finished, INPUT the word "END". The process displayed on the screen will be identical to what we saw before.

Can you see the potential for all this?

EXERCISE 39-1: Change line 5∅ of the sort program to list the names in reverse alphabetical order.

Learned in Chapter 39

Miscellaneous

Sorting

Search and Sort

Multi-DIMension Arrays

We have learned that an array is nothing more than a temporary parking area for lots of numbers, or alphabet characters, or both. In addition, we are able to compare string contents outside the matrix (or array) with those inside it.

An array which only has one dimension, that is, just one long line-up of parking places, is sometimes called a *vector*. We can take that same one-dimensional array and cut it into, say, four equal chunks, and position those chunks side by side. We then call it a two-dimensional array — since the parking places are lined up in *rows* and *columns* (or *streets* and *avenues*). Not a single thing has changed about its DATA holding or processing abilities. Only the addresses of the parking places (or elements or memory cells) have changed.

Enter this NEW program:

```
10 DIM M(52)
20 FOR V = 1 TO 52
30   PRINT V
40 NEXT V
```

Any array with more than 11 elements (counting 0) must be DIMensioned.

. . .and RUN.

The RUN simply shows us the 52 storage positions and their numbers (addresses). They are all lined up in a single row, so they can be called a vector. What it didn't show us was the *contents* of those memory cells. Let's change the program and find out what's being stored:

```
30  PRINT V,M(V)
```

. . .and RUN.

Hmmmm. Every cell is storing the number 0. Why? Because every value is initialized at zero on power-up, and by typing RUN, we find this out. It acts just like all the other numeric or string variables we have encountered. Now we know both how to find the *address* of each memory cell, and how to find its *contents*.

Let's cut our 52-cell array into 4 equal strips, and line them up side by side. That would make. . .ah. . .er. . .13 rows each containing um. . .4 cells. . .right?

That's 13 rows by 4 columns.

Or 4 columns containing 13 cells. A "two-dimensional array" has *rows* and *columns*. Let's start over with this NEW program:

```
10  DIM M(13,4)
20  FOR R = 1 TO 13
30   FOR C = 1 TO 4
40    PRINT R;C,
50   NEXT C
60  NEXT R
```

Model II add 55 PRINT.

. . .and RUN.

And there we see the addresses of all 52 cells displayed on the screen at the same time. Again, nothing has changed from the earlier vector array containing the same 52 cells. We just rearranged the furniture and gave it different addresses. They read:

11   means "first *row*, first *column*".

83   means "eighth *row*, third *column*".

     etc.

To find out what each of these cells is holding in the way of DATA, change line 4Ø to:

```
4Ø          PRINT M(R,C),
```

    . . .and RUN.

See, the contents remain unchanged. They are still at their initialized value of zero since we have made no arrangement to store information in them. Isn't this easy (so far)?

Memory cells have to be "loaded" with DATA to be of value. This can be done by READing the DATA in from DATA lines, by INPUTing it via the keyboard or from a previously recorded DATA disk or tape. We will load our matrix from DATA lines imbedded in the program.

Add these DATA lines:

```
1ØØ DATA 1,2,3,4,5,6,7,8,9,1Ø,11,12,13,14,15,16
11Ø DATA 17,18,19,2Ø,21,22,23,24,25,26,27,28,29
12Ø DATA 3Ø,31,32,33,34,35,36,37,38,39,4Ø,41,42
12Ø DATA 43,44,45,46,47,48,49,5Ø,51,52
```

and this line to READ the DATA into matrix cells:

```
35 READ M(R,C)
```

    . . .and RUN.

Here we see the DATA nicely arranged in the matrix, and each matrix position has a specific address. Let's stay in the command mode for a minute and "poll" or "interrogate" several matrix positions and see what they are holding. Ask:

```
PRINT M(2,3)
```

Write down 7, the answer. We'll RUN the program again later and check it.

```
PRINT M(11,14)
```

It says *that* cell holds the number 44.

```
PRINT M(3,5)
```

Subscript out of range? Why did we get that? Oh, there is no column 5? No wonder.

Let's RUN the program again and check the screen, counting down the rows and over the columns to see if our answers match up.

Mine did — how about yours?

Row 2 Col. 3 = 7, Row 9 Col. 4 = 44.

As an aside, type:

```
CLEAR
```

then, at the command level, check any matrix memory spot again.

```
PRINT M(2,2)
```

and we get 0. CLEAR re-initialized *all* cells to zero, along with all other variables. We can of course reload them by RUNning again, then:

```
PRINT M(2,2)
```
                                                            Row 2 Col. 2 = 6.

> *EXERCISE 40-1:* Change line 35 to a LET statement that fills the array with the same numbers without the use of DATA lines. (Be sure to restore the program back to its original self when you're finished.)

Okay, Now What Do We Do With It?

Good question. Everything we learned in the last chapter on arrays applies. We've only rearranged the deck chairs on this Titanic — the end result is unaffected.

At this point, what we've learned is best utilized for calling up and loading relatively unchanging DATA. It is placed in a matrix so it can be accessed and compared, processed or otherwise put to work. Typical applications are:

1. Technical tables: Instead of repeatedly looking up the same information in tables, store those tables in DATA lines and let the computer look them up, do the calculations and give us the final answer. Works great, and the time saved quickly pays for the computer.

2. Price quotes: I've seen this approach used by a lumber yard to furnish fast quotes on materials, and by a PRINTing shop for fast quoting of all sorts of PRINTed materials. In the latter case, the program is written so simply that the customer bellys right up to the counter, answers the computer's questions, and gets his printing price quote right there on the screen. The latest prices on all the paper products and PRINTing costs are held in DATA lines and "spun up" into the Matrix at the beginning of the day. The customer responds to a "Menu" on the screen, and answers the questions. The quote is calculated, and PRINTed on the screen and on a PRINTer.

When DATA is loaded in externally, either via the keyboard, disk, or tape, we obviously don't want to have to go through *that* loading process each time we want an answer. It's important, therefore, to never let execution END. Always have it come back to a screen "Menu" of choices, or at least a simple INPUT statement. If an END is hit, the matrix crashes and the DATA has to be reloaded.

String Matrices

So far, we have seen mainly numbers in our arrays. We can also use them to hold letters or words, using the same rules learned in earlier chapters on strings, and on CLEARing enough space for the strings. We have to give string matrices string names. Make these subtle changes in your resident program:

```
10 DIM M$(13,4)
35  READ M$(R,C)
40 PRINT M$(R,C),
```

. . .and RUN.

Absolutely no difference! We now have a string matrix. The data was all numeric, but it was handled beautifully.

Now let's change our DATA and try it again. Change:

```
20 FOR R = 1 TO 6
100 DATA ALPHA,BRAVO,CHARLIE,DELTA,ECHO,FOXTROT
110 DATA GOLF,HOTEL,INDIA,JULIETTE,KILO,LIMA,MIKE
120 DATA NOVEMBER,OSCAR,PAPA,QUEBEC,ROMEO,SIERRA
130 DATA TANGO,UNIFORM,VICTOR,WHISKEY,XRAY
```

. . .and RUN.

Really no difference between the string matrix and the previous numeric ones, except it handles words. Stop for a moment and contemplate the string-comparing and string-handling techniques we learned a few chapters ago. Your mind should be RUNning flat-out at this point, considering the possibilities.

How About Mixing Strings and Numerics?

(Sounds good — I'll have one on the rocks)

Oh! Funny you should ask. That's why we ran all numbers in a string matrix, then all words with that same program. They mix very well, as long as the mixer is a string matrix and not a numeric one.

We have one final program. It is not meant to be a practical one, but could be expanded to INPUT the DATA from disk or tape and be quite usable. It demonstrates a few important possibilities and is worth entering and studying.

The Objective

The objective of this demo program is to allow a church treasurer to keep track of who gave what, when. We could do the same thing with a service club, or any organization that has a membership and dues. We want to be able to access every member's record by name, and get a readout on his status.

Let's start the program with the DATA. Type this in the NEW program:

```
1000 REM *DATA FILE *
1010 DATA 07.1082, JONES, 15
1020 DATA 07.0182, SMITH, 87
1030 DATA 07.1082, BROWN, 24
1040 DATA 07.1082, JOHNSON, 53
1050 DATA 07.1082, ANDERSON, 42
```

Analyzing the DATA, we find that we've employed several techniques. The first number in each DATA line employs "data compression", that is, "encoding" several pieces of information into one number. This number contains the month, date and year in one six-digit number. (Using string techniques, we could easily strip them apart again if we wished, for special reports.) Single precision will hold the six digits accurately.

The second thing we've done with this first number is protect the leading $\emptyset$. Since months below October are represented by only one digit, the leading $\emptyset$ would be lost on these months and the number changed to only five digits.

There are other ways to get around that problem, but we will throw in a decimal point just to act as an unmovable reference.

The second element in each DATA line is the *name*. We could put in the full name, but if we used a comma we'd, of course, have to enclose the name in quotes.

The third element of each DATA line holds the amount of money given on that date.

Obviously, a full DATA set would contain many entries for each Sunday, and many Sundays in a row. We don't need to enter that much DATA to demonstrate the principles involved so we'll just keep it short and to the point.

We now have to READ this DATA into a string matrix, displaying it on the screen as we go. Add:

```
5 CLS
10 FOR E = 1 TO 5 : PRINT E,        'TODAYS ENTRY
20   FOR D = 1 TO 3
30     REM ENTRY DATA : DATE, NAME, TITHE
40     READ R$(E,D)
50     PRINT R$(E,D),
60   NEXT D
70 NEXT E
100 PRINT : PRINT "ENTRY #","DATE","NAME","TITHE $"
```

. . .and RUN.

Very good. The matrix is loaded, and confirmed on the screen. We see the first five bookkeeping entries from July 1, 1982.

Now that we know it loads OK, we can remove some of the software. Change these lines:

```
10 FOR E = 1 TO 5                        'TODAYS ENTRY
```

Delete line 5Ø.

   . . .and RUN.

Good. We still get the heading, but the display is gone. Now, how can we interrogate the matrix to pull an individual member's record? Guess we first have to ask a question. Type:

```
90 INPUT"WHOSE RECORD ARE YOU SEEKING";N$
```

   . . .and RUN.

Seems to work OK. We will just answer the question with any member's name as it appears in the DATA lines. Then we have to scan the matrix and compare N$ (the name we INPUT) with each element, R$(E,D), until we find a match. This means setting up the FOR-NEXT loops again and scanning every element. Add:

```
110 FOR E = 1 TO 5
120  IF R$(E,2) = N$ THEN 150
130 NEXT E
140 PRINT "NOT IN THE FILE" : GOTO 90
150 PRINT E, R$(E,1), R$(E,2), R$(E,3)
160 PRINT : GOTO 90
```

   . . .and RUN.

Try names that are in the DATA lines, and those that are not. Lines 140 and 160 have built-in defaults back to the question.

The key line is 150. It PRINTs four things:

   E, obviously, the entry number on that date.

   R$(E,1), not so obviously, the contents of the memory cell just *preceding* the one containing the member's name.

   R$(E,2), the cell containing the name.

   R$(E,3), the cell following it.

If you have trouble visualizing what line 150 is doing, add this temporary line. It PRINTs the address of each DATA element just below it, and is very helpful:

```
155 PRINT E, E;1, E;2, E;3
```

. . .and RUN.

Implications

Again, the preceding program was not written to be a model of programming style and efficiency — but to be a good learning program. You should now sit by the bank of the creek and think through how you would modify it to load in, say, 1000 lines of DATA from cassette tape via an INPUT statement. Then, add more DATA each Sunday and shoot that updated DATA back out to tape for reuse the following Sunday, or in between as needed. It is possible and marginally practical to use your TRS-80 for this application. (With disk it is routine, though we have more sophisticated techniques for handling large files.)

EXERCISE 40-2: Write a program that fills a two-dimensional string array with:

JONES, C.	10439	100.00
ROTH, J.	10023	87.24
BAKER, H.	12936	398.34
HARMIN, D.	10422	23.17

Don't forget to keep the rest of the information on each row with the original name. This exercise will be a challenge. Think it through carefully.

EXERCISE 40-3: If you survived Exercise 40-2, try sorting the array in increasing order by the numbers in Column 3.

Learned in Chapter 40

Miscellaneous

Multi-Dimension Arrays

String Arrays

Advanced Graphics

Model II users, skip this chapter.

The uses of PRINT@ go well beyond the simple display formatting we have seen so far. Used in conjunction with the CHR$ function, PRINT@ can speed up our graphic displays by a factor of six in some applications. That's right, six times as fast as SET.

How can that be? Well, to answer that question, we need to recall the set of ASCII characters discussed in Chapter 22. Sure, you remember (if not, better take a brief glance to refresh your memory cells). The codes from 128 to 191 represent graphic characters. Let's take a closer look at this range of characters with this NEW program:

```
10 CLS
20 FOR I=128 TO 191
30 IF I=8*INT(I/8) PRINT
40 PRINT I;CHR$(I)"   ";
50 NEXT I
60 GOTO 60
```

  . . .and RUN.

The characters are composed of the very same SET rectangles we have been using all along. From Figure 1 we can see that the rectangles are arranged in groups of six — three rows and two columns. By PRINTing these characters, we can light as many as six rectangles in one statement. It would take up to six SET statements to do the same thing. The gain in speed is considerable.

TRS-80 Video Display Worksheet

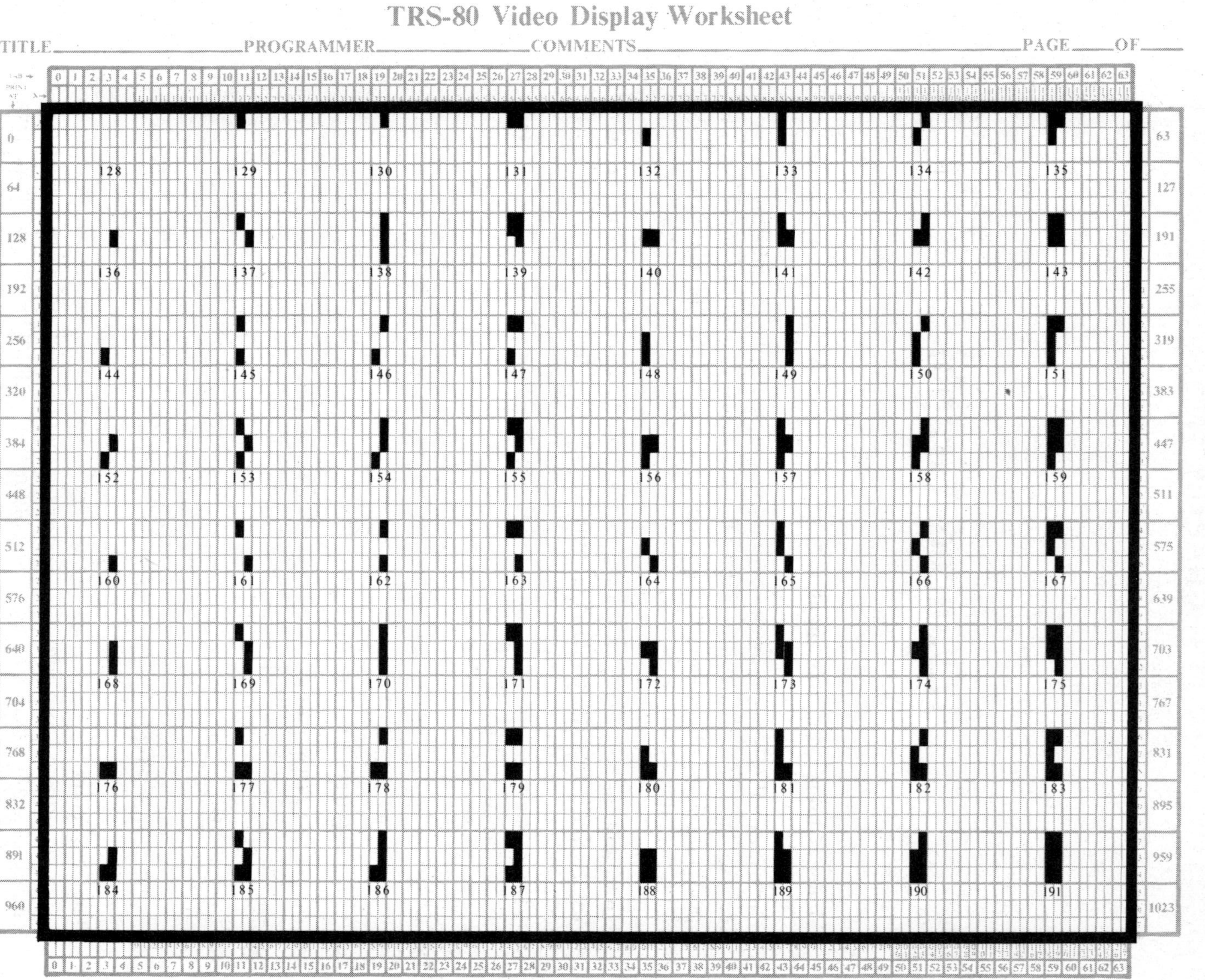

Figure 1

Skeptical? Nonsense. Bring out your stop watch and we'll take these two methods out for a spin. First the SET approach.

```
10 CLS
20 FOR Y=0 TO 23 : FOR X=0 TO 127
30   SET(X,Y)
40 NEXT X : NEXT Y
50 GOTO 50
```

. . .and RUN.

Okay, we can fill up half the screen in about 22 seconds. Contrast that with the results of using the PRINT statement and graphic character 191 (all 6 rectangles lit):

```
10 CLS
20 FOR P=0 TO 511
30   PRINT CHR$(191);
40 NEXT P
50 GOTO 50
```

. . .and RUN.

Ahhhh. Just about 4 seconds. The message is clear: PRINTing graphic characters is *a lot* faster than SETting them.

> *EXERCISE 41-1:* See if you can fill the entire screen using CHR$(191). Hint: You have 1023 PRINT positions to fill.

Dilemma

This puts us on the horns of a real dilemma. We've seen how convenient the SET statement is for things like plotting math functions, and yet we now see just how slow SET is when compared to PRINTing graphic characters. So which method should we use?

Before we make a hasty decision, let's take a closer look at printing graphic characters.

To emphasize the speed with which we can PRINT characters, our first task will be to store the following graphic figure (Figure 2) in a BASIC program so that it can be displayed in the blink of an eye.

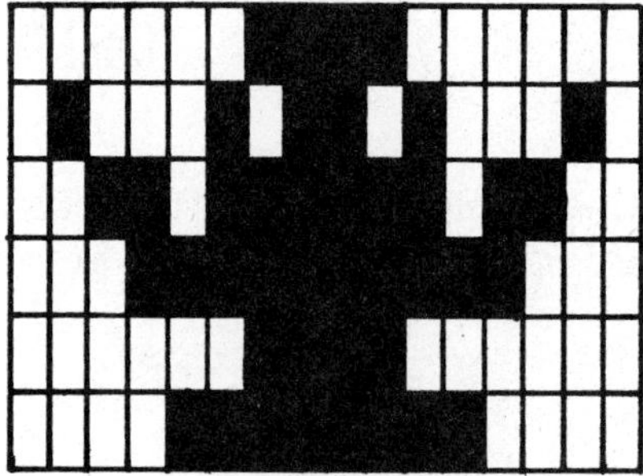

Figure 2

Sound impossible? Well, it's not. Just pay attention.

To achieve this kind of speed, we must store the entire figure in a single variable using string concatenation. (Yes, we covered concatenation earlier. See Chapter 24.) If we are successful, we can then print the entire figure *instantaneously* anywhere on the screen with the PRINT@ statement. Amazing!

Graphic Codes

Before we build the string, let's bog ourselves down for just a moment in the details of translating the figure from the video display sheet into a BASIC program. There are a few noteworthy tricks we should be aware of.

First in line in the trick department is the pattern of the graphic characters themselves. One way to convert Figure 2 into the appropriate ASCII numbers is to use the chart in Figure 1. But searching for each character takes time. Fortunately, there is a simple way to calculate the ASCII number associated with any of the graphic characters, without a chart.

Suppose that we are looking for the code number for the following character:

Figure 3

Here's the way we would proceed. Assign the following values to each of the six rectangles:

<table>
<tr><td>1</td><td>2</td></tr>
<tr><td>4</td><td>8</td></tr>
<tr><td>16</td><td>32</td></tr>
</table>

Figure 4

Memorize this pattern! It is easy and *very* useful.

To calculate the code number associated with any graphic character, we add the numeric values of each of the lit rectangles to 128. Since the lit rectangles in Figure 3 are labeled 2 and 4, we get:

$$128 + 2 + 4 = 134$$

Check this against the chart in Figure 1. It works! Now try:

Figure 5

Well, rectangles 16 and 32 are lit, so 128 + 16 + 32 = 176. Nothing to it! Once you recognize the pattern, it is easy to calculate the number for any graphic character.

Now we can practice on our graphic figure. Go ahead, try translating a few characters from Figure 2 before you peek. There is no time like the present to learn.

For those who don't need the practice, the two rows are composed of codes:

    136 176 168 187 183 148 176 132
    128 130 179 191 191 179 129 128

Building the String

Our next task is to use these code numbers to build a string variable. At first blush, we might be tempted to use a brute force method like:

```
10 LPRINT   X$=CHR$(136)+CHR$(176)+CHR$(168)+...
```

But this is supposed to be a classy operation. Why not place the numbers in DATA statements and READ them into the program? (I think we've stumbled on something here.) Enter this NEW program:

```
10 CLS : CLEAR 300 : DEFSTR X
30 FOR I=1 TO 8 : READ N : X=X + CHR$(N) : NEXT I
70 DATA 136,176,168,187,183,148,176,132
150 PRINT@410,X
```

        . . .and RUN.

Line 10 clears the screen, reserves string space and defines X to be a string variable. In line 30, each code number is read into N. It is then converted to a graphic character via the CHR$ function and added to the end of the string variable X. (Remember, X is defined to be a string variable in line 10). Line 70 holds the DATA, and X is printed in line 130.

Check your program output against the top row of Figure 2.

Cursor Control Codes

Add the second row with:

```
5Ø FOR I=1 TO 8 : READ N : X=X + CHR$(N) : NEXT I
8Ø DATA 128,13Ø,179,191,191,179,129,128
```

. . .and RUN.

Oops! The figure calls for two rows, one on top of the other, but our string prints everything in one row. How can we position the second row directly under the first without using two separate strings? Everyone back to the ASCII chart in Appendix B. Pay particular attention to codes 24 to 27. They are the solution to our problem. By adding the appropriate cursor motion codes into the middle of our string, we can move the second row of characters exactly where it belongs.

Let's see, after the first row is printed, we need to move the cursor down once, then left eight times. Add:

```
4Ø X = X + CHR$(26) + STRING$(8,24)
```

That ought to do the trick. RUN the program to make sure we are on the right track. Voila! Our very own creature.

Notice how quickly the figure is displayed once the string is assembled in memory. Try displaying the same figure with SET statements. There is no comparison. We have just unlocked the secret of high speed graphics with BASIC.

But Can It Fly?

Some people just don't know when to quit. I suppose you want the figure to flap its wings (those ARE wings, aren't they?) and zoom around the screen like a loony bird.

Before we start this adventure, you should be aware that we are working with a SLOW language. BASIC is very easy to use, but its interpretive nature makes it the sloth of computer languages. Unfortunately, animation requires speed. Our alternatives? Use assembly language – ARRRGGH, work only with SET and RESET and a single bouncing dot (who cares?) or continue with the "string packing" technique we used above. The latter technique requires extra programming effort, but it is the only way to generate fast graphics in BASIC. So much for the rationale.

Our method of achieving the animation will be to create several packed string variables identical to the first one, except that the wings will be in slightly different positions. By displaying these strings in rapid-fire succession, we will create the illusion of motion. This idea is not new. It is the same process used to create animated cartoons.

The other two figures (or frames) we will use are shown in Figure 6.

Figure 6

Loading an Array

Instead of storing these figures in separate variable names, let's turn X into a string array. Change lines 3∅-5∅ to:

```
3∅ FOR I=1 TO 8:READ N:X(J)=X(J) + CHR$(N):NEXT

4∅ X(J)=X(J) + CHR$(26) + STRING$(8,24)

5∅ FOR I=1 TO 8:READ N:X(J)=X(J) + CHR$(N):NEXT
```

Now we can add the looping instructions needed to read in DATA for all three strings:

```
2∅ FOR J=1 TO 3

6∅ NEXT J : X(4)=X(2)
```

and the DATA:

```
90 DATA 128,128,168,187,183,148,128,128
100 DATA 131,131,179,191,191,179,131,131
110 DATA 128,128,168,187,183,148,128,128
120 DATA 160,142,179,191,191,179,141,144
```

and finally, instructions to display the figure:

```
150 FOR J=1 TO 4:PRINT@410,X(J);
220 FOR I=1 TO 40:NEXT I:NEXT J
230 GOTO 150
```

. . .and RUN.

Up, up, and away. Our computer acts like a series of flash cards. Line 22Ø adds a delay to control the speed of animation.

Save this program on tape or disk as we will use it in a later chapter.

EXERCISE 41-2: List the graphic codes that make up the following figure, then pretend that it is a snail:

And In Conclusion . . .

If you have been paying attention, you should now have no trouble deciding which graphic techniques are best for you. We know that SET and RESET are super for plotting with X,Y coordinates, as long as speed is not essential.

They can even be used for the simple animation of small figures. However, where speed is required to deal with large figures, the power of PRINT@ used with string packing is the only way to fly.

For an in-depth look at graphics on the TRS-80, see *TRS-80 Graphics for the Model I and Model III*, by D. A. Kater and S. J. Thomas, Byte Books.

Learned in Chapter 41

Techniques

String Packing

Animation

Array Loading

Miscellaneous

Graphic character

code pattern

Cursor control codes

Graphic INKEY$

Model II users, skip the next two chapters.

The implications of instantaneous (well, nearly instantaneous) input are not limited to the applications shown thus far. This capability adds a new dimension to the area of games and animation programming. Using INKEY$, we can write game programs with real-time response to keyboard input.

As an example of this use of INKEY$, let's bring back the wing flapping monstrosity we created. Here is the listing:

```
10 CLS:CLEAR 300:DEFSTR X
20 FOR J=1 TO 3
30 FOR I=1 TO 8:READ N : X(J)=X(J)+CHR$(N):NEXTI
40 X(J)=X(J)+CHR$(26)+STRING$(8,24)
50 FOR I=1 TO 8:READ N : X(J)=X(J)+CHR$(N):NEXTI
60 NEXT J:X(4)=X(2)
70 DATA 136,176,168,187,183,148,176,132
```

```
80  DATA 128,130,179,191,191,179,129,128
90  DATA 128,128,168,187,183,148,128,128
100 DATA 131,131,179,191,191,179,131,131
110 DATA 128,128,168,187,183,148,128,128
120 DATA 160,142,179,191,191,179,141,144
150 FOR J=1 TO 4:PRINT@410,X(J);
220 FOR I=1 TO 40:NEXT I:NEXT J
230 GOTO 150
```

We are going to use INKEY$ and the arrow keys to move the figure around the screen. So our first step will be to change the PRINT@ position into a variable. Change:

```
10  CLS:CLEAR 300:DEFSTR X:P=410
150 FOR J=1 TO 4:PRINT@P,X(J);
```

    . . .and RUN.

Next, we'll speed up the graphics a bit:

```
220 FOR I=1 TO 10:NEXT I:NEXT J
```

    . . .and RUN.

Because of the way the PRINT@ locations are laid out, changes in the position variable, P, will have to be made according to:

Left P=P-1

Right P=P+1

Down P=P+64

Up   P=P-64

Horizontal positions on the video screen differ by one. Vertical positions differ by 64. Make sure this is clear before proceeding.

Since we want to direct the movement from the keyboard, we need to associate the above changes in P with the correct arrow keys. A bit of experimenting shows that the arrow keys return the following ASCII values:

Left 8

Right 9

Down 10

Up   91

So, the proper matchups are:

Left   8: P=P-1

Right 9: P=P+1

Down   10: P=P+64

Up   91: P=P-64

We can add this information to the BASIC program as follows. Add:

```
130 P=P+K
160 X=INKEY$:IF X="" THEN 210
170 K=0:V=ASC(X):IF V=8 THEN K=K-1
180 IF V=9 THEN K=K+1
190 IF V=10 THEN K=K+64
200 IF V=91 THEN K=K-64
230 GOTO 130
```

Don't RUN yet.

In line 16Ø, keyboard input is stored in the string variable X. In line 17Ø, V is set to the ASC value of X. This value is compared to the ASCII numbers returned by each of the four arrow keys in lines 17Ø through 2ØØ, and K is changed accordingly. Then back in line 13Ø, the screen position variable P is adjusted by K.

I'll bet you forgot about testing for our figure floating off the edge of the screen. Stick with us kid, we wouldn't steer you wrong.

Add:

```
210 IF P+K>888 OR P+K<0  THEN P=P-K:GOTO 140
```

It pays to plan ahead. *Now* you can RUN it. Press the arrow keys to move the figure around the screen.

Argggg! Well, we can only plan ahead so far. Forgot one tiny little detail. Can't leave a messy trail behind our flying friend, can we?

Add line 14Ø:

```
140 CLS
```

. . .and RUN.

There it is: a flying creature that would give King Kong fits. All due to the INKEY$ function and our clever programming.

I think that's just about enough for this chapter.

> *EXERCISE 42-1:* Write a program using INKEY$ to control game paddle (STRING$(8,14Ø)) movement back and forth across the bottom of the screen with the left and right arrows. Protect the screen borders.

Learned in Chapter 42

Miscellaneous

Real time input

Part VII

Miscellaneous

PEEK and POKE

Model II users skip this chapter.

PEEK and POKE are BASIC words that allow us to do non-BASIC things. They provide the means whereby we can PEEK into the innards of the computer's memory and, if we wish, POKE in new information.

It is not our purpose here to become an expert in machine language programming, nor on how the computer works. We have to approach this and related topics a little gingerly, lest we fall over the edge into a computer abyss (or is it an abysmal computer?).

We do know, however, that computers do their thing entirely by the manipulation of numbers. Therefore, when we PEEK at the contents of memory, guess what we'll find? Numbers? Very good! (Ummmyaas).

Figure 7

Model I and III Memory Map		
Decimal Address	**Hex Address**	**Function**
65535	FFFF	END "48K" SYSTEMS
49151	BFFF	END "32K" SYSTEMS

Model I and III Memory Map

Decimal Address	Hex Address	Function
32767	7FFF	END "16K" SYSTEMS
20479	4FFF	END "4K" SYSTEMS
17385 (17129MI)	43E9 (42E9)	PROGRAM AND USER MEMORY
17384 (17128)	43E8 (42E8	RESERVED FOR SYSTEM USE
16384	4000	
16383	3FFF	VIDEO MEMORY
15360	3C00	
15359	3BFF	RESERVED FOR SYSTEM
12288	3000	INPUT/OUTPUT
12287	2FFF	TRS-80 BASIC READ
0	0000	ONLY MEMORY (ROM)

Figure 7

The Memory Map in Figure 7 shows that large chunks of the computer's memory are reserved or "mapped" for very specific uses. The BASIC ROM, for example, uses byte addresses 0 through 12287. (All numbers we talk about here are decimals, not hex, octal, binary or Sanskrit.)

Turn the machine off to clear out memory, wait a minute, turn it back on, bring up BASICA and type in this NEW program:

```
20 N=0
40 PRINT N, PEEK(N), CHR$(PEEK(N))
50 N=N+1
60 GOTO 40
```

Let's analyze the program before RUNning it.

Line 2∅ sets the *beginning* address where we want to start PEEKing. As Figure 7 shows, there are lots of good places to go spelunking, and we can change line 2∅ to start wherever we want.

Line 4∅ PRINTs three things:

1. The address — that is, the number of the byte, the contents of which we are PEEKing (the offset into the SEGment).

2. The contents of that byte, expressed as a decimal number between 0 and 255.

3. The contents of that address converted to its ASCII character. (Many of the ASCII characters are not PRINTable. Go back to the Chapter on ASCII if *your* memory has grown dim.)

Okay, now RUN the program, being ready to freeze it with `SHIFT` @ if you see something interesting. It can also be stopped at any time with the `BREAK` key, and restarted with CONT without having to start all over again with N at 0.

Didn't see anything interesting? What did you find starting at address 261? You have to be able to read vertically as the letters swish by.

When the letters jump to double-width, hit `BREAK` , then `CLEAR` , then CONT, as they are too hard to read when so large. Change N to start at different places in memory and PEEK to your heart's delight. You can't goof up anything by just PEEKing. It's indiscriminate POKEing that gets you into trouble.

The command level is very handy for resetting the starting address. We can change the value of N by just typing:

```
N=5∅∅∅
```

for example, then:

```
CONT
```

instead of RUN.

When done PEEKing, and having seen far more information than can possibly be absorbed, rework line 4Ø to read simply:

```
4Ø PRINT CHR$(PEEK(N));
```

. . .and RUN.

It PRINTs only the ASCII characters, horizontally, and is the ideal program to RUN when friends visit. Just act casual about the whole display and avoid any direct questions. Makes a great background piece for a science fiction movie.

When you find an interesting spot, hit `BREAK` , then

```
PRINT N
```

at the command level to find out where in memory we are PEEKing. (Don't you wish we could explore the corners of our minds as easily?)

CONTinue on when ready.

Having degenerated from PEEKing to leering, we are ready to see what else we can do.

Careless POKEing Can Leave Holes. . .

Before POKEing, we'd better see that we're not POKEing a stick into a hornet's nest. It's with the greatest of ease that we destroy a program in memory by POKEing around where we shouldn't.

Obviously, there is no use POKEing the ROM area since ROM stands for Read Only Memory. It's not changeable. The rest of the "Memory mapped" area, from 12288 thru 17384 (17128 on the Model I) is reserved for specific things, so best not to POKE in there while we're just bungling around. Anything above 17384 should be available memory, unless taken up with our BASIC program or required for processing. With such a short program as ours we surely can't goof anything up. Can we?

Let's PEEK around 20000 and see if anything is going on there. Change these two program lines to:

```
2Ø N = 2ØØØØ
```

```
40 PRINT N; PEEK(N),
```

. . .and RUN.

20000	19	20001	68	20002	184	20003	48
20004	5	20005	62	20006	194	20007	195
20008	9	20009	68	20010	58	20011	218
20012	78	20013	245	20014	205	20015	138
20016	80	20017	122	20018	50	20019	86
20020	78	20021	241	20022	198	20023	48
20024	50	20025	227	20026	78	20027	62
20028	1	20029	50	20030	239	20031	78
20032	33	20033	220	20034	78	20035	205
20036	27	20037	2	20038	62	20039	2
20040	50	20041	238	20042	78	20043	33
20044	238	20045	78	20046	126	20047	52
20048	95	20049	58	20050	218	20051	78
20052	79	20053	22	20054	0	20055	33
20056	0	20057	67	20058	205	20059	117

Model I may show slightly different results.

What we see are the address numbers and their contents, in easy-to-read parallel rows.

Great! Let's change our program and **POKE** in some information, then do something with it. Make it read:

```
10 REM * POKE PROGRAM *
20 N = 20000
30 READ D
40 POKE N,D
50 N = N + 1
```

Disk BASIC users change line 20 to N = 3000.

```
60 IF N = 20011 THEN END
70 GOTO 30
100 DATA 80,69,69,75,45,65,45,66,79,79,33
```
30011 Disk BASIC.

Before RUNning, let's analyze it.

Line 20 initializes the starting address at 2000 (or 3000).

Line 30 READs a number from the DATA line.

Line 40 POKEs the DATA "D" into address "N".

Line 50 increments the address number by one.

Line 60 ENDs execution after we've POKEd in all 11 pieces of DATA.

Line 70 sends us back for more DATA.

Line 100 holds the DATA we are going to POKE into memory.

   . . .now RUN.

Well, that was sure fast. I wonder what it did? How can we find out? Should we PEEK at it? Yes, but let's leave the old program in and just start a new one at 200.

```
200 REM * PEEK PROGRAM *
210 FOR N=20000 TO 20010
220 PRINT N, PEEK(N)
230 NEXT N
```
30000 to 30010 Disk BASIC.

   . . .and RUN 200.

```
20000     80
20001     69
20002     69
20003     75
```

```
20004    45
20005    65
20006    45
20007    66
20008    79
20009    79
20010    33
```

How about that? We really *did* change the contents of those memory locations. We shot the numbers from our DATA line right into memory. Now if we only knew what those numbers stood for. Wonder. . .if we changed them to ASCII characters, would they tell us anything?

Add:

```
205 CLS
220  PRINT@470+N-20000,CHR$(PEEK(N));     N - 30000 Disk BASIC.
```

to PRINT at a certain location on the screen

   . . .and RUN 200.

And that's how PEEK and POKE work.

> *EXERCISE 43-1:* Display the word POKE centered in the top line of the video display using the POKE statement instead of PRINT@. Hint: POKEing characters to RAM memory locations 15360 — 16383 has virtually the same effect as printing to screen locations 0 — 1023. Just add 15360 to the desired PRINT@ location.

Learned in Chapter 43

Statements	Functions	Miscellaneous
POKE	PEEK	Memory Map

Model III POKE Features

Changing Cassette Speed

Model III users have the option of selecting either high or low cassette speed when powering up. For compatibility with the Model I tape format, use low speed. Otherwise, use high speed. . .it's much more reliable.

Restarting BASIC to change the Model III cassette speed will, of course, erase any program in memory.

Fortunately, there is another way to change speed. Model III memory location 16913 is the key. When this location contains a zero, low speed is used. When it contains a non-zero value, the high speed is used.

To select low speed from BASIC without disturbing a current program in memory, type:

```
POKE 16913,0
```

To select the high speed use:

```
POKE 16913,1
```

or any other non-zero number.

Special Characters

Now that we are well-versed in POKEing characters to the video display (see Exercise 43-1), Model III owners arc in for another surprise. There is one more set of foreign characters hidden away in the Model III character generator. Unlike any of the other ASCII codes, this set cannot be printed in the normal fashion using the CHR$ function. It can only be accessed by more devious means as we shall see.

Just as the Special and Kana character sets are hidden among the ASCII codes (192 − 255), the foreign characters reside in the ASCII domain, in the lower reaches (0 − 31).

How do we display these characters on the screen? Instead of using codes like PRINT CHR$(21) and PRINT CHR$(22) to swap character sets in and out, as we did earlier, the foreign character set is activated only when the POKE statement is used. When the codes from 0 to 31 are used with CHR$, we get action characters such as cursor motion and character width. When POKEd, we get foreign characters.

Let's POKE these characters onto the screen so they can see the light of day. We'll put the computer in double-width, and place the characters in the first row of the screen. Recall from the memory map that the video display starts at location 15360. We will POKE code 0 in address 15360, 1 in 15362, 2 in 15364, etc. Hang on, here we go. Enter this NEW program:

```
10 CLS
20 PRINT CHR$(23)
30 FOR P=0 TO 31
40 POKE 15360 + P*2, P
50 NEXT P : PRINT
```

   . . .and RUN.

There they are! All the foreign symbols we dreamed about but were afraid to ask. (Kan du snakke Norsk?)

Learned in Chapter 44

Miscellaneous

Cassette Speed Changes

Foreign Character Set

Video Display Memory

Logical Operators
(AND, OR, and NOT)

In classical mathematics (fancy words for simple ideas), there exist what are known as the "logical AND", the "logical OR", and the "logical NOT".

So The One Cow Said To The Other Cow . . .

In Figure 8, if gate A AND gate B AND gate C are open, the cow can move from pasture #1 to pasture #2. If any gate is closed, the cow's path is blocked.

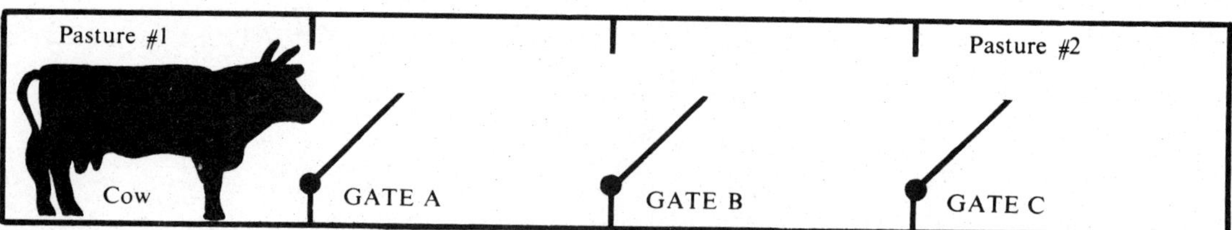

Figure 8

The principle is called "logical AND".

In Figure 9, if gate X OR gate Y OR gate Z is open, then old Bess can move from pasture #3 to #4. That principle is called "logical OR". These ideas are both pretty logical. If the cow can figure them out, surely we can!

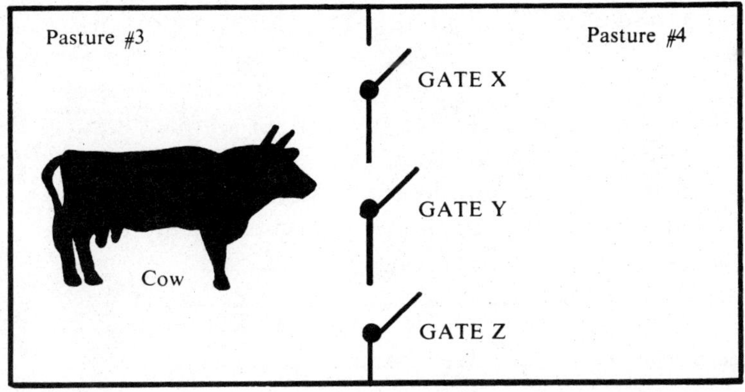

Figure 9

Using these ideas is very simple. Type this NEW program:

```
10  INPUT "IS GATE 'A' OPEN"; A$
20  INPUT "IS GATE 'B' OPEN"; B$
30  INPUT "IS GATE 'C' OPEN"; C$
40  PRINT
50  IF A$="Y" AND B$="Y" AND C$="Y" THEN 80
60  PRINT "OLD BESSIE CAN'T GET TO PASTURE #2."
70  END
80  PRINT "ALL GATES ARE OPEN. OLD BESSIE IS FREE TO ROAM."
```

. . .and RUN.

Answer (Y/N) the questions differently during RUNs to see how the logical AND works in line 50.

Where Is The Logic In All This?

You should by now understand every line in the program, except perhaps line 50.

Lines 10, 20, and 30 INPUT the gate positions as *open* (which we defined as equal to "Y") or *closed* (defined as "N"). We could have defined them the other way around and rewritten line 50 to match, if we'd wanted to.

Line 50 is the key. It reads, literally, "If gate A is *open*, AND gate B is *open*,

AND gate C is *open*, then go to line 8Ø." If any one gate is closed, report that fact by defaulting to line 6Ø.

Imagine how this simple logic could be used to create a super-simple "computer" consisting of only an electric switch on each gate. Add a battery and put a light bulb in the farmer's house. The bulb could indicate whether the gates are all open. Such a "gate-checking" computer would have only three memory cells — the switches.

> Hmm. It would do the job a lot cheaper than a TRS-80. . .but would be awfully hard to play Blackjack with.

EXERCISE 45-1: Using the above program as a model, and the "OR logic" seen in Figure 9, write a program which will report Bess' status as determined by the position of Gates X, Y and Z.

Teacher's Pet

Here is a simple program which uses > instead of the equals sign in a logical test. The student passes if he has a final grade over 60, OR a midterm grade over 70 AND a homework grade over 75. Enter this NEW program, RUN it a few times, and see how efficiently the logical OR and logical AND tests work in the same program line (4Ø).

```
1Ø INPUT "FINAL GRADE"; F
2Ø INPUT "MIDTERM GRADE"; M
3Ø INPUT "HOMEWORK GRADE"; H
4Ø IF (F > 6Ø OR M > 7Ø) AND H > 75 THEN 7Ø
5Ø PRINT "FAILED"
6Ø END
7Ø PRINT "PASSED"
```

Does this give you some idea of the power and convenience of logical math? The actual grade numbers could, of course, be set at any level.

Logical Variations

This next program example mixes equal, greater-than and less-than signs in the same program. It determines and reports whether the two numbers we INPUT are both positive, both negative, or have different signs.

Analyze the program. Note the parentheses. Although they are not necessary, they tell us to shift our thinking to "logical". Type it in and RUN.

```
10  INPUT "FIRST NUMBER IS"; X
20  INPUT "SECOND NUMBER IS"; Y
30  IF (X>=0) AND (Y>=0) THEN 70
40  IF (X<0) AND (Y<0) THEN 90
50  PRINT "OPPOSITE SIGNS"
60  END
70  PRINT "BOTH POSITIVE OR ZERO"
80  END
90  PRINT "BOTH NEGATIVE"
```

With Graphics Too, Yet

> Model II users skip to "And In Conclusion".

Yes, the logical symbols also work along with the graphic statements. See if you can figure out the surprise which will be caused by the logical AND in line 40. Type this NEW program in, and RUN.

```
10  CLS
20  FOR X = 0 TO 127
30   FOR Y = 0 TO 47
40    IF (X>=64) AND (Y>=24) THEN 60
50    SET(X,Y)
60   NEXT Y
70  NEXT X
99  GOTO 99
```

What will happen if we replace the AND in line 4∅ with an OR? After you think you have it figured out, do it and see the result.

Use BREAK to get out of the program's endless loop.

Did you guess right?

There's More?

Oh, yes — the only limit is your imagination. See how easily the logical notation makes the drawing of lines? Type and RUN this NEW one:

```
1∅ CLS
2∅ FOR X = ∅ TO 127
3∅  FOR Y = ∅ TO 47
4∅   IF (X>=64) OR (Y>=24) THEN 6∅
5∅    SET(X,Y)
6∅   NEXT Y
7∅ NEXT X
99 GOTO 99
```

What happens to the program if we replace OR with AND? Sketch your estimated result, then change line 4∅ and try it.

Hope you got it right. If not, it really sneaked up on you, didn't it!

Using the INT function we can create an elaborate checkerboard. The reasoning is:

In the horizontal dimension:

The INT(X/16)*16-X will equal 0 when X equals 0, 16, 32, 48, 64, 80, 96, and 112.

In the vertical dimension:

The INT(Y/6)*6-Y will equal 0 when Y equals 0, 6, 12, 18, 24, 30, 36, and 42.

Oh come on, it's very simple if you take the time and think it through!

Replace the old line 4Ø with:

```
4Ø IF ((INT(X/16)*16-X)=Ø) OR ((INT(Y/6)*6-Y)=Ø) THEN 6Ø.
```

and you will create an elaborate eight-by-eight checkerboard.

And on and on it goes. . .

And In Conclusion

Logical math is worth the hassle. As one last fun program, enter and RUN this "Midnight Inspection". Line 1ØØ checks each response for a NO answer (instead of a YES). Using logical OR, it branches to the "no-go" statement (line 12Ø) if any one of the tests is negative ("N").

```
1Ø CLS
2Ø PRINT "ANSWER THESE QUESTIONS WITH 'Y' OR 'N'."
3Ø PRINT
4Ø INPUT "HAS THE CAT BEEN PUT OUT"; A$
5Ø INPUT "IS THE PORCH LIGHT TURNED OFF"; B$
6Ø INPUT "ARE ALL THE DOORS AND WINDOWS LOCKED"; C$
7Ø INPUT "IS THE TELEVISION TURNED OFF"; D$
8Ø INPUT "DID YOU TURN THE THERMOSTAT DOWN"; E$
9Ø PRINT : PRINT
1ØØ IF A$="N" OR B$="N" OR C$="N" OR D$="N" OR E$="N" THEN 12Ø
11Ø PRINT "          GOODNIGHT": END
12Ø PRINT "SOMETHING HAS NOT BEEN DONE. DO NOT GO TO BED"
13Ø PRINT "UNTIL YOU FIND THE PROBLEM!"
14Ø GOTO 4Ø
```

In most cases, AND and OR statements are interchangeable if other parts of a program are rewritten to accommodate the switch.

> **Note: Not for Model II.**
>
> *EXERCISE 45-2:* Rewrite line 4∅ in the checkerboard program to produce a black-on-white checkerboard instead of white-on-black.

NOT

In addition to the logical AND and OR functions, we have what is called logical NOT. Here is how it can be used:

```
1  CLS : PRINT
1∅  INPUT "ENTER A NUMBER"; N
2∅  L = NOT(N>5)
3∅  IF L = ∅ GOTO 5∅
4∅  PRINT "N WAS NOT GREATER THAN 5" : PRINT : LIST
5∅  PRINT "N WAS GREATER THAN 5" : PRINT : LIST
```

Line 2∅ is obviously the key one, containing NOT. If the statement in line 2∅ is *true* (namely that N is NOT larger than 5), the computer makes the value of L = −1. The test in line 3∅ then fails.

If, on the other hand, N is larger than 5, the statement is false and the computer makes the values of L = 0.

True = -1 and False = 0. (Time for the primal scream, again. All together now. . .)

Order of Operations

When trying to figure out which gets calculated first in the thick of a "humongous" equation, here's the pecking order:

Those operations buried deepest inside the parentheses get resolved first. The idea is to clear the parentheses as quickly as possible. When it all becomes a big tie, here's the order:

1. Exponentation — a number raised to a power.

2. Negation, that is, a number having its sign changed. Typically, a number multiplied times -1.

3. Multiplication and division — from left to right.

4. Addition and subtraction — from left to right.

5. Less than, greater than, equals, less or equal to, greater or equal to, not equal to — from left to right.

6. The logical NOT.

7. The logical AND.

8. The logical OR.

Learned in Chapter 45

Miscellaneous
Logical AND
Logical OR
Logical NOT
Order of operations

A Study of Obscurities

Model II users may want to skip this chapter, realizing that your BASIC does not support PEEK or POKE.

TRS-80 BASIC has some features that are not used by most beginning programmers. Their use requires special applications and knowledge which are really beyond the scope of this book. In the interest of completeness, abbreviated descriptions of what they are and how they are used are included in this chapter.

USR

The USR function has a variety of uses, most of them having little to do with BASIC. It allows us to "call" or "gosub" a program written in assembly language, and "return" back to our BASIC program when it's finished. To make much sense of USR you'll need assembly language skills — not a part of this book. Model I users will have a chance to see USR in action in Appendix C dealing with the "Real Time Clock". We use it there almost like a simple toggle switch to turn the clock on and off when we want.

In its simplified form we might think of

```
X=USR(1)
```

as meaning "turn it on",

and

```
X=USR(0)
```

as meaning "turn if off".

What it *actually* means, of course, is determined by the function of the machine language program it's "calling".

HEX	Most Significant Bytes		Least Significant Bytes	
CODE	IV	III	II	I
0	0	0	0	0
1	4096	256	16	1
2	8192	512	32	2
3	12288	768	48	3
4	16384	1024	64	4
5	20480	1280	80	5
6	24576	1536	96	6
7	28672	1792	112	7
8	32768	2048	128	8
9	36864	2304	144	9
A	40960	2560	160	10
B	45056	2816	176	11
C	49152	3072	192	12
D	53248	3328	208	13
E	57344	3584	224	14
F	61440	3840	240	15

Figure 10
Hex-to-Decimal Conversion Chart
Decimal Value = IV + III + II + I

Without getting out too deep in the water, memory addresses 16526 and 16527 are inspected by USR to find out where in memory we have stored a machine language program.

If it starts at 32000, for example, we have to express 32000 in HEXadecimal, then split that HEX number into its *least* and *most significant* bytes, convert those bytes separately back to decimal, and POKE that information into 16526 and 16527. (Are you really sure you want to go through with this?)

Looking at the HEX-to-Decimal conversion chart (Figure 10), any ace digital engineer can readily see that 32000 equals 7530 HEX. We divide 7530 into 30 and 75, the least and most significant bytes, respectively. By converting them back to decimal using the same chart, we get:

30 = LSB = 48 decimal,

and

75=MSB=117 decimal.

Ummm yaas!

Now, we POKE that starting address into our BASIC program, something like this:

```
10 POKE 16526,48 : POKE 16527,117
```

Disk users must use DEFUSR. See your TRSDOS Manual.

and we're set to call our non-existent machine language program at 32000 from BASIC by simply saying:

```
X=USR(1)
```

That's as far as we're going to press our luck on this one right now. We don't want to leave so terror-stricken that we won't continue.

Machine and Assembly language programming books are readily available for that small percentage of readers who want to pursue the subject. You at least have a sufficient introduction to nod your head and smile knowingly (and say ummm. . .yaas) when others try to impress you with their knowledge of these things.

INP

Note: Not on Model II.

The TRS-80 has 256 "ports" or channels of communication with the "outside world". They are numbered from 0 to 255. Because this subject is worthy of an entire book itself, we will only learn enough here to get an elementary "feel" for it.

CompuSoft® Publishing has an excellent book titled *Controlling The World With Your TRS-80* (soon to be released by your favorite author) which takes the beginner all the way through advanced applications of the TRS-80 using digital information INPut and OUTput via these 256 ports.

Only one of these ports in the TRS-80 will be considered here. Port number 255 controls the cassette recorder. All other ports are available to take in information or send it out via the bus connector at the back of the computer. (Just look now — no fiddling please.)

You're not going to "Control The World" with what you learn about ports in this chapter, but enter this program and you may be surprised at what INP can do.

```
10 OUT 255,0                    'RESETS PORT TO ZERO
20 S = INP(255) : PRINT S,
30 IF S>127 GOTO 50
40 PRINT "NO DATA COMING FROM CASSETTE" : GOTO 10
50 PRINT,"DATA IS FLOWING FROM CASSETTE" : GOTO 10
```

Now, place a program tape in the recorder (BLACKJACK will do nicely). Set the volume where you usually do. Remove the REM motor control plug, and press PLAY. Type RUN.

Haha! Didn't expect that, did you? Here's how it works:

Line 1Ø disregard for right now.

Line 2Ø looks at port #255 and reads a coded message, then prints that code.

Line 3Ø tests that code number. If it is greater than 127, *execution branches to line 5Ø.* If not, it defaults to line 4Ø. Execution returns to line 1Ø where we begin the "polling" of the port again.

Astute observers have probably noted that there is a definite pattern to the numbers displayed. Why these particular numbers appear is beyond the scope of this book. The point is, DATA either *is* or *isn't* flowing, and this is what INP reads, and acts upon.

If you want to have a little fun, play the tape again but adjust the volume control very carefully (down around 2) so that variations in data flow are sensed and appear as changes in the message on the screen. Doesn't take much imagination to go from this point to different kinds of visual displays.

One more view of INP. Enter this NEW program, and RUN.

```
1Ø FOR N = Ø TO 255

2Ø PRINT N; INP(N),

3Ø NEXT N
```

This program scans all 256 ports and gives us their status.

OUT

Let's see what OUT does. Remove the cassette from the recorder, and leave the hatch open so you can see the drive hub. Press the PLAY key, and type in this program:

```
1Ø INPUT"2 = ON  &  Ø = OFF";N

2Ø OUT 236,N

3Ø GOTO 1Ø
```

---

4 = on for Model I, out 255,N for Model I.

. . .and RUN, responding to the INPUT? and watching the drive hub.

We are sending directions OUT to port 236, the recorder port, and telling the motor to be either ON or OFF.

---

155 for Model I .

That's a sample of what OUT does. Nuff said.

Oh yes, the OUT in line 1Ø of the section on INP? Well, you see there's this little rubber band inside the computer that has to be pulled to reset the. . .

VARPTR

While VARPTR (short for VARiable PoinTeR) is found in this TRS-80 BASIC, it's about as far from main line BASIC as anything we have.

Take a Deep Breath

If a variable is numeric, VARPTR tells us the location of the first byte of the number stored in that variable.

If it's a string variable, VARPTR tells us where in memory the INDEX to a given variable is located. Read that last line carefully. We don't want anyone getting lost. VARPTR doesn't have the common decency to point to the *contents* of a string variable in memory. Instead, it points to a three-byte "index" to the variable. The three bytes contain:

1. The *length* of the string.

2. The least significant byte of the *starting location* of the string.

3. The most significant byte of the *starting location* of the string.

To actually find the *contents* of the string variable, we have to calculate the location using bytes two and three of the *index* to that variable. Sound complicated? Well, it is a bit tricky, but an example should clarify matters quite nicely.

Enter this NEW program:

```
1Ø REM * STRING VARIABLE LOCATER *
2Ø CLS
3Ø A$ = "123456"
4Ø X = VARPTR(A$)
45 PRINT "INDEX TO A$ IS AT";X
```

. . .and RUN.

Line 4∅ uses VARPTR to store the location of the index to A$ in X. Then line 45 prints it.

We haven't found the contents of A$ yet, just the index. Hang in there. Add:

```
5Ø L = PEEK(X+1) + 256*PEEK(X+2)
55 PRINT "A$ IS HIDING AT LOCATION";L
```

. . .and RUN.

So that's where the little rascal is. Line 5∅ uses some fancy footwork to convert bytes two and three of the index into the actual location of A$. Line 55, of course, prints its value.

How could we prove that we have found the correct location? Sure. PEEK at the contents of A$ and compare it with "123456". Add:

```
6Ø FOR I=L TO L+5
7Ø PRINT CHR$(PEEK(I));
8Ø NEXT I : PRINT
```

. . .and RUN.

Satisfied?

Now, knowing where a variable is located in memory may not seem too useful at first blush, but it has some surprising consequences. Once we have found the location of a string variable, we can modify its contents. Try this one on for size:

```
7Ø READ N : POKE I,N
8Ø NEXT I : PRINT A$ : PRINT
9Ø DATA 136,181,182,191,185,176
```

. . .and RUN.

Surprise! We have just poked graphic codes into an unsuspecting "normal" string variable and transformed it into a pictorial masterpiece. (You recognize the snail from an earlier chapter, don't you?)

Type:

```
PRINT A$
```

to be sure you weren't just dreaming. Yes, it really happened. We have actually modified the contents of A$. These computers can be down right fun once you get to know them.

Now type:

```
LIST
```

Did we do that to line 3Ø? I'm afraid so. A messy listing doesn't affect the program, and it's a small price to pay for this capability.

Model III users won't see a messy listing.

Let us leave you with this thought. We packed a "dummy" string with only six graphic codes. A string variable *can* hold up to 255 characters (nearly one-fourth of the video display). Just imagine what we can do with a single string packed with up to 255 cursor control codes, space compression codes, graphic codes, and special character sets! If that doesn't push your cardiovascular system to overload, you might as well trade the 80 in for a calculator.

For More Information

See *TRS-80 Graphics for the Model I and Model III*, by D. A. Kater and S. J. Thomas, for a full account of this string-packing technique.

EXERCISE 46-1: Modify the current program using cursor motion codes (24-27) and a 13-character dummy string to store the following two-line figure in A$:

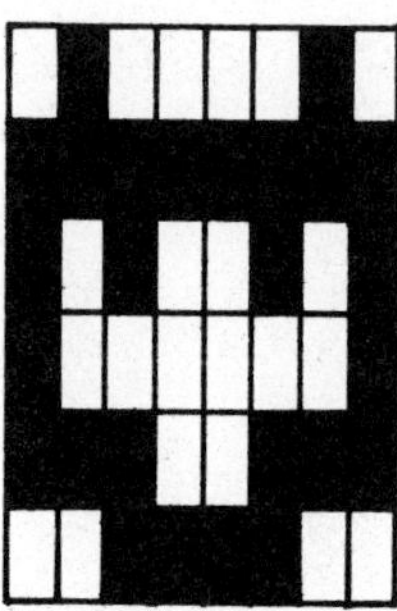

Learned in Chapter 46

Statements

OUT

Functions

USR

INP

VARPTR

Part VIII

Program Control

Flowcharting

Most of the programs we wrote so far were simple, but they met fairly simple needs. Suppose we want to write a program to play chess or bridge, evaluate complicated investment alternatives, keep records for a bowling league or a small business, or do stress calculations for a new building? How would we go about writing a complex program like that?

Answer: We break down the big program into a series of smaller programs. This is called *modular programming* and the individual programs are called *modules*. But how are the modules related — and how do we write them, anyway?

Module is just a 75-cent word for "section" or "building block".

One way to plan a program is to make a picture displaying its logic. Remember, a picture is worth a thousand words (or is it the other way around?). The picture that programmers use is called a *flowchart*. Flowcharts are so widely used that programmers have devised standard symbols. There are many specialized symbols in use, but we will examine only the most common ones.

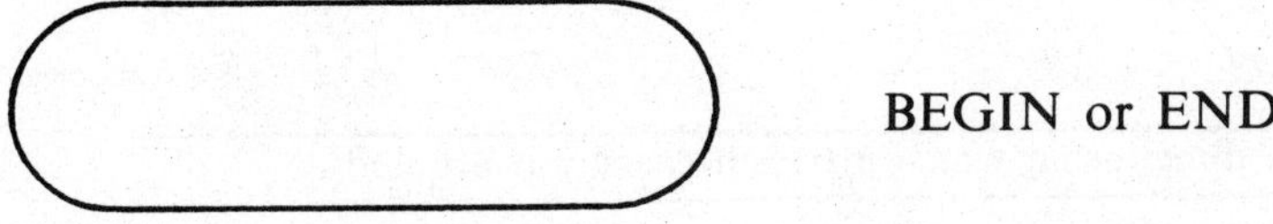

BEGIN or END

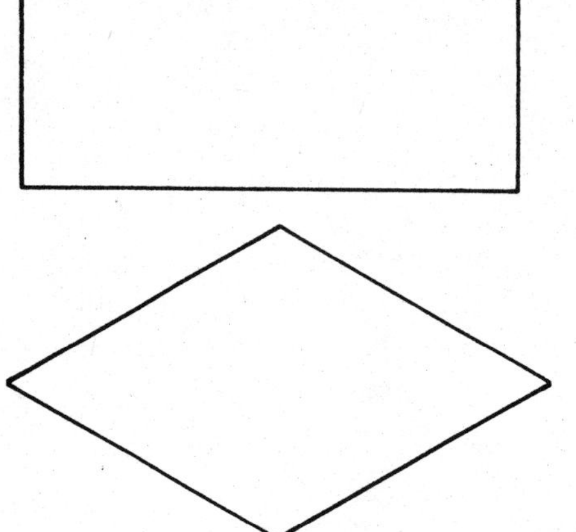

PROCESSING BLOCK (encloses something the computer does without making any decisions)

DECISION DIAMOND (branches off in different directions, depending on the decision it makes)

Each decision point asks a question such as, "Is A larger than B?" or *"Have all the cards been dealt?"* The different branches are marked by YES or NO.

Another useful symbol is:

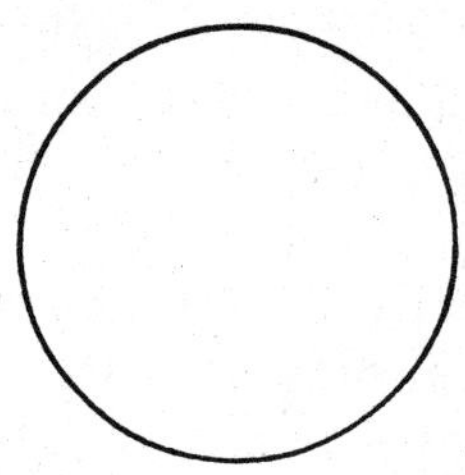

CONTINUATION

The circle usually has a number inside it which corresponds to a number on another page if the flowchart is too large for a single sheet.

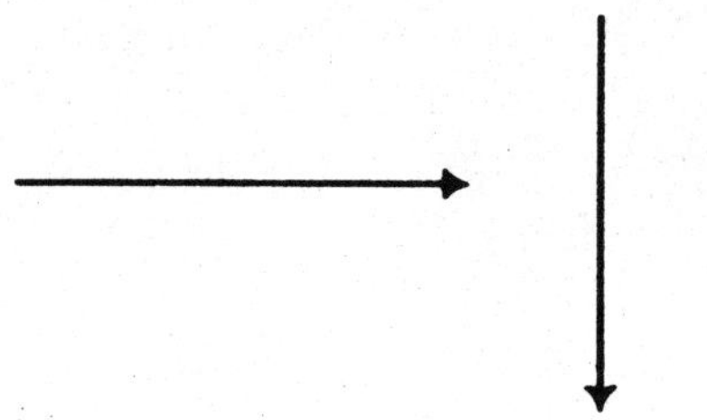

CONNECTOR ARROWS

Arrows indicate the direction in which program execution proceeds.

Flowcharts are most helpful in designing programs when they are kept simple. A cluttered flowchart is hard to read and usually isn't much more helpful than an ordinary written program LISTing. A good flowchart is also helpful for "documentation", to give us (or others) a picture of how the program works — for later on, when we've forgotten.

There are no hard-and-fast rules about what goes into a flowchart and what doesn't. A flowchart is supposed to help, not be more work than it's worth. It helps us plan the *logic* of our program. When it STOPs helping and makes us feel like we're back in arts and crafts designing mosaics, then we've gone as far as the flowchart will take us (or more typically, it's passed its point of usefulness).

Let's look at some examples. Suppose we want to grade a five-question test by comparing each of the *students'* answers with the *correct* answer. We will put the correct answers in a DATA statement in the program, enter a student's answers through the keyboard, compare (grade) them, then PRINT the % of correct answers. This procedure will be repeated until all the students' papers are graded.

The flowchart might look like Figure 11.

This flowchart has three decision diamonds. In the first, the computer determines if an answer is correct. In the second, the computer determines if all the questions in a single student's paper have been graded. The third one terminates execution when all the tests have been graded.

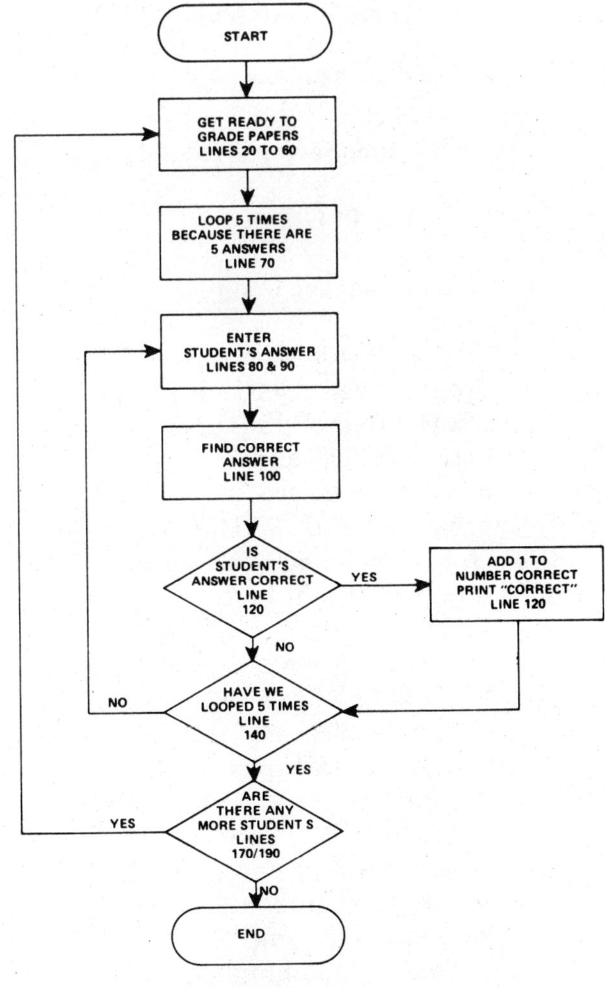

Figure 11

For more complicated problems, we may want to subdivide the flowchart into larger modules. A *master flowchart* will then show the relationship between the flowcharts of individual programs.

For example, let's say we want to write a program that calculates the *return* on various investments. The options might be:

1. Certificate of Deposit

2. Bank Savings Account

3. Credit Union

4. Mortgage Loan

The main (or Control) program will select one of these four options using an INPUT question, execute the correct subprogram, and PRINT the answer. Its flowchart might be like Figure 12.

We could now separately flowchart each of the individual programs in the blocks. The Certificate of Deposit program would, for example, have to contain the rate of return, size of deposit, and number

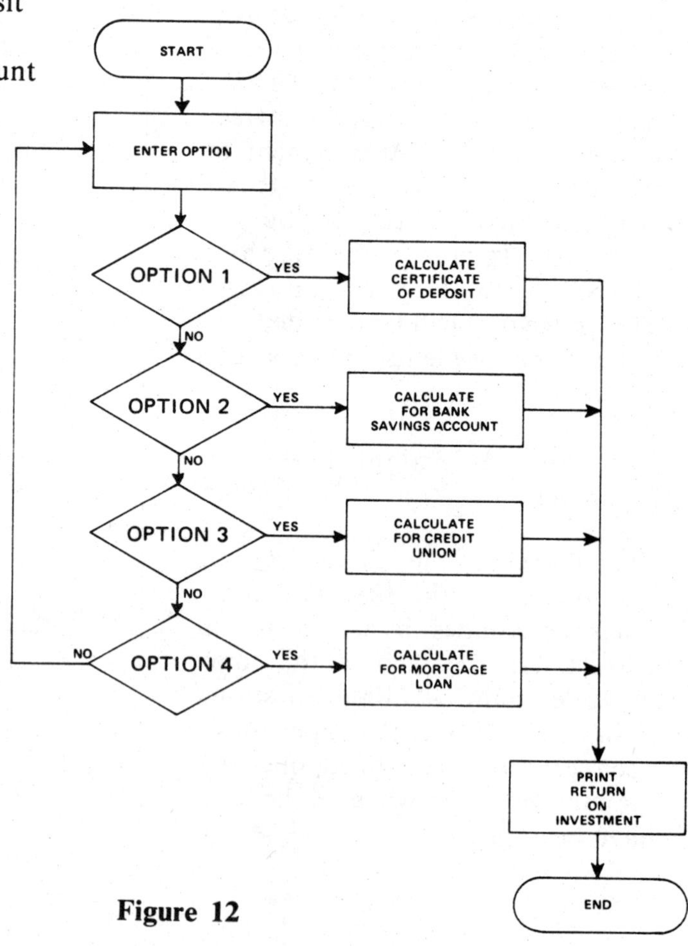

Figure 12

of years in which the certificate matures. The order in which that program INPUTs data and performs the calculations would be specified in its own flowchart.

> *EXERCISE 47-2:* Write the master program as flowcharted, with a branch to a program to calculate the return on a Bank Savings Account paying simple interest.

> *EXERCISE 47-3:* Choose a program from an early chapter and design your own flowchart.

Learned in Chapter 47

Miscellaneous

Flowcharting

Debugging Programs

Quick — The Raid!

By now, the computer has given us plenty of nasty messages. We know something's wrong, but it isn't always obvious exactly where or why.

How do we find it? The answer is simple — *be very systematic*. Even experienced programmers make lots of silly mistakes. . .but the experience teaches us how to locate mistakes quickly.

Hardware, Cockpit or Software?

The first step in the "debugging" process is to isolate the problem as being either:

1. A hardware problem,

2. An operator problem, or

3. A software problem.

Is It Farther To Ft. Worth or By Bus?

Starting with the least likely possibility. . ."Is the computer itself working properly?" Chances are very high that the computer is working perfectly. There are several very fast ways to find out.

A. Type:

```
PRINT MEM
```

If there is no program loaded into memory, the answer should be:

```
15314
```

or the correct value noted for your system. If there is a program loaded, the answer should be some value *less* than 15314.

If the answer is *more* than 15314 (assuming, of course, we have not added more memory), there may be trouble. Or, it's possible that the answer is a NEGATIVE number. . .same solution.

Possible Solution

In either of the above cases, shut the computer off completely. (Or, as they say in the big time, "Take it all the way down.") Let it sit for a full minute before turning it on again.

Yes, we will lose any program in memory, but at this point it's probably shot anyway. You could try to SAVE it before turning off the machine if it makes you feel any better.

Turn the machine back ON, type NEW and try the PRINT MEM test again. If the results are the same, there is probably a chip failure that will require professional troubleshooting and replacement.

B. One last try:

Before full panic sets in, type NEW and enter this program. It assigns every free memory location in RAM a specific value, then reads that value back out onto the screen.

Type very carefully:

```
5 DIM A(3765)
10 FOR X=1 TO 3765 : A(X)=X : NEXT X
20 FOR Y=1 TO 3765 : PRINT A(Y);
30 IF A(Y)-A(Y-1)<>1 PRINT "BAD"
40 NEXT Y
```

Model II use 8344.

For 16k Model I use 3835.

. . .and RUN.

After a *short* wait for the array to "spin-up", the monitor should display:

1 2 3 4 5 6 7 8 (etc. through 3765).

. . .or the appropriate number.

If the word "BAD" appears on the screen, we *may* have found the problem.

You will probably want to enter this test program into your computer, try it out *before you need it*, then save it on disk or tape and hope that you won't. . .(need it, that is).

Video Display Problems?

The Video Display is very similar to a television set. It has adjustments for brightness, contrast, horizontal and vertical sync, etc. If these fail to give the desired display, the problem could be in the computer.

Horizontal and vertical centering and "jitter" can be controlled by simple internal computer adjustments, but you have to know where to adjust. Don't mess with it, or you could end up goofing up the voltage regulators instead, and wiping out the entire lineup of integrated circuits. Very expensive fiddling around!

Besides. . .As the warranty points out, **opening the case voids your warranty.**

Idiot Here — What's Your Excuse?

Of course *you* don't make silly mistakes!

Now that that's settled,

1. Is everything plugged in? Correctly? Firmly?

2. Are the recorder batteries fresh (if you're using batteries)?

3. Have you avoided the recorder ground loop problems by using Aux and Earphone separately? (CTR recorder only.)

With the CTR recorders it's a good idea to plug in either Aux or Earphone — but not both. Connecting both can produce "ground loop" problems resulting in unwanted hum.

---

4. Is the recorder volume level properly set?

5. Is the recorder tone switch on "high"?

6. Are you using "legal" commands?

IF so. . .

Go walk the dog, then check it all over again.

If. . .Then

If the trouble was not found in the cockpit or with the hardware, there is probably something wrong with your program. Dump out the troublesome program. LOAD in one that is known to work and RUN it as a final hardware and operator check.

Common Errors

Let's look at some of the common sources of "computer-detected errors".

1. Assume the error is in a **PRINT**, or **INPUT** statement. Did you:

   a. Forget one of the needed pair of quotation marks?

Example:

```
10 PRINT "ANSWER IS, X : GOTO 5
```

ERROR: No ending quotation mark after IS.

> Yes, I know it's OK if the missing quote is the last character in the line.

b. Use an illegal variable name?

Example:

```
10 INPUT 6G
```

ERROR: Must be recognizable by the computer.

c. Forget a semicolon or comma separating variables or text, or bury the semicolon or comma inside quotation marks?

Example:

```
10 PRINT "THE VALUE IS "V X
```

ERROR: A semicolon is missing between V and X (so the variables are not properly separated).

d. Forget the line number, accidentally mix a letter in with the number, or use a line number larger than 65529?

Example:

```
72B3 PRINT "BAD LINE NUMBER."
```

└─ERROR

e. Accidentally have a double quotation mark in your text?

Example:

```
10 PRINT "HE SAID "HELLO THERE.""
```

f. Type a line more than 255 characters long?

g. Misspell PRINT or INPUT *(it happens!)*?

h. Accidentally type a stray character in the line, especially an extra comma or semicolon?

2. If the error is in a **READ** statement, almost all the previous possibilities apply, plus:

a. Is there really a **DATA** statement for the computer to read? Remember, it will only read a piece of **DATA** once unless it is RESTOREd.

Example:

```
10 READ X,Y,Z
20 DATA 2,5
```

ERROR: There are only two numbers for the computer to read.
If we mean for Z to be zero, we must say so.

```
20 DATA 2,5,0
```

3. If the bad area is a **FOR-NEXT** loop, most of the previous possibilities also apply, plus:

a. Do we have a **NEXT** statement to match the **FOR**?

Example:

```
10 FOR A=1 TO N
```

ERROR: Where's the NEXT A?

Some of these FOR-NEXT loop errors won't cause actual error messages; instead, your program may wind up in endless loops, requiring the use of the ▮BREAK▮ key.

---

b. Do you have all the requirements for a loop — a starting point, an ending point, a variable name, and a STEP size if it's not 1?

Example:

```
10 A=1 TO N
```

ERROR: Must have a FOR and a NEXT.

c. Did you accidentally nest two loops using the same variable in both loops?

Example:

```
10 FOR X=1 TO 5
20  FOR X=1 TO 3
30   PRINT X
40  NEXT X
50 NEXT X
```

ERROR: The nested loops must have different variables.

d. Does a variable in a loop have the same letter as the loop counter?

Example:

```
10 A=22
20 FOR R=1 TO 5
30  R=18
40   Y=R*A
50    PRINT Y
60 NEXT R
```

ERROR: The value of R was changed by another R inside the loop, and NEXT R was overRUN, since 18 is larger than 5.

e. Did you nest loops incorrectly with one not completely inside the other?

Example:

```
1Ø FOR X=1 TO 6
2Ø  FOR Y=1 TO 8
3Ø   SET (X,Y)
4Ø  NEXT X
5Ø NEXT Y
```

4. If the goofed-up statement is an IF-THEN or GOTO:

   a. Does the line number specified by the THEN or GOTO really exist? Be especially careful of this error when you eliminate a line in the process of "improving" or "cleaning up" a program.

5. The ERROR comes back as ?OM (Out of Memory) but the PRINT MEM indicates there is room left in memory. If we get an ?OM and are using an array, **extra room (up to hundreds of bytes) has to be left for processing.** You have probably overRUN the amount of available memory.

6. The ERROR comes back as ?BS (subscript out of range).

   a. Did you exceed the limits of one of the built-in functions?

   b. Did one of the values on the line exceed the maximum or minimum size for numbers?

   c. Did you tell the computer to divide by zero? (The computer isn't about to let you get away with that one!)

To find out whether you did any of these things, PRINT (in immediate mode) the values for all the variables used in the offending line. If you still don't see the error, try carrying out the operations indicated on the line. For example, the error may occur during a multiplication of two very large numbers.

> PRINT in calculator mode (no line number).

These certainly aren't all the possible errors one can make, but at least they give us some idea where to look first. Since we can't completely avoid silly errors, it's necessary to be able to recover from them as quickly as possible.

By the way. . .a one-semester course in beginning typing can do wonders for your programming speed and typing accuracy.

From The Ridiculous To The Sublime

All the computer can tell us is that we have (or have not) followed all of its rules. Assuming we have followed all the rules, the computer will not ask "questions" — even if we're asking it to do something that's quite silly and isn't at all what we intended. It will dutifully put out garbage all day long if we feed it garbage — even though we follow its rules. If the program has no obvious errors, what might be the matter?

Typical "unreported" errors are:

1. Accidentally reinitializing a variable — particularly easy when using loops.

   Example:

```
10 FOR N=1 TO 3
20   READ A
30   PRINT A
40   RESTORE
50 NEXT N
60 DATA 1,2,3
```

2. Reversing conditions (i.e., using "=" when we mean "<>", or "greater than" when we mean "less than").

3. Accidentally including "equals", as in "less than or equals", when you really mean only "less than".

4. Confusing similarly-named variables, particularly the variable A, the string A\$, and the array A(X). *They are not at all related.*

5. Forgetting the order of program execution — from left to right on each line, but multiplications and divisions always having priority before additions and subtractions. And intrinsic functions (INT, RND, ABS, etc.) having priority over everything else.

6. Counting incorrectly in loops. FOR I=0 TO 7 causes the loop to be executed *eight*, not seven, times.

7. Using the same variable accidentally in two different places. This is okay if we don't need the old variable any more, but disastrous if we do. Be especially careful when combining programs or using the special subroutines.

But how do we spot these errors if the computer doesn't point them out? Use common sense and let the computer help you. The rules to follow are:

1. Isolate the error. Insert temporary "flags". Add STOP, END, and extra PRINT statements until you track the error down to one or two lines.

Examples of useful flags:
   299 PRINT "   line #299"
   399 IF X <0 THEN PRINT "X OUT OF RANGE AT #399":STOP

---

2. Make your "tests" as simple as possible. Don't add complications until you've found the error.

3. Check simple cases by hand to test your logic, but let the computer do the hard work. Don't try to wade through complex calculations with pencil and paper. You'll introduce more new mistakes than you'll find. Use the calculator mode, or a separate hand calculator to do that work.

Line 299 will help you check whether the line immediately following line 299 is executed. This helps you follow program flow. Line 399 might be used to locate the point where X goes out of range.

---

4. Remember that we can force the computer to start RUNning a program at any line number we choose. Just type RUN### (where ### represents the desired line number). This is a useful tool for working

your way back through a program. You give the variables acceptable values using calculator-mode statements, and then RUN the program starting from some point midway through the program flow. If the answers are what we expect, then the error is before the "test point" you've created. Otherwise, the error is after the test point.

Although the details would be different for your program, these techniques can be applied easily.

---

5. Remember also that it's not necessary to LIST the entire program just to get a look at the one section of it. Just type:

```
LIST###-###
```

---

where ### tells the computer on which lines you'd like to start and end the LIST.

---

6. Practice "defensive programming". Just because a program "works okay", don't assume it's dependable. Programs that accept INPUT data and process it can be especially deceptive. Make a point of checking a new program at all the critical places.

Examples: A square root program should be checked for INPUTs less than or equal to zero. Math functions we have programmed should be checked at points where the function is undefined, such as TAN(90°).

Beware Of Creeping Elegance

Programs can grow to become more and more elegant with the ego reinforcement of the programmer as success follows success. With this "creeping elegance" comes increased chance of silly errors. It's fun to let your mind wander and add on some more program here, and some more there, but it's easy to lose sight of the purpose of the program. It is at times like this when the flow chart is ignored and the trouble begins. Nuff said.

We'll leave some space here to make notes on your own debugging and troubleshooting ideas. . .

Share them with us too. . .especially if you come up with some really neat ones.

Learned in Chapter 48

Miscellaneous

Defensive programming

Computer-detected ERRORs

Flags

Hardware check-out procedures

Chasing Bugs

We have seen that the EDITor is a powerful aid in changing programs once we find out what is wrong. In this and the next chapter, we will learn how to use the built-in diagnostic tools to help hunt down the actual errors.

Tron/Troff

The simplicity, but power, of TRON/TROFF is awesome. Enter this program:

```
10 FOR N = 1 TO 5
20 PRINT "SEE TRON RUN"
30 NEXT N
99 END
```

. . .and RUN, to be sure it's OK.

Now, type TRON (which stands for TRacer ON), then RUN. The screen should say:

```
<10><20>  SEE TRON RUN
<30><20>  SEE TRON RUN
<30><20>  SEE TRON RUN
<30><20>  SEE TRON RUN
```

[10][20] on Model II.

```
<30><20> SEE TRON RUN

<30><99>
```

What does it mean?

The numbers between < > ([ ] on Model II) are the program line numbers. TRON traces the sequence of program execution and prints each line number as it is "hit". How's that for powerful?

Now type TROFF (for TRacer OFF) and RUN.

The tracing has stopped and

```
SEE TRON RUN

SEE TRON RUN

SEE TRON RUN

SEE TRON RUN

SEE TRON RUN
```

appears in the usual way. It's the very essence of simplicity.

Since TRON and TROFF can be used as program *statements* as well as commands, the possibilities for troubleshooting program *logic* are endless. Our little demonstration program is short and error-free, but by adding the following lines and RUNning, you will see another way tracing is used.

```
5 TRON

35 TROFF
```

Imagine its value in a program with dozens or hundreds of program lines all tangled up with IF-THEN's, ON-GOTO's, etc. The errors that will drive you wild are those you can't see. Although all characters appear to be upper-case on the screen, it ain't necessarily so. Model I users can press the SHIFT key when typing a letter; the computer will store it as a *lower*-case letter (just the opposite of a regular typewriter). The computer has been trained to respond to both upper- and lower-case *letters* in many cases, as in the word PRINT.

Type NEW.

Enter a 1Ø (line 1Ø) and then hold a [SHIFT] key down and type the rest of this line:

`1Ø PRINT "HELLO THERE LOWER CASE"`

and continue to hold [SHIFT] down while typing RUN.

Worked just fine, didn't it? We don't use those lower case letters for anything else anyway.

Model I users have a special problem with the @ key. Enter this program, but hold down the [SHIFT] key as you type the @.

Model II users will not experience this problem since @ is [SHIFT] "2" on the keyboard.

`1 CLS`

`1Ø PRINT@55,"MISTAKE HERE"`

`. . .and RUN.`

Aha! The Model I screen shows a plain old @ but the computer doesn't recognize it, sends us an error message and throws us to the EDITor.

Works fine with some Disk BASICs.

An L displays a fine looking program line. Do a

`S@`   (*without* the [SHIFT] key)

and watch it SEARCH right over the @. Try again but hold down [SHIFT] . It snags it, and a simple

`C@`   (*without* [SHIFT])

changes it to what we need. The above is a *very common* error since we use [SHIFT] @ so often to freeze listings and runs.

The EDITor is a great tool to spot such errors, especially in very long lines where retyping would be tedious or hazardous. Simply step through the entire line SEARCHing for each character in turn. If you hit a lower-case character, the SEARCH will pass right over it, and you've found the bug.

Try it! It really works.

Another nasty little invisible bug can be caused by hitting the down arrow
(⬇) key by accident when typing in a program line or when the EDITor is in
INSERT mode.

`CTRL` -J is the linefeed on Model II.

The result of either can be that parts of the program are scattered all over the
screen. If severe enough, even a LISTing won't divulge the exact problem.
Often the best solution is to just retype the offending line.

Clear the memory with NEW, then type:

```
10 PRINT "DOWN ARROW ⬇ ⬇ ⬇ ⬇ ⬇ DILEMMA"
```

and experiment with the ⬇ in both AUTO and EDITor modes, and with and
without the `SHIFT` key.

Model II use `CTRL` -J.

As a little aside, the ⬇ can be used to frustrate and slow down "program-
peekers" who insist on LISTing your favorite program to find the secret formula.

Type in this program:

```
10 REM * SECRET EQUATION HIDER *
20 REM * THE NEXT LINE HAS THE EQUATION *
30 X=1234567890/987654321 + 1234567890 - 9876543210
```

(Insert 16 ⬇'s before pressing `ENTER`.)

```
40 PRINT"THE ANSWER IS";X
50 PRINT"MISSED THE SECRET FORMULA, DIDN'T YOU!"
99 END
```

. . .and RUN.

Then LIST. The LISTing at line 3∅ should whiz by so fast you can't read it.
The only way to really freeze and analyze it is to first discover the line

number which has the hidden arrows, then go into EDITor there and step through each character one at a time. It's not at all foolproof, but slows the interloper down. Makes it even harder if you give the "secret" line an unusual line number that's harder to guess.

Learned in Chapter 49

Commands/Statements

TRON

TROFF

Chasing the ERRORs

TRS-80 BASIC contains 23 different ERROR messages to assist us in troubleshooting programming or operating problems. (There are 66 on the Model II. Note that numbers 24-29 and 66 are undefined. Refer to Appendix H.) We'll LIST them for your reference. There are so many we need a separate chapter plus an appendix just to understand what they mean.

Let's quietly tiptoe into the hall of ERRORs by typing this NEW little test program:

```
1 CLS
10 REM * TESTING ERROR CODES *
20 INPUT"WHAT ERROR CODE NUMBER SHALL WE CHECK";N
30 ERROR N
```

RUN the program a number of times (entering numbers between 1 and 23), forcing the computer to PRINT out the message for various types of ERRORs. Don't waste time trying to understand them now. You can study them in detail in Appendix H.

Enter numbers between 1 and 66 on Model II.

The only new word above is in line 30. ERROR has little real use in life except as above, PRINTing the error message from its code number.

TRS-80 ERROR CODES
Models I and III

Code	Abbreviation	Error
1	NF	NEXT without FOR
2	SN	Syntax ERROR
3	RG	RETURN without GOSUB
4	OD	Out of DATA
5	FC	Illegal function call
6	OV	Overflow
7	OM	Out of memory
8	UL	Undefined line number
9	BS	Subscript out of range
10	DD	ReDIMensioned array
11	/∅	Division by zero
12	ID	Illegal direct
13	TM	Type mismatch
14	OS	Out of string space
15	LS	String too long
16	ST	String formula too complex
17	CN	Can't continue
18	NR	No RESUME
19	RW	RESUME without ERROR
20	UE	Unprintable error
21	MO	Missing operand
22	FD	Bad file DATA
23	L3	Disk BASIC only

ERROR Trapping

The **ON ERROR GOTO** statement is of more value, and we should use it when we think we're on the trail of a specific type of ERROR, but are not sure.

Suppose we suspect that someplace in the program there is an accidental division by zero, and it's goofing up the results. Type in this NEW test program:

```
10 ON ERROR GOTO 70
20 PRINT
30 INPUT"WHAT NUMBER SHALL WE DIVIDE 100 BY";N
40 A = 100/N
50 PRINT "100 DIVIDED BY";N; "=";A
60 GOTO 10
70 PRINT "DIVISION BY ZERO IS ILLEGAL - MAYBE EVEN
IMPOSSIBBLE!"
99 END
```

. . .and RUN.

Try positive values and negative values, then try a Ø.

ON ERROR GOTO is acting much as our old friend **ON X GOTO** did, so there are no big surprises here.

Change line 1Ø to a REM line and try assorted values, ending with Ø. Again, no big surprise. An ERROR message was delivered, pinpointing both the nature and location of the ERROR, and execution was terminated with a READY.

Change line 1Ø back to:

```
10 ON ERROR GOTO 70
```

and add:

```
8Ø RESUME 2Ø
```

. . .and RUN with various values, including Ø.

Notice that even though the computer was forced to operate with an ER-ROR (division of zero), execution did not terminate. The ERROR message was delivered but the computer kept on going, thanks to RESUME. This is the essence of good ERROR trapping — identifying the ERROR without "crashing" the program. There may be several interrelated ERRORs that can be found easily only by continuing the RUN.

Change line 8Ø to:

```
8Ø RESUME NEXT
```

. . .and RUN.

Although the results are similar to those obtained with RESUME 2Ø, there is a subtle difference.

RESUME NEXT causes execution to RESUME at the *next* line immediately following the line which made the ERROR. Thus line 5Ø is PRINTed, even though (in this case) it gives a wrong answer. RESUME 2Ø directed execution to a very specific line. With a little head-scratching we can quickly see how both of these features can be used in difficult debugging situations.

Next, change line 8Ø to simply:

```
8Ø RESUME
```

. . .and RUN.

As you see, RESUME by itself (or RESUME Ø) sends execution back to the line in which the ERROR is being made. (If you are having difficulty visualizing what is taking place in any of these examples, just turn on TRON and it becomes as easy as following a road map.)

More Variations On The Theme

Change line 8Ø back to:

```
8Ø RESUME 2Ø
```

and add line 75:

```
75 PRINT"ERROR IS IN LINE #";ERL
```

. . .and RUN.

ERL is a "reserved" word that PRINTs the *line number* in which the ER-ROR occurs. For my money, this little jewel in combination with ON ER-ROR GOTO to snag 'em, and RESUME NEXT (or RESUME line number) to keep the program from crashing, makes this whole hassle worthwhile.

ERR

A final esoteric touch may be obtained by adding the ERR (not ERL) state-ment. ERR produces a number which, when divided by 2 and increased by 1 (oh, swell), brings us back to the ERROR code number. We've gone almost full cycle.

Model II uses ERR, not ERR/2 + 1.

Add line 77:

```
77 PRINT"AND ERROR CODE IS";ERR/2+1          ERR on Model II.
```

. . .and RUN.

Finally, to complete this loop begun several pages ago, add:

```
78 PRINT "WHICH STANDS FOR" : ERROR ERR/2+1          ERR on Model II.
```

. . .and RUN.

Which brings us back to Do, a deer, a female deer. . .(it must be time to STOP this book — getting too silly!).

We should note in passing that when using ERR, strange moonbeams sometimes affect the computer. The interpreter temporarily takes on slightly different characteristics at the command level. We deliberately won't elaborate on them here as they don't seem harmful and will probably be ironed out in future versions of the interpreter. Just thought it should be mentioned though, lest you suspect the saucers have been flying again.

A very useful application of the ERROR traps we've learned allows the program to automatically LIST itself if there is an ERROR. It requires the addition of two temporary program lines using all three ERROR statements.

From Appendix H (which covers the error messages) comes the example of what happens when there is an ERROR in a FOR-NEXT loop. Type in:

```
10 FOR A = 1 TO 5
20 PRINT "THERE IS NO 'NEXT A'"
30 NEXT Z
```

    . . .and RUN.

In this simple program the computer responds with:

```
?NF ERROR IN 30.
```

There is a FOR-NEXT Error in line 30. By adding the following lines we can approximate the same result, plus cause an automatic program LISTing:

```
5 ON ERROR GOTO 100
```

    to "set" the ERROR trap,

```
99 END
```

    to END execution if all is well,

```
100 PRINT ERL,ERR/2+1 : LIST                    ERL, ERR : LIST on Model II.
```

    to PRINT the line # with the ERROR, the ERROR code (which can be found in Appendix H) and to LIST the program (or LIST ##-##).

Try this routine. If all is well in the program, nothing will seem different. If there is an ERROR, it will be trapped as you can see on the screen.

EXERCISE 50-1: Enter the following NEW program:

```
20 CLS
30 FOR I=1 TO 10
40 X = RND(21)-1 : F = X-10/X
50 PRINT I, "X=" X, "F(X)=" F;
60 IF F<0 THEN PUNT ELSE PRINT
70 NEXT I
80 INPUT "PRESS ENTER TO CONTINUE"; Z : GOTO 20
```

Write an ERROR-trapping routine that recovers from both ER-RORs and PRINTs:

```
ATTEMPTED DIVISION BY ZERO IN LINE ##
```

or

```
SYNTAX ERROR IN LINE ##
```

as appropriate.

HINT — Syntax ERROR is code 2, and Out of DATA is code 11.

Learned in Chapter 50

Statements	Functions	Miscellaneous
ON ERROR	ERL	Error Codes
GOTO	ERR	
RESUME		

515 RETURN ELSE GOTO 527
520 REM * SUPER PROGRAM *
527 END

Sample Answers For Exercises

Answers To Exercises

SAMPLE ANSWER FOR EXERCISE 3-1:

```
EDIT 1Ø ENTER


SPACE        Move one space to right
C            CHANGE next character
R            new character
2ST          SEARCH for 2nd T
7D           DELETE next 7 characters
SF           Search for next F
4D           Delete next 4 characters
SN           Search for next N
4C           CHANGE next 4 characters
MPUT         the new characters
SE           SEARCH for next E
2C           CHANGE next 2 characters
AM           the new characters
LL           to LIST the edited program for inspection
ENTER        to leave the EDITOR mode
```

SAMPLE ANSWER FOR EXERCISE 5-1:

```
50 PRINT D
```

SAMPLE RUN FOR EXERCISE 5-1:

```
6000
```

Note: You may have used a different line number in your answer but the way to get the answer printed on the screen is by using the PRINT statement. If you didn't get it right the first time, don't be discouraged. Type in line 50 above and RUN the program. Then return to Chapter 5 and continue.

SAMPLE ANSWER FOR EXERCISE 5-2:

```
10 REM * TIME SOLUTION KNOWING DISTANCE AND RATE *
20 D = 6000
30 R = 500
40 T = D / R
50 PRINT "THE TIME REQUIRED IS "; T ;"HOURS."
```

Note: Remember to ENTER each line.

SAMPLE RUN FOR EXERCISE 5-2:

```
THE TIME REQUIRED IS 12 HOURS.
```

Note: In order to arrive at the formula in line 40, it is necessary to transpose D = R * T and express in terms of T.

SAMPLE ANSWER FOR EXERCISE 5-3:

```
10 REM * CIRCUMFERENCE SOLUTION *
20 P = 3.14
```

```
30  D = 35
40  C = P * D
50  PRINT "THE CIRCLE'S CIRCUMFERENCE IS"; C ;"FEET."
```

SAMPLE RUN FOR EXERCISE 5-3:

```
THE CIRCLE'S CIRCUMFERENCE IS 109.9 FEET.
```

Note: Since π is not included in TRS-80 BASIC, we have to set a variable (in this case P was used) equal to the value of pi (3.14).

SAMPLE ANSWER FOR EXERCISE 5-4:

```
10  REM * CIRCULAR AREA SOLUTION *
20  P = 3.14
30  R = 5
40  A = P * R * R
50  PRINT "THE CIRCLE'S AREA IS"; A ;SQUARE INCHES."
```

SAMPLE RUN FOR EXERCISE 5-4:

```
THE CIRCLE'S AREA IS 78.5 SQUARE INCHES.
```

Note: Some BASICs do not have a function which means "raise to the power" to handle R^2 (TRS-80 BASIC does). In easy cases like this one, we can simply use R times R EXPONENTIATION function as we proceed.

SAMPLE ANSWER FOR EXERCISE 5-5:

A bare-minimum effort might look like this: (C = checks, D = deposits, B = old balance, N = new balance.)

```
10  B = 225
20  C = 17 + 35 + 225
30  D = 40 + 200
```

```
40 N = B - C + D
50 PRINT "YOUR NEW BALANCE IS $"; N
```

SAMPLE RUN FOR EXERCISE 5-5:

```
YOUR NEW BALANCE IS $ 188
```

SAMPLE ANSWER FOR EXERCISE 6-1:

```
10 REM * CAR MILES SOLUTION PROGRAM *
20 N = 1000000
30 D = 10000
40 T = N * D
50 PRINT "THE TOTAL NUMBER OF MILES DRIVEN IS";T
```

SAMPLE RUN FOR EXERCISE 6-1:

```
THE TOTAL NUMBER OF MILES DRIVEN IS 1E+10
```

Note: As discussed earlier, this answer is the number 1 followed by ten zeros. 10,000,000,000. Ten Billion. The computer will not print any numbers over 999,999 without converting them to exponential notation.

SAMPLE ANSWER FOR EXERCISE 6-2:

```
20 N = 1E+6
30 D = 1E+4
```

SAMPLE RUN FOR EXERCISE 6-2:

```
THE TOTAL NUMBER OF MILES DRIVEN IS 1E+10
```

Note: The answer came out exactly the same as before, meaning we not only receive answers in SSN, but can also use it in our programs.

SAMPLE ANSWER FOR EXERCISE 7-1:

```
10 REM * FAHRENHEIT TO CELSIUS CONVERSION *
20 F = 65
30 C = (F - 32) * (5 / 9)
40 PRINT F; "DEGREES FAHRENHEIT ="; C ;"DEGREES CELSIUS."
```

SAMPLE RUN FOR EXERCISE 7-1:

```
65 DEGREES FAHRENHEIT = 18.33333 DEGREES CELSIUS.
```

Observe carefully how the parentheses were placed. As a general rule, when in doubt — use parentheses. The worst they can do is slow down calculating the answer by a few millionths of a second.

SAMPLE ANSWER FOR EXERCISE 7-2:

```
30 C = F - 32 * (5 / 9)
```

SAMPLE RUN FOR EXERCISE 7-2:

```
65 DEGREES FAHRENHEIT = 47.22222 DEGREES CELSIUS.
```

Note how silently and dutifully the computer came up with the *wrong* answer. It has done as we directed, and we directed it wrong.

A common phrase in computer circles is GIGO (pronounced "gee-goe"). It stands for "Garbage In — Garbage Out". We have given the computer garbage and it gave it back to us by way of a wrong answer.

Phrased another way, "Never in the history of mankind has there been a machine capable of making so many mistakes so rapidly and confidently." A computer is worthless unless it is programmed correctly.

SAMPLE ANSWER FOR EXERCISE 7-3:

```
30 C = (F - 32) * 5 / 9
```

SAMPLE RUN FOR EXERCISE 7-3:

```
65 DEGREES FAHRENHEIT = 18.33333 DEGREES CELSIUS.
```

SAMPLE ANSWER FOR EXERCISE 7-4:

Two possible answers:
```
30 - (9 - 8) - (7 - 6) = 28
30 - (9 - (8 - (7 - 6))) = 28
```

Sample programs:

```
10 A = 30 - (9 - (8 - (7 - 6)))
20 PRINT A
```

Or line 10 might be:

```
10 A = 30 - (9 - 8) - (7 - 6)
```

Try a few on your own.

SAMPLE ANSWER FOR EXERCISE 8-1:

```
10 A = 5
20 IF A <> 5 THEN 50
30 PRINT "A EQUALS 5"
40 END
50 PRINT "A DOES NOT EQUAL 5"
```

SAMPLE RUN FOR EXERCISE 8-1:

```
A EQUALS 5
```

SAMPLE ANSWER FOR EXERCISE 8-2:

```
10 A = 6
20 IF A <> 5 THEN 50
30 PRINT "A EQUALS 5"
40 END
50 PRINT "A DOES NOT EQUAL 5"
60 IF A < 5 THEN 90
70 PRINT "A IS LARGER THAN 5"
80 END
90 PRINT "A IS SMALLER THAN 5"
```

SAMPLE RUN FOR EXERCISE 8-2:

```
A DOES NOT EQUAL 5
A IS LARGER THAN 5
```

Note: We had to put in another END statement (line 8Ø) to keep the program from running on to line 9Ø after printing line 7Ø.

SAMPLE ANSWER FOR EXERCISE 13-1:

```
1 CLS
2 INPUT "HOW MANY SECONDS DELAY DO YOU WISH"; S
3 P = 800
4 D = S * P
5 FOR X = 1 TO D
6 NEXT X
```

```
7 PRINT "DELAY IS OVER.   TOOK"; S ;" SECONDS."
```

Explanation:

Line 2 used the INPUT statement to obtain desired delay, S, in seconds.

Line 3 defined P, the number of passes required for a one-second delay.

Line 4 multiplied the delay for one second times the number of seconds desired, and called that product D.

Line 5 began the FOR-NEXT loop from 1 to whatever is required.

Line 6 is the other half of the loop.

Line 7 reports that the delay is over, and prints S, the number of seconds. Obviously, S is only as accurate as the program itself since it merely copies the value of S you entered in line 2.

SAMPLE ANSWER FOR EXERCISE 13-2:

```
60 PRINT "RATE", "TIME", "DISTANCE"
65 PRINT "(MPH)", "(HOURS)", "(MILES)"
```

If you honestly had trouble with this one, better go back and start all over because you've missed the real basics.

SAMPLE ANSWER FOR EXERCISE 13-3:

```
5 CLS
10 PRINT "    ***   SALARY   RATE   CHART   ***"
20 PRINT
30 PRINT "YEAR", "MONTH", "WEEK", "DAY"
```

```
40 PRINT
50 FOR Y = 5000 TO 25000 STEP 1000
55 REM * CONVERT YEARLY INCOME INTO MONTHLY *
60 M = Y / 12
65 REM * CONVERT YEARLY INCOME INTO WEEKLY *
70 W = Y / 52
75 REM * CONVERT WEEKLY INCOME INTO DAILY *
80 D = W / 5
100 PRINT Y, M, W, D
110 NEXT Y
```

SAMPLE RUN FOR EXERCISE 13-3:

```
***   S A L A R Y   R A T E   C H A R T   ***


YEAR              MONTH            WEEK              DAY


5000              416.667          96.1539           19.2308
6000              500              115.385           23.0769
7000              583.333          134.615           26.9231
```

SAMPLE ANSWER FOR EXERCISE 13-4:

```
10 R = .01
20 D = 1
30 T = .01
35 CLS
40 PRINT "DAY ", "DAILY ", "TOTAL"
50 PRINT "  #", "RATE ", "EARNED "
60 PRINT
70 PRINT D, R, T
```

```
80 IF R > 1E+06 THEN END
90 R = 2 * R
100 D = D + 1
110 T = T + R
120 GOTO 70
```

SAMPLE RUN FOR EXERCISE 13-4:

DAY #	DAILY RATE	TOTAL EARNED
1	.01	.01
2	.02	.03
3	.04	.07
4	.08	.15
5	.16	.31
6	.32	.63

SAMPLE ANSWER FOR EXERCISE 13-5:

```
1 REM * FIND THE LARGEST AREA *
5 CLS
10 PRINT "WIRE FENCE", "LENGTH ", "WIDTH ", "AREA "
20 PRINT " (FEET)", "(FEET)", "(FEET)", "(SQ. FEET)"
30 F = 1000
40 FOR L = 0 TO 500 STEP 50
50   W = (F - 2 * L) / 2
60   A = L * W
70    PRINT F, L, W, A
80   NEXT L
90 END
```

SAMPLE RUN FOR EXERCISE 13-5:

WIRE FENCE (FEET)	LENGTH (FEET)	WIDTH (FEET)	AREA (SQ. FEET)
1000	1	499	499
1000	51	449	22899
1000	101	399	40299
1000	151	349	52699
1000	201	299	60099

etc...

ADDENDUM TO EXERCISE 13-5:

Here's a program that lets the computer do the comparing:

```
5 CLS
9 REM
10 M = 0
14 REM * SET DESIRED LENGTH AT ZERO *
15 N = 0
19 REM * F IS TOTAL FEET OF FENCE AVAILABLE *
20 F = 1000
24 REM * L IS LENGTH OF ONE SIDE OF RECTANGLE *
25 FOR L = 0 TO 500 STEP 50
29 REM * W IS WIDTH OF ONE SIDE OF RECTANGLE *
30 W = (F - 2 * L) / 2
35 A = W * L
39 REM * COMPARE  A WITH CURRENT MAXIMUM. REPLACE IF
NECESSARY   *
40 IF A <= M THEN GOTO 55
45 M = A
49 REM * ALSO UPDATE CURRENT DESIRED LENGTH *
```

```
50 N = L
55 NEXT L
60 PRINT "FOR LARGEST AREA USE THESE DIMENSIONS:"
65 PRINT N;  "FT.BY";  500-N; "FT. FOR TOTAL AREA OF"; M;
"SQ. FT."
```

SAMPLE RUN FOR ADDENDUM TO EXERCISE 13-5:

```
FOR LARGEST AREA USE THESE DIMENSIONS:
  250 FT. BY 250 FT. FOR TOTAL AREA OF 62500 SQ.FT.
```

SAMPLE ANSWER FOR OPTIONAL EXERCISE 13-6:

```
10 REM * FINDS OPTIMUM LOAD TO SOURCE MATCH *
20 CLS
30 PRINT "LOAD ", "CIRCUIT ", "SOURCE ", "LOAD "
40 PRINT "RESISTANCE ", "POWER ", "POWER ", "POWER "
50 PRINT "(OHMS) ", "(WATTS) ", "(WATTS) ", "(WATTS) "
60 PRINT
70 FOR R = 1 TO 20
80   I = 120 / (10 + R)
90   C = I * I * (10 + R)
100   S = I * I * 10
110   L = I * I * R
120   PRINT R, C, S, L
130 NEXT R
```

SAMPLE RUN FOR OPTIONAL EXERCISE 13-6:

```
LOAD              CIRCUIT           SOURCE            LOAD
RESISTANCE        POWER             POWER             POWER
(OHMS)            (WATTS)           (WATTS)           (WATTS)


1                 1309.09           1190.08           119.008
2                 1200              1000              200
3                 1107.69           852.071           255.621

etc...
```

SAMPLE ANSWER FOR EXERCISE 14-1:

```
10 PRINT "THE ",  "TOTAL ",  "SPENT "
20 PRINT "BUDGET              YEAR'S                 THIS"
30 PRINT TAB(0); "CATEGORY"; TAB(16); "BUDGET"; TAB(32);
"MONTH"
```

SAMPLE ANSWER FOR EXERCISE 14-2:

```
30 PRINT TAB(1);  "YEAR  "; TAB(12); "MONTH  "; TAB(25);
35 "WEEK";
40 PRINT TAB(38); "DAY "; TAB(51); "HOUR "
85 REM * CONVERT WEEKLY INCOME INTO HOURLY *
90 H = W/40
100 PRINT TAB(0); Y;TAB(11); M;TAB(24); W;TAB(37); D;
```

SAMPLE RUN FOR 14-2:

```
***          S A L A R Y   R A T E   C H A R T   ***


YEAR          MONTH          WEEK          DAY          HOUR


5000          416.667        96.1539       19.2308       2.40385
6000          500            115.385       23.0769       2.88462
                             etc...
```

SAMPLE ANSWER FOR EXERCISE 14-3:

```
30 PRINT "INTER "; TAB(10); "LOAD" ;TAB(21); "CIRCUIT ";
35 PRINT TAB(36); "SOURCE "; TAB(51); "LOAD "
40 PRINT "RESIST "; TAB(10); "RESIST "; TAB(21); "POWER ";
45 PRINT TAB(36); "POWER "; TAB(51); "POWER "
50 PRINT "(OHMS)" ;TAB(10); "(OHMS)"; TAB(21); "(WATTS) ";
55 PRINT TAB(36); "(WATTS)"; TAB(51); "(WATTS)"
120 PRINT "   10"; TAB(11); R; TAB(20); C; TAB(35);
S; TAB(50); L
```

SAMPLE RUN FOR EXERCISE 14-3:

```
INTER        LOAD          CIRCUIT       SOURCE        LOAD
RESIST       RESIST        POWER         POWER         POWER
(OHMS)       (OHMS)        (WATTS)       (WATTS)       (WATTS)


 10           1           1309.09       1190.08       119.008
 10           2           1200          1000          200
 10           3           1107.69       852.071       255.621
            etc...
```

SAMPLE ANSWER FOR EXERCISE 15-1:

```
10 FOR A = 1 TO 3
20   PRINT "A LOOP"
30    FOR B = 1 TO 2
40     PRINT " ","B LOOP"
42      FOR C = 1 TO 4
44       PRINT " "," ","C LOOP"
48       NEXT C
50    NEXT B
60 NEXT A
```

SAMPLE ANSWER FOR EXERCISE 15-2:

The program will be the same as the answer to Exercise 15-1 with the following additions:

```
45          FOR D = 1 TO 5
46           PRINT " "," "," ","D LOOP"
47          NEXT D
```

Note: To get the full impact of this "4-deep" nesting, stop the RUN frequently to examine the nesting relationships between each of the loops.

SAMPLE ANSWER FOR EXERCISE 16-1:

Addition of the following single line gives a nice clean printout with all values "rounded" to their integer value:

```
55 A = INT(A)
```

Worth all the effort to learn it, wasn't it?

SAMPLE ANSWER FOR EXERCISE 16-2:

```
55 A = INT(10 * A) / 10
```

When 3.14159 was multiplied times 10 it became 31.4159. The INTeger value of 31.4159 is 31. 31 divided by 10 is 3.1., etc.

SAMPLE ANSWER FOR EXERCISE 16-3:

This was almost too easy.

```
55 A = INT(100) * A) / 100
```

SAMPLE ANSWER FOR EXERCISE 17-1:

```
10 INPUT "TYPE ANY NUMBER";X
20 T = SGN(X)
30 ON T+2 GOTO 50,60,70
45 END
50 PRINT "THE NUMBER IS NEGATIVE."
55 END
60 PRINT "THE NUMBER IS ZERO."
65 END
70 PRINT "THE NUMBER IS POSITIVE."
```

SAMPLE ANSWER FOR EXERCISE 21-1:

```
EDIT 1Ø ENTER
KF          KILL up to next F
X           eXtend the line
I*I:NEXTI   new characters
SHIFT [     leave INSERT mode (optional)
LL          check line before leaving EDIT mode (optional)
ENTER       leave EDIT mode
```

SAMPLE ANSWER FOR EXERCISE 22-1:

```
1Ø CLS
2Ø FOR N=Ø TO 63
3Ø PRINT "SPACE"; CHR$(N+192); "COMPRESSION"
4Ø NEXT N
```

SAMPLE ANSWER FOR EXERCISE 22-2:

```
1Ø PRINT CHR$(84);CHR$(82);CHR$(83);CHR$(45);CHR$(56);
CHR$(48)
```

SAMPLE ANSWER FOR EXERCISE 22-3:

```
1Ø INPUT "ENTER A NUMBER"; A$
2Ø A = ASC(A$)
3Ø IF A<47 THEN 1Ø
4Ø IF A>57 THEN 1Ø
5Ø PRINT "ASCII VALUE OF "; A$; " IS"A
```

SAMPLE ANSWER FOR EXERCISE 23-1:

```
10 CLS
20 INPUT "FIRST STRING": A$
30 INPUT "SECOND STRING": B$
40 PRINT : PRINT "ALPHABETICAL ORDER:"
50 IF A$<B$ THEN PRINT A$,B$ : END
60 PRINT B$,A$
```

SAMPLE ANSWER FOR EXERCISE 24-1:

```
10 CLS
20 INPUT "INPUT STRING";A$
30 IF LEN(A$)>10 THEN PRINT "THE 10 CHARACTER LIMIT WAS
EXCEEDED."
```

SAMPLE ANSWER FOR EXERCISE 24-2:

```
10 CLS
20 INPUT "ENTER PASSWORD"; A$
30 FOR X=1 TO 11
40 READ N
50 P$ = P$ + CHR$(N)
60 NEXT X
70 IF A$ = P$ THEN 100
80 PRINT "WRONG PASSWORD, GET LOST MAXWELL SMART"
```

```
90 END
100 PRINT "CORRECT PASSWORD, YOU MAY ENTER"
110 DATA 79,80,69,78,32,83,69,83,65,77,69
```

SAMPLE ANSWER FOR EXERCISE 25-1:

```
10 CLS
20 INPUT "INPUT YOUR STREET ADDRESS"; A$
30 A = VAL(A$)
40 PRINT : PRINT"YOUR NEIGHBOR'S STREET NUMBER IS "; A+4
50 PRINT : LIST
```

SAMPLE ANSWER FOR EXERCISE 25-2:

```
10 CLS
20 FOR X=101 TO 120
30 A$ = STR$(X)
40 PRINT A$+"WT",
50 NEXT X
60 PRINT : LIST
```

SAMPLE RUN FOR EXERCISE 25-2:

101WT	102WT	103WT	104WT
105WT	106WT	107WT	108WT
109WT	110WT	111WT	112WT
113WT	114WT	115WT	116WT
117WT	118WT	119WT	120WT

SAMPLE ANSWER FOR EXERCISE 26-1:

```
10 CLS
20 INPUT "ISN'T THIS A SMART COMPUTER";A$
30 B$ = LEFT$(A$,1)
40 IF B$="Y" THEN PRINT "AFFIRMATIVE" : END
50 IF B$="N" THEN PRINT "NEGATIVE" : END
60 PRINT "THIS IS A YES OR NO QUESTION"
70 GOTO 20
```

SAMPLE ANSWER FOR EXERCISE 26-2:

```
10 CLS : MAX$=""
20 FOR I=1 TO 3
30 READ A$
40 N$ = MID$(A$,2,3)
50 IF N$>MAX$ THEN MAX$=N$ : P$=A$
60 NEXT I
70 PRINT"THE PART  NUMBER WITH THE LARGEST  NUMERIC PORTION
IS ";P$
80 PRINT:LIST
90 DATA N106WT,A208FM,Z154DX
```

SAMPLE ANSWER FOR EXERCISE 26-3:

```
Choice C: P-
```

SAMPLE ANSWER FOR EXERCISE 26-4:

```
1 CLS
10 A$ = STRING$(30,42)
20 PRINT TAB(32-LEN(A$)/2);A$
```

SAMPLE ANSWER FOR EXERCISE 28-1:

```
10 CLS
20 A = 5 : B = 12
30 C = SQR( A[2 + B[2)
40 PRINT "THE SQUARE ROOT OF";A;"SQUARED PLUS";B;"SQUARED
IS";C
50 PRINT : LIST
```

SAMPLE ANSWER FOR EXERCISE 28-2:

```
10 INPUT "ENTER A NUMBER"; N
20 PRINT "LOG( EXP(";N;")) =";  LOG(EXP(N))
30 PRINT "EXP( LOG(";N;")) =";  EXP(LOG(N))
40 PRINT
50 GOTO 10
```

SAMPLE ANSWER FOR EXERCISE 30-1:

```
10 INPUT "STARTING HORIZONTAL BLOCK (0 TO 127)"; H
20 INPUT "ENDING HORIZONTAL BLOCK (0 TO 127)"; I
30 INPUT "STARTING VERTICAL BLOCK (0 TO 47)"; V
40 INPUT "ENDING VERTICAL BLOCK (0 TO 47)"; W
```

```
50 CLS
60 FOR X = H TO I
70  FOR Y = V TO W
80   SET(X,Y)
90   NEXT Y
100  NEXT X
999 GOTO 999
```

SAMPLE ANSWER FOR EXERCISE 30-2:

The following lines are changed. The rest are the same.

```
50 FOR L = X TO X + K * 2 + 1
70 SET(L,Y+K+1)
90 FOR M = Y TO Y + K + 1
110 SET (X+K*2+1,M)
```

SAMPLE ANSWER FOR EXERCISE 31-1:

A. Move the dot up

```
10 INPUT "HORIZONTAL STARTING POINT (0 TO 127)"; X
20 INPUT "VERTICAL STARTING POINT (0 TO 46)"; Y
30 CLS
40 RESET(X,Y+1)
50 SET(X,Y)
60 Y = Y - 1
70 IF Y >= 0 GOTO 40
99 GOTO 99
```

B. Move the dot to the left

```
10  INPUT "HORIZONTAL STARTING POINT (1 TO 126)"; X
20  INPUT "VERTICAL STARTING POINT (0 TO 47)"; Y
30  CLS
40  RESET(X+1,Y)
50  SET(X,Y)
60  X = X - 1
70  IF X >= 0 THEN 40
99  GOTO 99
```

SAMPLE ANSWER FOR EXERCISE 32-1:

Insert the following lines:

```
95  P$ = "PING"
105  IF Y = 46 THEN 160
115  IF Y = 1 THEN 170
145  P$ = "    " : ON D+2 GOTO 160,,170          '4 SPACES
160  PRINT@928,P$;: GOTO 90
170  PRINT@160,P$;: GOTO 90
```

Note that P$ BOTH prints the "PING" and makes it disappear by printing blanks in its place.

SAMPLE ANSWER FOR EXERCISE 34-1:

Change line 110 to:

```
110  FOR X=0 TO 111 : FOR Y=3 TO 47
```

SAMPLE ANSWER FOR EXERCISE 36-1:

```
10 CLS : PRINT TAB(24)"CREDITS      TAX       TOTAL"
20 FOR I = 1 TO 3
30 READ A$,X,Y,Z
39 REM       1234567890123456789012345678901234567890123
40 U$ = "%                   %         ##.#        .#        ##.#"
50 PRINT USING U$ ; A$,X,Y,Z
60 NEXT I
70 READ A$,N
79 REM       1234567
80 V$ = "%  %      ###.##"
90 PRINT TAB(35); : PRINT USING V$; A$,N
100 DATA ASTRAL COMPUTER, 18.3, .7, 19.0
110 DATA BIOFEEDBACK ADAPTER, 1.8, 0, 1.8
120 DATA PERSONALITY MODULE, 7.2, .3, 7.5
130 DATA   "DUE:", 28.3
```

SAMPLE ANSWER FOR EXERCISE 37-1:

```
10 CLS : PRINT
20 A$="REVENUES" : B$="EXPENSES" : C$="ASSETS"
30 U$="   %       %        %       %        %       %"
40 PRINT USING U$; A$ , B$ , C$
50 A#=1203104.22 : B#=560143.80 : C=0
60 V$="######,###.##      ####,###.##       ######,###.##-"
70 PRINT USING V$; A# , C , A#
80 PRINT USING V$; C , B# , B#
90 PRINT : LIST
```

SAMPLE ANSWER FOR EXERCISE 38-1:

Add or change the following lines:

```
5 DIM A(210)
10 INPUT "WHICH CAR'S ENGINE, COLOR, & BODY STYLE DO YOU
   WANT TO KNOW" ; W
130 FOR B = 201 TO 210
135 READ A(B)
140 NEXT B
180 PRINT "LICENSE #", "ENGINE SIZE" ,"COLOR CODE" ,"BODY
    STYLE"
210 PRINT W , A(W) , A(W+100) , A(W+200)
400 DATA 20,20,10,20,30,20,30,10,20,20
```

SAMPLE ANSWER FOR EXERCISE 38-2:

DELETE lines 5Ø, 55, and 6Ø, and change line 3Ø to :

```
30 DIM A(52) : FOR C=1 TO 52 : A(C) = C : NEXT C
```

SAMPLE ANSWER FOR EXERCISE 39-1:

Change line 5Ø to:

```
50 IF A$(F)  = A$(S) THEN 90   'TEST FOR LARGER ASCII #
```

An alternate approach is to reverse the order of printing:

```
110 FOR D=N TO 1 STEP -1 : PRINT A$(D), : NEXT D
```

but that's not what we had in mind.

SAMPLE ANSWER FOR EXERCISE 40-1:

```
35 M(R,C)  =  4*(R-1) + C
```

SAMPLE ANSWER FOR EXERCISE 40-2:

```
10  CLS
20  FOR E=1 TO 4
30  FOR D=1 TO 3
40  REM ENTRY DATA :   NAME, NUMBER, $$$$
50  READ R$(E,D)
60  PRINT R$(E,D),
70  NEXT D : PRINT
80  NEXT E : PRINT
1000 REM * DATA FILE *
1010 DATA "JONES, C.", 10439, 100.00
1020 DATA "ROTH, J.", 10023, 87.24
1030 DATA "BAKER, H.", 12936, 398.34
1040 DATA "HARMON, D.", 10422, 23.17
```

SAMPLE ANSWER FOR EXERCISE 40-3:

Change these lines:

```
130  IF VAL(R$(F,3))<=VAL(R$(S,3))  THEN 190
210 PRINT : PRINT "NUMERIC SORT" : PRINT
```

SAMPLE ANSWER FOR EXERCISE 41-1:

```
10  CLS
20  FOR P=0 TO 1022
30  PRINT CHR$(191);
40  NEXT P
50  POKE 16383,191
60  GOTO 60
```

The only way to eliminate the automatic screen scroll at PRINT position 1023 is with the POKE statement as illustrated in line 50. POKE will be covered in detail in Part VII.

SAMPLE ANSWER FOR EXERCISE 41-2:

The graphic codes are:

136, 181, 182, 191, 185, 176

SAMPLE ANSWER FOR EXERCISE 42-1:

```
10  CLEAR 300 : P=990
20  X$ = STRING$(8,140)
30  P = P + K
40  CLS
50  PRINT@P,X$;
60  I$=INKEY$ : IF I$="" THEN 90
70  K=0 : V=ASC(I$) : IF V=8 THEN K=K-1
80  IF V=9 THEN K=K+1
90  IF P+K>1015 OR P+K<960 THEN P=P-K : GOTO 40
100 FOR I=1 TO 10 : NEXT I
110 GOTO 30
```

SAMPLE ANSWER FOR EXERCISE 43-1:

```
10 CLS
20 FOR P=31 TO 34
30 READ N : POKE 15360 + P, N
40 NEXT P : PRINT
50 DATA 80,79,75,69
```

SAMPLE ANSWER FOR EXERCISE 45-1:

```
10 INPUT "IS GATE 'X' OPEN"; A$
20 INPUT "IS GATE 'Y' OPEN"; B$
30 INPUT "IS GATE 'Z' OPEN"; C$
40 PRINT
50 IF A$="Y" OR B$="Y" OR C$="Y" THEN 80
60 PRINT "OLD BESSIE IS SECURE IN PASTURE #1."
70 END
80 PRINT "A GATE IS OPEN.   OLD BESSIE IS FREE TO ROAM."
```

SAMPLE ANSWER FOR EXERCISE 45-2:

Change line 40 to:

```
40 IF INT(X/16)*16-X<>0 AND INT(Y/6)*6-Y<>0 THEN 60
```

Here's one way to create (nearly) uniform boundaries:

```
40 IF INT(X/16)*16-X<>0 AND INT(Y/6)*6-Y<>0 THEN 55
55 IF Y=47 OR X=127 SET(X,Y)
```

SAMPLE ANSWER FOR EXERCISE 46-1:

```
10 REM * STRING VARIABLE LOCATER *
20 CLS
30 A$ = "1234567890123"
40 X = VARPTR(A$)
45 PRINT "INDEX TO A$ IS AT";X
50 L = PEEK(X+1) + 256*PEEK(X+2)
55 PRINT "A$ IS HIDING AT LOCATION";L
60 FOR I=L TO L+12
70 READ N : POKE I,N
80 NEXT I : PRINT A$ : PRINT
90 DATA 158,156,172,173,26,24,24,24,24
100 DATA 141,180,184,142
```

SAMPLE ANSWER FOR EXERCISE 47-1:

```
10 REM * TEST GRADER *
20 CLS
30 PRINT "THIS IS A TEST GRADING PROGRAM"
```

```
40 PRINT "ENTER THE STUDENT'S FIVE ANSWERS AS REQUESTED"
50 RESTORE
60 N = 0
70 FOR I=1 TO 5
80 PRINT "ANSWER NUMBER";I;
90 INPUT A
100 READ B
110 PRINT A,B;
120 IF A=B THEN PRINT "CORRECT"; : N=N+1 ELSE PRINT,
"WRONG"
130 PRINT
140 NEXT I
150 PRINT N;"RIGHT OUT OF 5";
160 PRINT N/5 * 100;"%"
170 PRINT "ANY MORE TESTS TO GRADE";
180 INPUT "--1=YES,   2=NO";Z
190 IF Z=1 GOTO 50
200 DATA 65,23,17,56,39
```

SAMPLE ANSWER FOR EXERCISE 47-2:

```
100 CLS
110 PRINT : PRINT
120 PRINT "ENTER THE NUMBER OF ONE OF THE FOLLOWING
INVESTMENTS"
130 PRINT
140 PRINT "    1 - CERTIFICATE OF DEPOSIT"
150 PRINT "    2 - BANK SAVINGS ACCOUNT"
160 PRINT "    3 - CREDIT UNION"
```

```
170 PRINT "   4 - MORTGAGE LOAN"
180 PRINT : INPUT "INVESTMENT" ; F
190 ON F GOTO 1000, 2000, 3000, 4000
200 GOTO 100 : REM USED IF NUMBER NOT BETWEEN 1 AND 4
1000 REM * CERTIFICATE OF DEPOSIT PROGRAM GOES *
1010 PRINT "THE C. D. PROGRAM HAS YET TO BE WRITTEN."
1020 GOSUB 10000 : GOTO 100
2000 REM * BANK SAVINGS ACCOUNT PROGRAM *
2010 CLS : PRINT : PRINT "THIS ROUTINE CALCULATES SIMPLE
INTEREST ON"
2020 PRINT "DOLLARS HELD IN DEPOSIT FOR A SPECIFIED
PERIOD"
2030 PRINT "USING A SPECIFIED PERCENTAGE OF INTEREST." :
PRINT
2040 PRINT : INPUT "HOW LARGE IS THE DEPOSIT (IN DOLLARS)"
; P
2050 INPUT "HOW LONG WILL YOU LEAVE IT IN (IN DAYS)";D
2060 INPUT "WHAT INTEREST RATE DO YOU EXPECT (IN %)" ; R
2070 CLS : PRINT : PRINT : PRINT "FOR A STARTING PRINCIPAL
OF $" ; P ; "AT A"
2080 PRINT "RATE OF " ; R ; "  % FOR " ; D ; "  DAYS. THE
INTEREST "
2090 PRINT "AMOUNTS TO $" ;
2100 REM INTEREST = (% / YR) / (DAYS / YR) * DAYS *
PRINCIPAL
2200 I = R  / 100 / 365 * D * P
2300 PRINT : PRINT "    " , "    " ; I
2400 END
3000 REM * CREDIT UNION PROGRAM GOES HERE *
```

```
3010 PRINT "THE C. U. PROGRAM HAS YET TO BE WRITTEN."
3020 GOSUB 10000 : GOTO 100
4000 REM * MORTGAGE LOAN PROGRAM GOES HERE *
4010 PRINT "THE M. L. PROGRAM HAS YET TO BE WRITTEN."
4020 GOSUB 10000 : GOTO 100
10000 FOR I = 1 TO 1000 : NEXT I : RETURN
```

SAMPLE ANSWER FOR EXERCISE 50-1:

```
10 ON ERROR GOTO 100
20 CLS
30 FOR I=1 TO 10
40 X = RND(21)-1 : F = X-10/X
50 PRINT I, "X=" X,"F(X)=" F;
60 IF F<0 THEN PUNT ELSE PRINT
70 NEXT I
80 INPUT "PRESS ENTER TO CONTINUE";Z : GOTO 20
100 IF ERR/2+1=2 THEN 140          Model II use ERR=2
110 IF ERR/2+1=11 THEN 130         Model II use ERR=11
120 PRINT "ERROR" : END
130 PRINT "ATTEMPTED DIVISION BY ZERO IN LINE ";ERL :
    RESUME NEXT
140 PRINT:PRINT "SYNTAX ERROR IN LINE ";ERL:RESUME NEXT
```

Prepared User Programs

Prepared User Programs

12-Hour Clock

```
1 REM * COPYRIGHT (C) 1982 BY D.A. LIEN. ALL RIGHTS
RESERVED. *
3 REM        <<<<< 12-HOUR CLOCK >>>>>
10 INPUT "THE HOUR IS"; E
20 F = INT(E/10) : E = E - (F*10)
30 INPUT "THE MINUTES ARE"; C
40 D = INT(C/10) : C = C - (D*10)
50 INPUT "THE SECONDS ARE"; A
60 CLS : PRINT CHR$(23)      'MODEL II USE CHR$(31)
70 B = INT(A/10) : A = A - (B*10)
80 FOR N=1 TO 400 : NEXT N       'Adjust for your system
90 A = A + 1
100 IF A>9 THEN 120
110 GOTO 310
120 A = 0
130 B = B + 1
140 IF B>5 THEN 160
150 GOTO 310
160 B = 0
170 C = C + 1
180 IF C>9 THEN 200
190 GOTO 310
200 C = 0
210 D = D + 1
```

```
220  IF  D>5  THEN  240
230  GOTO  310
240  D = 0
250  E = E + 1
260  IF  E>9  THEN  280
270  GOTO  300
280  E=0
290  F = F + 1
300  IF  (F=1)  AND  (E=3)  THEN  A=0 :B=0 :C=0 :D=0 :E=1 :F=0
310  PRINT@456,  F; E;  ":"; D; C;  ":"; B; A
320  GOTO  80
```

Checksum For Business

For those responsible for inventory numbers or check clearing and balancing in business, a checksum is a most useful testing "code". This simple program calculates error-free checksums almost instantly. It is designed for 6-digit numbers and so can be used for stock number verification or other applications.

```
1 REM * COPYRIGHT (C) 1982 BY D.A. LIEN. ALL RIGHTS
RESERVED. *
3 REM                   <<<<< CHECKSUM FOR BUSINESS >>>>>
10  PRINT
20  INPUT  "THE FIRST DIGIT IS "; A
30  INPUT  "THE SECOND DIGIT IS "; B
40  INPUT  "THE THIRD DIGIT IS "; C
50  INPUT  "THE FOURTH DIGIT IS "; D
60  INPUT  "THE FIFTH DIGIT IS "; E
70  INPUT  "THE SIXTH DIGIT IS "; F
80  PRINT
90  PRINT "THE NUMBER IS "; A ; B ; C ; D ; E ; F
100  S = A + 2 * B + C + 2 * D + E + 2 * F
110  T = INT(S / 10)
120  U = S - T * 10
130  S = T + U
140  IF S>9 THEN 110
150  PRINT "     THE CHECKDIGIT IS "; S
```

Design Program For Cubical Quad Antenna

The cubical quad is an exceptionally fine antenna for use in receiving and transmitting ham, citizen band, short wave broadcasting, industrial, public service radio, and television signals. It is rotatable, being well-balanced and lightweight.

Electrically, it consists of two loops of wire, one of which is fed with coaxial cable or twin lead, the other simply soldered together at its ends. Figure 13 is an illustration of a quad.

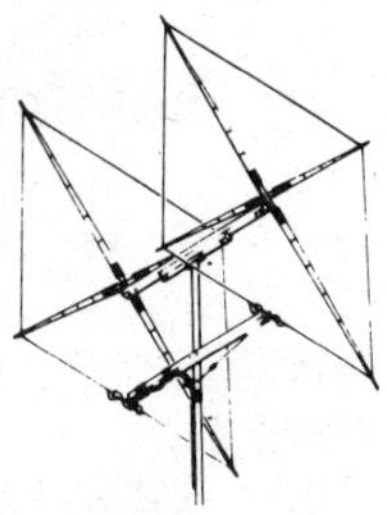

Figure 13

The program inputs only your desired operating frequency. It then calculates and outputs all the mechanical dimensions needed so you can construct your own quad. Happy designing!

```
1 REM * COPYRIGHT (C) 1982 BY D.A. LIEN. ALL RIGHTS
RESERVED. *
3 REM  <<<<< DESIGN PROGRAM FOR CUBICAL QUAD ANTENNA >>>>>
10 CLS
20 PRINT "CUSTOM DESIGNING YOUR OWN HIGH GAIN
ANTENNA>>-->>"
30 PRINT
40 INPUT "CENTER FREQUENCY (IN MEGAHERTZ) = " ; F
50 CLS
60 PRINT ">-->    C U B I C A L    Q U A D    A N T E N N A
<--<"
70 PRINT
80 E = .985 * F
90 G = 1.033 * F
100 D = 1000 / F
110 R = 1032 / F
120 B = 118 / F
130 X = (2 * (R * R / 64))
140 S = SQR(X)
150 X = (S * S + (B * B / 4))
160 P = SQR(X)
170 X = ((R * R / 64) + 75 * 75 / (F * F * 4))
180 T = SQR(X)
190 X = ((R * R / 64) + 125 * 125 / (F * F * 4))
200 U = SQR(X)
```

```
210 W = 468 / F
220 PRINT "THE DESIGN CENTER FREQUENCY IS" ; F ; "MHZ.
THIS 2
230 PRINT "ELEMENT QUAD SHOULD EXHIBIT A STANDING WAVE
RATIO"
240 PRINT "OF 2:1 OR LESS OVER THE FREQUENCY RANGE FROM" ;
E ; "TO"
250 PRINT G ; "MHZ WHEN USED WITH 50 TO 75 OHM FEED LINE."
260 PRINT
270 PRINT "THE BOOM LENGTH CAN VARY BETWEEN" ; 75 / F ;
"FEET AND"
280 PRINT 125 / F ; "FEET WITH LITTLE EFFECT. A LENGTH OF"
; B
290 PRINT "FEET IS OPTIMUM."
300 PRINT
310 PRINT "TOTAL LENGTH OF THE WIRE IN THE DRIVEN ELEMENT
IS" ; D
320 PRINT "FEET, WHICH COMES TO" ; D / 4 ; "FEET ON EACH
SIDE."
340 GOSUB 1000
360 PRINT "TOTAL LENGTH OF WIRE IN THE REFLECTOR ELEMENT
IS" ; R
370 PRINT "FEET, WHICH IS";R/4;"FEET ON EACH SIDE."
380 PRINT
390 PRINT "THE MINIMUM LENGTH OF BAMBOO, FIBERGLASS OR
OTHER"
400 PRINT "STRONG INSULATING MATERIAL USED IN EACH
SPREADER"
410 PRINT "WILL BE" ; S ; "FEET, MEASURED FROM THE CENTER
OF THE"
420 PRINT "BOOM.  IF A SPIDER (BOOMLESS) QUAD MOUNT IS
USED,"
430 PRINT "EACH SPREADER WILL HAVE TO BE AT LEAST" ; P ;
"FEET."
440 PRINT
450 PRINT "THE TURNING RADIUS (FOR TREE CLEARANCE, ETC)
WILL VARY"
460 PRINT "BETWEEN" ; T ; "FEET AND" ; U ; "FEET,
DEPENDING ON THE LENGTH"
470 PRINT "OF THE BOOM."
500 GOSUB 1000 : CLS
510 PRINT "THIS QUAD ANTENNA WILL WORK WELL EVEN AT LOW
HEIGHTS"
```

```
520 PRINT "ABOVE THE GROUND, BUT IT WORKS BEST WHEN UP  IN
THE AIR"
530 PRINT "A HALF-WAVELENGTH  --- " ; W ; "FEET, OR MORE."
540 PRINT
550 PRINT "THE FRONT-TO-BACK RATIO (ABILITY TO REDUCE
UNWANTED"
560 PRINT "SIGNALS FROM THE OPPOSITE DIRECTION) SHOULD
EXCEED 10"
570 PRINT "DECIBELS FROM ABOUT" ; .97 * F ; "TO" ; 1.03 *
F ; "MEGAHERTZ,"
580 PRINT "APPROACHING 25 DB AT" ; F ; "MEGAHERTZ."
590 PRINT
600 PRINT "     * * * * *     G O O D   D X    * * * * *"
999 GOTO 999
1000 PRINT@970,; : INPUT "PRESS <ENTER> TO CONTINUE";A$
1010 CLS : RETURN
```

Speed Reading

Your computer is your own personal Tachistoscope, a device used to practice speed reading. Study this sample program carefully to see how easy it is to substitute your own reading material at whatever reading level you want. The variable time loop lets you input the desired reading speed in words-per-minute.

```
1 REM * COPYRIGHT (C) 1982 BY D.A. LIEN. ALL RIGHTS
RESERVED. *
3 REM             <<<<< SPEED READING PROGRAM >>>>>
10 GOTO 40
20 FOR I=1 TO B : NEXT I : PRINT@448, : RETURN    ' 800
FOR MODEL II
30 REM AUDIO PROMPT GOES BEFORE RETURN IN ABOVE LINE.
40 INPUT "HOW MANY WORDS PER MINUTE DO YOU READ";W
50 B = (12 * 60 / W) * 400
60 REM 400 = # OF FOR/NEXT LOOPS IN ONE SECOND
70 REM ADJUST THE 400 IN LINE 20 TO MATCH YOUR SYSTEM
80 CLS : GOSUB 20
```

```
90 PRINT@488,                          ' 850 FOR MODEL II
100 PRINT "FIRST PARAGRAPH FROM 'GONE WITH THE WIND'." :
GOSUB 20
110 PRINT "     SCARLETT O'HARA WAS NOT BEAUTIFUL, BUT MEN
SELDOM      " : GOSUB 20
120 PRINT "REALIZED IT WHEN CAUGHT BY HER OWN CHARM AS THE
TARLETON " : GOSUB 20
130 PRINT "TWINS WERE.   IN HER FACE WERE TOO SHARPLY
BLENDED THE      " : GOSUB 20
140 PRINT "DELICATE FEATURES OF HER MOTHER, A COAST
ARISTOCRAT OF    " : GOSUB 20
150 PRINT "FRENCH DESCENT, AND THE HEAVY ONES OF HER
FLORID IRISH    " : GOSUB 20
160 PRINT "FATHER.   BUT IT WAS AN ARRESTING FACE, POINTED
OF CHIN,  " : GOSUB 20
170 PRINT "SQUARE OF JAW.   HER EYES WERE PALE GREEN
WITHOUT A TOUCH " : GOSUB 20
180 PRINT "OF HAZEL, STARRED WITH BRISTLY BLACK LASHES AND
SLIGHTLY " : GOSUB 20
190 PRINT "TILTED AT THE ENDS.   ABOVE THEM, HER THICK
BLACK BROWS    " : GOSUB 20
200 PRINT "SLANTED UPWARDS, CUTTING A STARTLING OBLIQUE
LINE IN HER " : GOSUB 20
210 PRINT "MAGNOLIA-WHITE SKIN---THAT SKIN SO PRIZED BY
SOUTHERN       " : GOSUB 20
220 PRINT "WOMEN AND SO CAREFULLY GUARDED WITH BONNETS,
VEILS, AND   " : GOSUB 20
230 PRINT "MITTENS AGAINST HOT GEORGIA SUNS." : GOSUB 20
```

The Wheel of Fortune (Or. . .Never Give a Sucker an Even Break)

Modeled after the large wheels of fortune found at carnivals and other such gatherings, this graphics program accurately replicates its odds.   The numbers are read from a DATA bank and "rotated" through "windows" as the wheel is "spun".   As commonly played, a $1 bet on any number (1, 2, 5, 10, 20, or 40, the joker and TRS-80) returns those amounts, if that number comes up.   If not, it's a cheap education.

```
1 REM * COPYRIGHT (C) 1982 BY D.A. LIEN. ALL RIGHTS
RESERVED. *
3 REM                   <<<<< THE WHEEL OF FORTUNE >>>>>
4 REM          NOT FOR THE MODEL II.
```

```
10 DIM A(60)
20 CLS
30 PRINT "STEP RIGHT UP, STRANGER.    TRY YOUR HAND AT THE"
: PRINT : PRINT
40 PRINT "          W H E E L   O F   F O R T U N E" :
PRINT : PRINT
50 PRINT "PAYOFFS IN DOLLARS FOR A $1 BET ARE 1, 2, 5, 10,
20."
60 PRINT : PRINT "SPECIALS ARE THE JOKER(13) AND
TRS-80(80), EACH PAYING 40."
70 PRINT : PRINT "ENTER YOUR CHOICE AS A  1, 2, 5, 10, 13,
20, OR 80";
80 INPUT G
90 IF G=1 OR G=2 OR G=5 OR G=10 OR G=13 OR G=20 OR G=80
THEN 100 ELSE 70
100 CLS : PRINT@24, "WHEEL OF FORTUNE"
110 T = 65
120 P = RND(54)
130 RESTORE : FOR I=1 TO 54 : READ A(I) : NEXT I
140 RESTORE  : FOR I=55 TO 60 : READ A(I) : NEXT I
150 X = 0 : Y = 18 : GOSUB 490
160 X = 18 : Y = 12 : GOSUB 490
170 X = 36 : Y = 9 : GOSUB 490
180 X = 56 : Y = 6 : GOSUB 490
190 X = 76 : Y = 9 : GOSUB 490
200 X = 94 : Y = 12 : GOSUB 490
210 X = 112 : Y = 18 : GOSUB 490
220 PRINT@92, ">>----->>" ;
230 PRINT@594, "ROUND & ROUND IT GOES . . ." ;
240 PRINT@729, "JOKER (13) &"
250 PRINT@794, "TRS-80 (80)"
260 PRINT@856, "BOTH PAY 40 TO 1"
270 FOR S=1 TO 100 + RND(2)
280 PRINT@450, A(P) :: PRINT@331, A(P+1) :: PRINT@276,
A(P+2) ;
290 PRINT@222, A(P+3) ;
300 PRINT@296, A(P+4); : PRINT@369, A(P+5); : PRINT@506,
A(P+6) ;
310 IF S<T THEN 360
320 R = (S - T) * (S - T) * (S - T) / T
330 IF S>98 PRINT@594, "       PAYOFFS GO TO THE      " :
GOTO 350
340 PRINT@594, "      ALMOST THERE . . .           " ;
350 IF S<102 FOR Z=1 TO R : NEXT Z
```

```
360 P = P - 1 : IF P=0 THEN P = 54
370 NEXT S : PRINT TAB(29); : Q = A(P+4) : GOSUB 460 : X =
0
380 PRINT TAB(22); "YOUR CHOICE WAS "; : Q = G : GOSUB 460
390 PRINT TAB(23); : IF G = A(P+4) PRINT "YOU WIN AT" ; O
; "TO 1" : GOTO 410
400 PRINT "       YOU LOSE.      "
410 PRINT@985,; : INPUT "PRESS <ENTER>";A$
420 GOTO 20
430 DATA
1,2,80,1,5,1,2,1,10,1,2,1,5,1,2,1,5,1,2,1,20,1,2,10
440 DATA 1,2,1,5,1,2,1,5,1,2,13,1,2,1,10,1,2,1,2
450 DATA 1,20,1,2,5,1,2,10,1,2,5
460 O = Q : IF (Q = 13) = (Q = 80) PRINT " " ; Q : RETURN
470 O = 40 : A$ = "JOKER" : IF Q=80 THEN A$ = "TRS-80"
480 PRINT A$ : RETURN
490 FOR I=0 TO 7
500 SET(X,I + Y) : SET(X + 1,I + Y)
510 SET(X + 14,I + Y) : SET(X + 15,I + Y)
520 GOTO 550
530 NEXT I
540 FOR I=0 TO 7
550 SET(I * 2 + X,Y) : SET(I * 2 + 1 + X,Y)
560 SET(I * 2 + X,7 +Y) : SET(I * 2 + 1 + X,7 + Y)
570 NEXT I
580 RETURN
```

Dow-Jones Industrial Average Forecaster

There is no guarantee that this program will make you instantly wealthy, but
it is an example of converting a financial magazine article into a usable computer program. The article describing the market premises on which this
program is built appeared in Forbes Magazine.

```
1 REM * COPYRIGHT (C) 1982 BY D.A. LIEN. ALL RIGHTS
RESERVED. *
3 REM  <<<<< DOW-JONES INDUSTRIAL AVERAGE FORECASTER >>>>>
20 PRINT "*** PROJECTS TARGET DOW-JONES INDUSTRIAL AVERAGE
AS A"
```

```
30 PRINT "FUNCTION OF YEARS DJI EARNINGS AND INFLATION
RATE ***"
40 PRINT
50 REM * K = COST OF MONEY.   ASSUME 3% *
60 K = .03
70 REM * P = RISK PREMIUM OF STOCKS OVER BONDS.   ASSUME 1%
*
80 P = .01
90 PRINT "DO YOU KNOW YEARS PROJECTED EARNINGS OF 30 DJI
(Y/N)" ;
100 INPUT A$
110 IF A$ = "Y" THEN 300
120 PRINT
130 PRINT "THIS METHOD WILL GIVE AN EARNINGS APPROXIMATION
USING"
140 PRINT "THE NEWSPAPER PRICES AND P/E RATIOS. BETTER
FORECASTS"
150 PRINT "OF EACH COMPANIES EARNINGS MAY GIVE AN
IMPROVED"
160 PRINT "OVERALL FORECAST."
170 PRINT
180 D = 0
190 FOR N=1 TO 30
200 READ A$
210 PRINT "WHAT IS THE CURRENT PRICE OF >--> " ; A$ ; "
<--<" ;
220 INPUT P
230 PRINT "THE CURRENT P/E RATIO " ;
240 INPUT R
250 E = P / R
260 D = E + D
270 NEXT N
280 PRINT
290 GOTO 340
300 PRINT "WHAT IS THE TOTAL PROJECTED EARNINGS FOR 1
SHARE OF" ;
310 PRINT " EACH" ;
320 INPUT D
330 REM * I = ESTIMATED INFLATION RATE *
340 PRINT "WHAT PERCENTAGE IS THE INFLATION RATE";
350 INPUT I
360 T = D / (K + P + I * .01)
370 R = T / D
380 PRINT
```

```
390 PRINT "INFL. RATE","DJI EARN.","PROJ DJ AVE","AVE/EARN
RATIO"
400 PRINT
410 PRINT I , D , T , R
420 DATA ALLIED CHEM,ALCOA,AMER BRANDS,AMER CAN,A.T. & T
430 DATA BETH STEEL,CHRYSLER,DUPONT,E. KODAK,ESMARK,EXXON
440 DATA G.E.,GEN FOODS,GEN MOTORS,GOODYEAR,INCO
450 DATA INT. HARV.,INT. PAPER,JOHNS-MAN,MINN
MM,OWENS-ILLS
460 DATA PROCTER & G,SEARS,STD OIL CAL,TEXACO,UNION
CARBIDE
470 DATA U.S. STEEL,UNITED TECHNOL.,WESTINGHOUSE,WOOLWORTH
```

On a Snowy Evening. . .by Robert Frost

Who says computers only make stuffy mathematical calculations and are not for folks who appreciate the better things? If this one doesn't grab you, nothing will.

```
1 REM * COPYRIGHT (C) 1982 BY D.A. LIEN. ALL RIGHTS
RESERVED. *
3 REM                <<<<< ON A SNOWY EVENING . . .  >>>>>
4 REM            NOT FOR THE MODEL II.
10 CLS
20 PRINT@7, "ON A SNOWY EVENING     . . . . . BY ROBERT
FROST" ;
30 FOR N=1 TO 2000 : NEXT N
40 FOR Z=1 TO 300
50 SET(RND(127),RND(45)+2)
60 NEXT Z
70 I = 0
1000 PRINT@525, "WHOSE WOODS THESE ARE I THINK I KNOW." ;
1001 GOSUB 6000
1100 PRINT@525, "HIS HOUSE IS IN THE VILLAGE, THOUGH; " ;
1101 GOSUB 6000
1200 PRINT@525, "HE WILL NOT SEE ME STOPPING HERE      " ;
```

```
1201 GOSUB 6000
1300 PRINT@525, "TO WATCH HIS WOODS FILL UP WITH SNOW." ;
1301 GOSUB 6000
1400 PRINT@525, "MY LITTLE HORSE MUST THINK IT QUEER   " ;
1401 GOSUB 6000
1500 PRINT@525, "TO STOP WITHOUT A FARMHOUSE NEAR     " ;
1501 GOSUB 6000
1600 PRINT@525, "BETWEEN THE WOODS AND FROZEN LAKE" ;
1601 GOSUB 6000
1700 PRINT@525, "THE DARKEST EVENING OF THE YEAR. " ;
1701 GOSUB 6000
1800 PRINT@525, "HE GIVES HIS HARNESS BELL A SHAKE" ;
1801 GOSUB 6000
1900 PRINT@525, "TO ASK IF THERE IS SOME MISTAKE. " ;
1901 GOSUB 6000
2000 PRINT@525, "THE ONLY OTHER SOUND'S THE SWEEP" ;
2001 GOSUB 6000
2100 PRINT@525, "OF EASY WIND AND DOWNY FLAKE.    " ;
2101 GOSUB 6000
2200 PRINT@525, "THE WOODS ARE LOVELY, DARK, AND DEEP," ;
2201 GOSUB 6000
2300 PRINT@589, "BUT I HAVE PROMISES TO KEEP," ;
2305 I = 3
2310 GOSUB 6000
2400 PRINT@653, "AND MILES TO GO BEFORE I SLEEP," ;
2405 I = 6
2410 GOSUB 6000
2500 PRINT@717, "AND MILES TO GO BEFORE I SLEEP." ;
2505 I = 9
2510 GOSUB 6000
5000 SET(RND(127),RND(47))
5001 GOTO 5000
6000 FOR N=1 TO 20
6020 X = RND(127)
```

```
6030 Y = RND(47)
6070 IF Y = 24 + I GOTO 6020
6080 IF Y = 25 + I GOTO 6020
6090 IF Y = 26 + I GOTO 6020
6100 SET(X,Y)
6150 FOR A=1 TO 20 : NEXT A
6200 NEXT N
6300 RETURN
```

Termites

A malicious sense of humor helps on this one. Its avowed purpose is to demonstrate the graphic RESET(X,Y) function, turning off the "lights" in a random fashion, but it's not without other redeeming value. If you don't like to sit by the fire and watch it snow while reading good poetry, you can always watch the termites eat your house down.

```
1 REM * COPYRIGHT (C) 1982 BY D.A. LIEN. ALL RIGHTS
RESERVED. *
3 REM                         <<<<< TERMITES >>>>>
4 REM              NOT FOR THE MODEL II.
10 CLS : PRINT
20 FOR P=0 TO 958 : PRINT CHR$(191); : NEXT
30 POKE 16383,191
40 N = 5760
50 PRINT@5, "SEE THE TERMITES EAT.      ONLY";
60 PRINT@45, "BITES LEFT !";
70 X = RND(128) - 1
80 Y = RND(45) + 2
90 IF POINT(X,Y)=0 THEN 70
100 RESET(X,Y)
110 N = N - 1
120 PRINT@36, N;
130 IF N>0 THEN 70
999 GOTO 999
```

SORRY

SORRY is a popular board game by Parker Brothers. This program demonstrates how to load a deck of cards into a numerical array, draw them out in a random fashion, "reshuffle" the deck after the last card is drawn, and continue drawing. The program will pause between each drawing of the cards, allowing as much time as desired to actually move the pieces on your own SORRY board. Have fun!

```
1 REM * COPYRIGHT (C) 1982 BY D.A. LIEN. ALL RIGHTS
RESERVED. *
3 REM                   <<<<< SORRY >>>>>
10 CLS : RANDOM : DIM A(45)
20 PRINT "STAND BY FOR THE SHUFFLING OF THE DECK OF
CARDS."
30 PRINT : PRINT : PRINT
40 FOR N = 1 TO 45 : READ A(N) : NEXT N
50 PRINT : PRINT : PRINT
60 Y = 1
70 PRINT "SHUFFLING COMPLETED . . . . GAME BEGINS!" :
PRINT
80 R = INT(RND(45))
90 M = A(R)
100 IF M=0 THEN 80
110 A(R) = 0 : T = 0
120 FOR Z=1 TO 45
130 T = A(Z) + T
140 NEXT Z
150 PRINT TAB(25);"PRESS ENTER"; : INPUT A$
160 IF T=0 THEN 180
170 GOTO 210
180 PRINT "END OF DECK.   THE CARDS ARE BEING RESHUFFLED."
190 RESTORE
200 GOTO 30
210 IF Y<0 THEN 240
220 PRINT TAB(10); "RED"
230 GOTO 250
240 PRINT TAB(44); "GREEN"
250 IF M=13 THEN 270
260 PRINT TAB(B + 10); M
270 ON M GOTO  290,310,540,360,540,540,380,540
,540,410,430,540,450
280 GOTO 540
290 PRINT TAB(B);"MAY MOVE A NEW PIECE OUT"
300 GOTO 540
310 PRINT TAB(B);"MAY MOVE A NEW PIECE OUT"
320 PRINT : PRINT
330 PRINT TAB(B+5);"DRAW AGAIN . . ."
```

```
340  PRINT
350  GOTO 580
360  PRINT TAB(B);"MUST BACK UP  4  SPACES"
370  GOTO 540
380  PRINT TAB(B);"MAY SPLIT THE  7  BETWEEN"
390  PRINT TAB(B+3);" 2 PIECES"
400  GOTO 540
410  PRINT TAB(B);"MAY MOVE BACKWARDS  1  SPACE"
420  GOTO 540
430  PRINT TAB(B);"CAN SWAP PIECES WITH OPPONENT"
440  GOTO 540
450  PRINT : PRINT
460  IF B=0 THEN 510
470  PRINT "  GOTCHA             <<<====<<<     <<<====<<<";
480  PRINT TAB(49);"S O R R Y !"
490  PRINT : PRINT
500  GOTO 540
510  PRINT "S  O  R  R  Y  !     >>>====>>>     >>>====>>>"
;
520  PRINT TAB(55);"GOTCHA !"
530  PRINT : PRINT
540  FOR T=1 TO 1000 : NEXT T  : FOR X=1 TO 4
550  PRINT TAB(30); "*"
560  NEXT X
570  Y = Y * (-1)
580  IF Y>0 THEN B=0 ELSE B=35
590  GOTO 80
600  DATA
1,1,1,1,1,2,2,2,2,3,3,3,3,4,4,4,4,5,5,5,5,7,7,7,7,8,8
610  DATA
8,8,10,10,10,10,11,11,11,11,12,12,12,12,13,13,13,13
```

Craps

The game is as old as history. A testimonial to the intelligence and ingenuity of our ancient ancestors, it's an excellent way to demonstrate the running of twin Random Number Generators.

You don't need to know how to play the game — the computer will quickly teach you. . .there's one born every minute.

```
1 REM * COPYRIGHT (C) 1982 BY D.A. LIEN. ALL RIGHTS
RESERVED. *
```

```
3 REM                <<<<< CRAPS >>>>>
10 CLS : RANDOM
20 INPUT "PRESS <ENTER> TO CONTINUE";A$
30 CLS : GOSUB 150 : P = N
40 PRINT : PRINT "YOU ROLLED "; P, " ",
50 ON P GOTO 60,90,90,70,70,70,80,70,70,70,80,90
60 REM USED FOR THE ON STATEMENT IF P = 1   (WHICH IT
CAN'T)
70 PRINT "YOUR POINT IS"; N : GOTO 100
80 PRINT "YOU WIN!!" : PRINT : GOTO 20
90 PRINT "YOU LOSE." : PRINT : GOTO 20
100 GOSUB 150 : M = N
110 PRINT : PRINT "YOU ROLLED "; M,
120 IF P=M THEN 80
130 IF M=7 THEN 90
140 GOTO 100
150 A = RND(6) : B = RND(6) : N = A + B : RETURN
```

Fire When Ready, Gridley

```
1 REM * COPYRIGHT (C) 1982 BY D.A. LIEN. ALL RIGHTS
RESERVED. *
3 REM          <<<<< FIRE WHEN READY, GRIDLEY >>>>>
4 REM          NOT FOR THE MODEL II.
10 CLS
20 INPUT "ENTER YOUR INITIALS"; A$ : CLS : Z = 74 : FOR Y
= 18 TO 23
30 FOR X=Z TO 125 : SET(X,Y) : NEXT X : Z = Z + 2
40 NEXT Y : FOR P=554 TO 1004 STEP 64 : PRINT@P,
STRING$(21,191); : NEXT P
50 FOR P=356 TO 381 STEP 2 : PRINT@P,CHR$(188);CHR$(176);
: NEXT P : PRINT CHR$(188);
60 O = 0
70 FOR X=91 TO 121 STEP 5 : FOR Y=47 TO 35 STEP -1 :
RESET(X,Y) : NEXT Y : NEXT X
80 FOR X=91 TO 121 : RESET(X,34) : NEXT X
90 PRINT@687, A$; "'S CASTLE" ;
100 FOR X=74 TO 101 : SET(X,12) : SET(X,13) : NEXT X :
SET(100,11)
110 FOR X=86 TO 96 : SET(X,14) : SET(X,15) : NEXT X :
RESET(92,13) : RESET(93,13)
```

```
120 FOR Z=1 TO 2 : FOR X=2 TO 14 : FOR Y = 40 TO 43 :
SET(X,Y) : NEXT Y : NEXT X
130 FOR X=3 TO 13 STEP 2 : RESET(X,41) : NEXT X :
RESET(7,43) : RESET(8,43)
140 S$=STRING$(2,143) : R$=STRING$(2,128)
150 PRINT@293,R$; : RESET(100,11) : PRINT@307,S$; :
SET(104,11)
160 N = 100 : GOSUB 290
170 PRINT@293,S$; : PRINT@307,R$; : RESET(104,11) :
SET(100,11)
180 FOR X=71 TO 2 STEP -1 : P = X - 73 : Y = P * P / 150 +
12 : SET(X,Y) : SET(X-1,Y)
190 RESET(X+1,O) : RESET(X,O) : O = Y : NEXT X :
PRINT@771, "KAPOW!" ;
200 RESET(1,45) : RESET(2,45)
210 N = 500 : GOSUB 290
220 PRINT@800, "Z O T"; : PRINT@840, STRING$(35,176);
230 PRINT@840, ;
240 FOR I=1 TO 35 : PRINT CHR$(128); : NEXT I
250 FOR I=1 TO 30 : RESET(83+RND(4*Z),41+RND(2*Z)-Z*1) :
NEXT
260 FOR I=1 TO 30 : RESET(83+RND(6*Z),41+RND(4*Z)-Z*2) :
NEXT
270 N = 1000 : GOSUB 290 : PRINT@771, STRING$(35,128);
280 NEXT Z : GOTO 10
290 FOR X=1 TO N : NEXT X : RETURN
```

Automatic Ticket Number Drawer

Like to make a big splash at the next Rotary Club, County Fair, or other
ticket-drawing giveaway? This program uses the random number generator
to pick the lucky number(s) and eliminate charges of stuffing the ticket box,
besides giving the whole affair some pizazz. If your own number comes up
and you are charged with rigging the computer, you're on your own.

```
1 REM * COPYRIGHT (C) 1982 BY D.A. LIEN. ALL RIGHTS
RESERVED. *
3 REM    <<<<< AUTOMATIC TICKET NUMBER DRAWER >>>>>
10 CLS : RANDOM
20 REM * PICKS WINNER(S) BY DRAWING TICKET NUMBER *
30 REM * NO MORE THAT 32767 TICKETS CAN BE SOLD *
```

```
40 REM * BUT TICKET NUMBERS CAN RANGE TO 999999 & BEYOND *
50 INPUT "THE LOWEST TICKET NUMBER IS" ; B
60 PRINT
70 INPUT "THE HIGHEST TICKET NUMBER IS " ; H
80 PRINT
90 E = H - B + 1
100 IF E<32768 GOTO 120
110 PRINT "TOO MANY TICKETS SOLD!" : END
120 INPUT "HOW MANY WINNERS DO YOU WANT " ; W
130 CLS
140 IF W>E GOTO 280
150 PRINT : PRINT : PRINT : PRINT
160 PRINT " * A N D   T H E   W I N N I N G " ;
170 IF W>1 GOTO 200
180 PRINT " T I C K E T   I S *"
190 GOTO 210
200 PRINT " T I C K E T S   A R E   *"
210 PRINT
220 FOR N=1 TO W
230 Z = RND(E)
240 PRINT
250 PRINT TAB(12) ; ">------>>>   " ; Z + B - 1
260 NEXT N
270 END
280 CLS : PRINT : PRINT : PRINT : PRINT : PRINT : PRINT
290 PRINT TAB(8) ; " YOU CAN'T HAVE MORE WINNERS THAN" ;
300 PRINT " ENTRIES - DUMMY !"
```

House Security

```
1 REM * COPYRIGHT (C) 1982 BY D.A. LIEN. ALL RIGHTS
RESERVED. *
3 REM                    <<<<< HOUSE SECURITY >>>>>
10 CLS : DEFSTR A-E
20 PRINT "PLEASE ANSWER 'Y' OR 'N' TO THE FOLLOWING
QUESTIONS:"
30 PRINT
40 INPUT "IS THE FRONT DOOR LOCKED"; A
50 INPUT "IS THE BACK DOOR LOCKED"; B
60 INPUT "IS THE KITCHEN WINDOW CLOSED"; C
```

```
70 INPUT "IS THE BEDROOM WINDOW CLOSED AND LOCKED"; D
80 INPUT "IS THE GARAGE DOOR LOCKED"; E
90 PRINT : PRINT
100 IF A="Y" AND B="Y" AND C="Y" AND D="Y" AND E="Y" THEN
130
110 PRINT "HOUSE NOT LOCKED UP FOR THE NIGHT."
120 PRINT : PRINT "CHECK FOR AN UNLOCKED DOOR OR WINDOW."
: END
130 PRINT "HOUSE SECURITY CHECK SHOWS HOUSE LOCKED UP FOR
THE NIGHT." : END
```

Loan Amortization

This program provides a fully-developed installment plan for the repayment of small-to-moderate size loans, such as car or home improvement loans. It includes all instructions necessary. Use it with common sense; in the last payment period, amounts may be carried out to a fraction of a cent.

Challenge: Modify the program to eliminate fractional-cent payments, without changing the total amount paid as interest or principal.

```
1 REM * COPYRIGHT (C) 1982 BY D.A. LIEN. ALL RIGHTS
RESERVED. *
3 REM      <<<<< LOAN AMORTIZATION >>>>>
10 C = 0 : CLS : INPUT "PRINCIPAL"; P
20 INPUT "# OF PERIODS"; L
30 INPUT "INTEREST RATE"; R
40 I = R / 12 : I = I / 100
50 T = 1 : FOR X=1 TO L
60 T = T * (1 + I) : NEXT X : T = 1 / T
70 T = 1 - T
80 M = P * I / T
85 M = INT(M * 100 + .5) / 100
90 GOSUB 200
100 FOR Z=1 TO L
110 IF C<13 GOTO 120
115 INPUT "PRESS ENTER TO CONTINUE"; A$ : C = 0 : GOSUB
200
120 A = (INT(P * I * 100 + .5)) / 100
130 B = M - A : P = P - B
140 PRINT Z; : PRINT TAB(10); P; : PRINT TAB(20); M;
```

```
150 PRINT TAB(30); B; : PRINT TAB(40); A
160 C = C + 1 : NEXT Z
170 END
200 CLS : PRINT "PAYMENT  REMAINING  MONTHLY  PRINCIPAL
INTEREST"
210 PRINT "NUMBER   PRINCIPAL  PAYMENT  PAYMENT   PAYMENT"
220 RETURN
```

Slowpoke

The kiddies will enjoy this one. It tests reaction time. When the computer says "GO", you press the ENTER key to stop it. Then it's the next player's turn to RUN it. The player who stops it on the smallest number wins. Any player who gets a "SLOWPOKE" has to take the dog for a walk.

With a little easy rework of the PRINT statements it can be converted into a "drunkometer" reaction time tester.

To change the speed of the printing, you can add a short FOR-NEXT loop between Lines 11Ø and 12Ø.

```
1 REM * COPYRIGHT (C) 1982 BY D.A. LIEN. ALL RIGHTS
RESERVED. *
3 REM              <<<<< SLOWPOKE >>>>>
10 PRINT "   GET READY . . . . . . . . . ."
20 FOR B=1 TO 500 : NEXT B
30 PRINT : PRINT : PRINT
40 PRINT TAB(30), "GET SET . . . . . . . . ."
50 X = RND(1500)
60 FOR N=1 TO X : NEXT N
70 CLS
80 PRINT : PRINT : PRINT : PRINT : PRINT
90 PRINT TAB(30), "G  O    !   !   !"
100 FOR Z=1 TO 10
110 PRINT Z
120 NEXT Z
130 PRINT : PRINT : PRINT
140 PRINT "     S  L  O  W    P  O  K  E"
150 FOR N=1 TO 1000 : NEXT N
```

Test Grader Program.

```
1 REM * COPYRIGHT (C) 1982 BY D.A. LIEN. ALL RIGHTS
RESERVED. *
3 REM                    <<<<< TEST GRADER PROGRAM >>>>>
10 CLS : N = 10
20 PRINT "WOULD YOU LIKE TO INPUT THE ANSWER"
30 PRINT "ONE AT A TIME OR 5 AT A TIME (ENTER 1 OR
5)":INPUT T
40 IF (T=1) OR (T=5) THEN 60
50 GOTO 30
60 INPUT "ENTER THE STUDENT'S NAME (LAST NAME, FIRST
NAME)" ; A$ , B$
70 CLS : PRINT "TEST FOR " ; B$ ; "   " ; A$
80 RESTORE
90 R = 0
100 FOR I=1 TO N STEP T
110 PRINT "ENTER ANSWER"; : IF T=5 THEN PRINT "S
";I;"THROUGH ";
120 PRINT I + T - 1 ;
130 IF T=5 INPUT
A$(I),A$(I+1),A$(I+2),A$(I+3),A$(I+4) : GOTO 150
140 INPUT A$(I)
150 NEXT I
160 CLS
170 PRINT "RESULTS ON TEST FROM "; B$; " "; A$; ":"
180 FOR I = 1 TO N
190 PRINT A$(I),
200 READ Z$ : PRINT Z$,
210 IF A$(I) = Z$ PRINT "CORRECT:"; INT(R / N * 100
+ .5)
220 PRINT
230 NEXT I
240 PRINT "PERCENTAGE CORRECT:"; INT(R / N * 100 +
.5)
250 PRINT : GOTO 60
260 DATA 5,3,A,D,C,E,T,T,F,T
```

Appendices

Disk BASIC Systems

Doesn't Everyone Have Disk?

You are fortunate to have a disk system. So you had to sell the second car.
You're really computing in style!

Unfortunately, having a disk system is of only marginal help to the process
of learning Elementary and Intermediate BASIC. Sort of like having your
own Boeing 747 before mastering a Cessna 150.

Our non-disk Model I readers must wrestle with slow and marginally reliable
cassette tapes to store their programs and data. Model III users have a faster
and fairly reliable cassette system. Model II/16 users don't have a cassette
option. . .it's strictly disk. Since you have a highly reliable disk system you
may never experience the agony (and ecstasy?) of making a cassette system
work. Count your blessings!

There is no way we can more than *begin* to cover your disk system in this
book. The book is long already, and Disk BASIC (Advanced BASIC) is
covered in another CompuSoft® book. All we can do here is get you up and
running to meet the rest of the class waiting at Chapter 1. When necessary,
we'll have little side messages or return to this Appendix for special information.

Skip now to the section in this Appendix which deals with your specific TRS-
80.

Model I Disk
BASIC System — Part 1

Hook up all the parts and pieces per the manual which accompanies the system.

Turn the system ON in this order:

1. Disk drives (switches in the back)

2. Expansion Interface (switch in center front)

3. The Keyboard (switch on right rear)

Place the SYSTEM or DOS diskette (or a copy of it. . .see the big system manual) in Drive 0 (the one closest to the Expansion Interface on the disk drive cable) and close the door. Then hit the RESET button on the left rear of the keyboard.

A Real Turn On

If all the units are plugged into a Line Filter (RS #26-1451 is highly recommended), use *it* to turn on everything at the same time. The disk drive(s) will whir, and the screen should read:

```
TRSDOS-DISK OPERATING SYSTEM-VER 2.3

DOS READY

_
```

"DOS READY" tells us that we are at the *system* or *command* level. From here, we can do all sorts of things, but our mission in this book is *LEARNING BASIC*.

The most important thing we can do now at the system level is load the BASIC language into the computer's memory. Non-disk systems use the BASIC language "interpreter" inside the keyboard unit (Level II BASIC), but Level II BASIC does not know how to SAVE and LOAD programs on the disk drives. In order to use this capability, disk users must load an expanded version of BASIC (Disk BASIC) into memory from the TRSDOS diskette.

To do this, type:

BASIC `ENTER`

The computer responds with:

HOW MANY FILES? `ENTER`

The computer asks:

MEMORY SIZE?

Press `ENTER` again, and the computer says:

RADIO SHACK DISK BASIC VERSION 2.2
READY
>_

> Note: If we had answered the two preceding questions in certain ways we could do certain advanced things. We're still crawling, not yet even walking, so we just avoided the questions by typing `ENTER`.

The screen finally tells us that our Model I is ready to speak BASIC by saying:

READY
>_

Why Disk BASIC?

Disk BASIC has all the regular TRS-80 BASIC features plus a few special disk *commands*. We will be concerned in this book only with SAVE and LOAD and will learn about them in due course.

Just because you have a disk system doesn't mean you have to start right off using Disk BASIC. If, at this point, you would really rather learn the straight old BASIC like our non-disk readers, you can shut it all down, disconnect the Expansion Interface and drives, and chop the system down to minimum size.

As an alternative, after turning on the system, press the RESET button (located at the left rear of the keyboard) while holding down the ENTER key. You will get a simple:

`MEM SIZE?`

on the screen, and pressing ENTER will put you in non-disk Level II BASIC.

Users with an older Model I will see: MEMORY SIZE?

Neither of these options is especially recommended since you do have the disk system.

Turning the Disk System OFF

Always remove the diskette before turning the system OFF. Punishment for failure to do so might be a "zapped" disk, one with some of its information accidentally erased.

If you have Line Filter #26-1451, simply turn the whole works OFF by flipping its switch. If not, the switches must be flipped in reverse order:

The keyboard first

Followed by the Interface

Followed by the disk drive(s)

Back To the Book

With the system still on and

```
READY
```

giving us our cue, let's all mosey on back to Chapter 1 and meet the rest of the gang LEARNING TRS-80 BASIC at DISK FLAG #1.

Model I − Part 2

Suppose we want a LISTing of the programs on a diskette. The DOS command is:

```
DIR
```

In order to use DIR we must leave BASIC and return to DOS level. Typing DIR in BASIC simply gives us a SYNTAX ERROR. BASIC doesn't understand it.

When we leave BASIC for TRSDOS, we may lose any program in memory. The careful programmer will SAVE any program of value before leaving BASIC. Exit BASIC by typing:

```
CMD"S"
```

We know we're back at DOS by:

```
DOS READY
_
```

> Note: A less sophisticated way to get to DOS is by simply pressing the RESET key.

For a DIRectory listing of what's stored on Drive 0 type:

```
DIR
```

If you have more than one drive, use this format:

```
DIR :1
```
(don't forget the space)

for a directory of what's stored on Drive 1.

Quiz time! How do we get back to BASIC? Right! Just type:

```
BASIC
```

Cycle completed.

Model II Disk BASIC
System — Part 1

Unlike the other TRS-80's, the Model II is designed solely around disk storage of programs and data. It doesn't even know the meaning of the word cassette. There is no way we can learn Model II BASIC without using its disk.

A Real Turn On

We must use the diskette which came with the system, called the DOS or SYSTEM diskette, to teach the computer to understand BASIC before we can talk to it.

Plug in the computer, after referring to the manual which came with it. Do *not* insert a diskette, yet. Turn on the POWER switch.

> Note: If you have the expansion bay with additional drives, disconnect it first and insert the "terminator" per the big thick reference manual. We really have no need for more than a single drive and can do without the extra noise. If you want to leave the extra drives connected, be sure to turn them ON before turning ON the main computer, and OFF after turning it OFF.

After giving itself a perfunctory check-up, the computer will tell us to:

```
INSERT DISKETTE
```

Place the SYSTEM diskette (or a copy of it) in the built-in disk drive. Its label must be facing to the right. Close the door by moving the vertical bar to the left, toward the red light.

The factory original DOS diskette should be used *only* to make working copies. See the DOS Reference Manual for the FORMAT and BACKUP procedures.

The disk drive(s) will whir, and the screen will say:

```
INITIALIZING
```

along with a message telling how much memory we have. Momentarily it will display a title, a graphic insignia symbolizing Tandy Towers, a copyright notice, and ask us for the date:

```
Enter Date(MM/DD/YYYY)...............
```

Type in the date using this format:

```
09/28/1990
```
 followed by the `ENTER` key.

The next question is:

```
Enter Time(HH.MM.SS)................
```

We can either type the time in the format requested

```
08.42.35
```

or, if we want to skip the electric clock feature simply press `ENTER`. Note that the Model II runs on a 24-hour system, so 2:27 PM, for example, must be entered as 14.27.00.

The date and time are stored in memory for future reference, but have little value to us in our early study of BASIC.

The computer responds with:

```
TRSDOS READY
```

....

"TRSDOS READY" tells us that we are at the *system* or *command* level, not yet in BASIC. From here, we can do all sorts of things, but our subject in this book is *LEARNING BASIC*.

The Model II computer expects all its *commands* from us in capital letters, so we have to humor it. Press the `CAPS` key once and see that the red light in the key is lit.

The instructions which teach the Model II to speak BASIC are found on the diskette. To send these instructions to the computer we simply type:

`BASIC` `ENTER`

The computer responds with:

`TRS-80 Model II BASIC-80 Rev. 1.2a`

along with some other information and:

`READY`

`>`

Ready is our signal that the computer is speaking BASIC and we can use it like hundreds of thousands of other BASIC-speaking computers around the world.

Turn OFF

Always remove the diskette before turning the system OFF. Punishment for failure to do so might be a "zapped" disk, one with some of its information accidentally erased.

Then, turn the main computer OFF, followed by the expansion bay (if used), but not right now.

Back To the Book

With the system still **ON** and

`Ready`

`>`

giving us our cue, let's all mosey on back to Chapter 1 and meet the rest of the gang *LEARNING TRS-80 BASIC* at the DISK FLAG in Chapter 1.

Model II − Part 2

Suppose we want a LISTing of the programs on a diskette. The DOS command is:

```
DIR
```

In order to use DIR we must leave BASIC and return to DOS level. Typing DIR in BASIC simply gives us a ?SN Error. BASIC doesn't understand it.

When we leave BASIC for TRSDOS, we may lose any program in memory. The careful programmer will SAVE any program of value before leaving BASIC. Exit BASIC by typing:

```
SYSTEM
```

We know we're back at DOS by

```
TRSDOS READY
```

. . . .

For a DIRectory listing of what's stored on Drive 0 type:

```
DIR
```

If you have more than one drive, use this format:

```
DIR 1
```
(don't forget the space)

for a directory of what's stored on Drive 1.

Quiz time! How do we get back to BASIC? Right! Just type:

```
BASIC
```

Since the computer doesn't understand the DIR command while BASIC is in memory, and since going back and forth between BASIC and TRSDOS is inconvenient, BASIC requires that we use a slightly different procedure to execute DOS commands while BASIC is active. Enter:

```
SYSTEM"DIR"
```

to get a directory of Drive 0. Ah, yes. It's working like a charm. If you have more than one drive, use:

```
SYSTEM"DIR 1"    (don't forget the space)
```

to get a directory of Drive 1, for example.

Cycle completed.

Model III Disk BASIC
System — Part 1

A Real Turn On

Turn the computer ON with the power switch located under its right side. The disk drive(s) will whir for a few seconds. Place the SYSTEM diskette (or a *copy* of it) with its label up, in Drive 0 (the bottom drive), and close the door. Press the RESET button (the orange recessed button on the right side of the keyboard).

The disk drives will whir again, and the screen will display a title, a graphic insignia symbolizing the Model III computer, the number of drives connected, a copyright notice, and ask us for the date:

```
Enter Date(MM/DD/YY)?
```

Type in the date using this format:

```
09/28/90
```
followed by the `ENTER` key.

The next question is:

```
Enter Time(HH:MM:SS)?
```

Type in the time in this format:

```
08:42:35   ENTER
```

The date and time are stored in memory for future reference, but have little value to us in our early study of BASIC.

The computer finishes with:

```
TRSDOS Ready
```

. . . .

"TRSDOS Ready" tells us that we are at the *system* or *command* level. From here, we can do all sorts of things, but our mission in this book is *LEARNING BASIC.*

The instructions which teach the Model III to speak Disk BASIC are found on the diskette which we inserted. To send these instructions to the computer we simply type:

```
BASIC  [ENTER]
```

The computer responds with:

```
How Many Files?  [ENTER]
```

The computer then asks:

```
Memory Size?
```

Press [ENTER] again, and the computer will respond with:

```
TRS-80 Model III Disk BASIC Rev 1.3
```

along with more copyright information and finally:

```
READY
>
```

> Note: If we had answered the two preceding questions in certain ways, we could do certain advanced things. We're still crawling, not yet even walking, so we just avoided the questions by typing [ENTER] .

Why Disk BASIC?

Disk BASIC has all the regular TRS-80 BASIC features plus a few special disk commands. We will be concerned in this book only with SAVE and LOAD and will learn about them in due course.

Just because you have a disk system doesn't mean you have to start right off using Disk BASIC. If at this point you would really rather learn the straight old BASIC like our non-disk readers, as an alternative, after turning on the system, press the RESET button while holding down the ENTER key. This option isn't especially recommended since you have the disk system. On the other hand, the disks really aren't that much help *LEARNING BASIC*.

If you choose this option, read "Turning The Disk System Off" below, exercise the option, then return immediately to Chapter 1 and pick up the discussion at DISK FLAG #1.

Turning the Disk System OFF

Always remove the diskette before turning the system OFF. Punishment for failure to do so might be a "zapped" disk, one with some of its information accidentally erased.

Then, turn the computer OFF, but not right now.

Back To the Book

With the system still on and

```
READY
  >
```

giving us our cue, let's all mosey on back to Chapter 1 and join the rest of the group LEARNING TRS-80 BASIC at the disk in Chapter 1.

Model III – Part 2

Suppose we want a LISTing of the programs on a diskette.

The TRSDOS command is:

```
DIR
```

In order to use DIR we leave BASIC and return to TRSDOS Ready. Typing DIR in BASIC simply gives us a Syntax Error. BASIC doesn't understand it.

When we leave BASIC for TRSDOS we may lose any program in memory. The careful programmer will SAVE any program of value before leaving BASIC. Exit BASIC by typing:

```
CMD"S"
```

We know we're back at DOS by:

```
TRSDOS Ready
```

....

Note: A less sophisticated way to get to DOS is by simply pressing the RESET key.

For a DIRectory listing of what's stored on Drive 0 type:

```
DIR
```

If you have more than one drive, use this format:

```
DIR :1
```
(don't forget the space)

for a directory of what's on Drive 1.

Quiz time! How do we get back to BASIC? Right! Just type:

```
BASIC
```

Since the computer doesn't understand the DIR command while BASIC is in memory, and since going back and forth between BASIC and TRSDOS is inconvenient, there is a BASIC command which allows us to read a diskette's DIRectory without going to DOS.

`CMD"D:Ø"`

gives us a directory of Drive 0. If you have more than one drive, use:

`CMD"D:1"`   (don't forget the colon)

for a directory of Drive 1.

Cycle completed.

Diskette Diagrams
for Appendix A

MODEL I/III
DIAGRAM

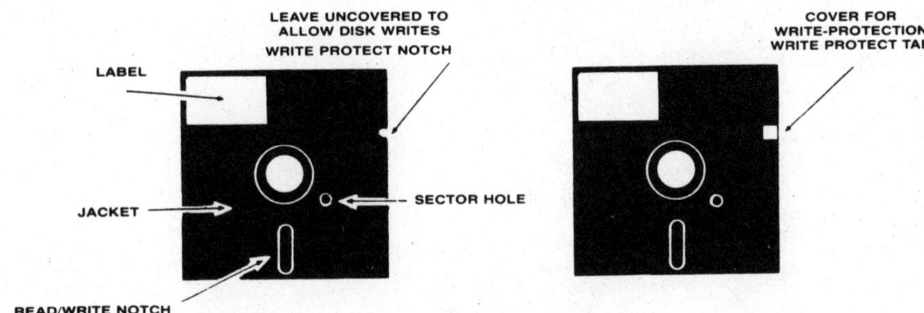

MODEL II
DIAGRAM

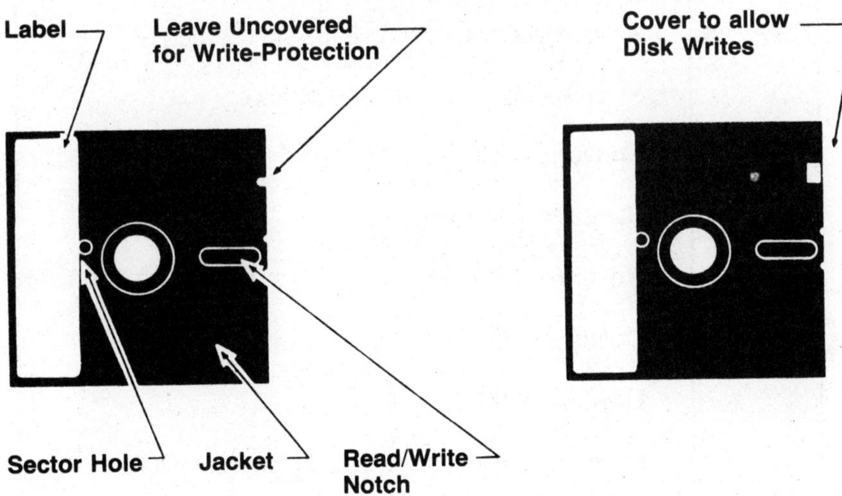

ASCII Code Tables

ASCII code numbers between 0 and 31 are used for special control purposes in the TRS-80:

MODELS I & III

Code	Function
0-7	None
8	Backspaces and erases current character
9	None
10-13	Carriage returns
14	Turns on cursor
15	Turns off cursor
16-20	None
21	Swap space compression/special characters
22	Swap special/alternate characters
23	Converts to 32 character mode
24	Backspace ← cursor
25	Advance → cursor
26	Downward ↓ linefeed
27	Upward ↑ linefeed
28	Home, return cursor to display position (0,0)
29	Move cursor to beginning of line
30	Erases to the end of the line
31	Clear to the end of the frame

Appendix B: ASCII Code Table — Model I / III

Decimal Code	ASCII Character	Decimal Code	ASCII Character	Decimal Code	ASCII Character
32	space	64	@	95	`
33	!	65	A	96	`
34	"	66	B	97	a
35	#	67	C	98	b
36	$	68	D	99	c
37	%	69	E	100	d
38	&	70	F	101	e
39	'	71	G	102	f
40	(	72	H	103	g
41	)	73	I	104	h
42	*	74	J	105	i
43	+	75	K	106	j
44	,	76	L	107	k
45	—	77	M	108	l
46	.	78	N	109	m
47	/	79	O	110	n
48	0	80	P	111	o
49	1	81	Q	112	p
50	2	82	R	113	q
51	3	83	S	114	r
52	r	84	T	115	s
53	5	85	U	116	t
54	6	86	V	117	u
55	7	87	W	118	v
56	8	88	X	119	w
57	9	89	Y	120	x
58	:	90	Z	121	y
59	;	91	↑ or [	122	z
60	<	92	↓ or /	123	{
61	=	93	← or]	124	\
62	>	94	→ or \	125	}
63	?			126	~

Note: Codes **96 thru 126** for the TRS-80 represent the lower-case forms of **64-95**; however, only upper-case characters are displayable on standard Model I machines.

Appendix B: ASCII Code Table — Model II

Code Dec.	Hex.	Character	Code Dec.	Hex.	Character	Code Dec.	Hex.	Character
00	00		34	22	"	72	48	H
01	01	Turns on blinking cursor	35	23	#	73	49	I
02	02	Turns off cursor	36	24	$	74	4A	J
03	03		37	25	%	75	4B	K
04	04	Turns on steady cursor	38	26	&	76	4C	L
05	05		39	27	'	77	4D	M
06	06		40	28	(	78	4E	N
07	07		41	29	)	79	4F	O
08	08	Backspaces cursor and erases character	42	2A	*	80	50	P
			43	2B	+	81	51	Q
09	09	Advances cursor to next 8-character boundary	44	2C	,	82	52	R
			45	2D	—	83	53	S
10	0A	Line feed	46	2E	.	84	54	T
11	0B		47	2F	/	85	55	U
12	0C		48	30	Ø	86	56	V
13	0D	Carriage return	49	31	1	87	57	W
14	0E		50	32	2	88	58	X
15	0F		51	33	3	89	59	Y
16	10		52	34	4	90	5A	Z
17	11		53	35	5	91	5B	[
18	12		54	36	6	92	5C	\
19	13		55	37	7	93	5D	]
20	14		56	38	8	94	5E	^
21	15		57	39	9	95	5F	—
22	16		58	3A	:	96	60	`
23	17	Erases to end of line	59	3B	;	97	61	a
24	18	Erases to end of screen	60	3C	<	98	62	b
25	19	Sets white-on-black mode	61	3D	=	99	63	c
26	1A	Sets black-on-white mode	62	3E	>	100	64	d
27	1B	Clears screen, homes cursor	63	3F	?	101	65	e
28	1C	Moves cursor back	64	40	@	102	66	f
29	1D	Moves cursor forward	65	41	A	103	67	g
30	1E	Sets 80-character mode and clears Display	66	42	B	104	68	h
			67	43	C	105	69	i
31	1F	Sets 40-character mode and clears Display	68	44	D	106	6A	j
			69	45	E	107	6B	k
32	20	Space	70	46	F	108	6C	l
33	21	!	71	47	G	109	6D	m

Model II (Continued)

Code		Character	Code		Character
Dec.	**Hex.**		**Dec.**	**Hex.**	
110	6E	n	147	93	
111	6F	o	148	94	
112	70	p	149	95	
113	71	q	150	96	
114	72	r	151	97	
115	73	s	152	98	
116	74	t	153	99	
117	75	u	154	9A	
118	76	v	155	9B	
119	77	w	156	9C	
120	78	x	157	9D	
121	79	y	158	9E	
122	7A	z	159	9F	↑
123	7B	{	160	A0	
124	7C	|	161	A1	!
125	7D	}	162	A2	"
126	7E	~	163	A3	#
127	7F	±	164	A4	$
128	80		165	A5	%
129	81		166	A6	&
130	82		167	A7	'
131	83		168	A8	(
132	84		169	A9	)
133	85		170	AA	*
134	86		171	AB	+
135	87		172	AC	,
136	88		173	AD	—
137	89		174	AE	.
138	8A		175	AF	/
139	8B		176	B0	0
140	8C		177	B1	1
141	8D		178	B2	2
142	8E		179	B3	3
143	8F		180	B4	4
144	90		181	B5	5
145	91		182	B6	6
146	92		183	B7	7
			184	B8	8

Model II (Continued)

Code		Character	Code		Character
Dec.	**Hex.**		**Dec.**	**Hex.**	
185	B9	9	225	E1	a
186	BA	:	226	E2	b
187	BB	;	227	E3	c
188	BC	{	228	E4	d
189	BD	=	229	E5	e
190	BE	}	230	E6	f
191	BF	?	231	E7	g
192	C0	@	232	E8	h
193	C1	A	233	E9	i
194	C2	B	234	EA	j
195	C3	C	235	EB	k
196	C4	D	236	EC	l
197	C5	E	237	ED	m
198	C6	F	238	EE	n
199	C7	G	239	EF	o
200	C8	H	240	F0	
201	C9	I	241	F1	
202	CA	J	242	F2	
203	CB	K	243	F3	
204	CC	L	244	F4	
205	CD	M	245	F5	
206	CE	N	246	F6	
207	CF	O	247	F7	
208	D0	P	248	F8	
209	D1	Q	249	F9	
210	D2	R	250	FA	
211	D3	S	251	FB	
212	D4	T	252	FC	Moves cursor left
213	D5	U	253	FD	Moves cursor right
214	D6	V	254	FE	Moves cursor up
215	D7	W	255	FF	Moves cursor down
216	D8	X			
217	D9	Y			
218	DA	Z			
219	DB	[			
220	DC	\			
221	DD	]			
222	DE	^			
223	DF	—			
224	E0	,			

The Expansion Interface
(Model I Only)

The TRS-80 can be connected directly to one Cassette Recorder and one additional device such as the Radio Shack Screen Printer. To use additional devices it becomes necessary to connect a "Black Box" that provides additional Input/Output jacks and can "talk" to each device. The TRS-80 Expansion Interface is such a box. It incorporates circuit cards which generate the necessary control signals, and has Input/Output jacks to operate up to four mini floppy drives, one printer, and two cassette recorders.

The Expansion Interface also has a digital clock circuit that can be read either by a machine language program (available free from Radio Shack) or the TRS-80 Disk Operating System (TRSDOS). Space is provided within the unit to install an additional circuit card to meet other specialized needs such as interfacing with RS-232 devices. Its most common use, however, is as a place to add an additional 16K or 32K bytes of memory, which adds to the 16K already inside the main computer case.

Setting It Up

Remove the Expansion Interface from its carton along with the ribbon cable, power supply, instruction book and other goodies. Some units are supplied with a buffer (a plastic box with ribbon cable attached at both ends) which is easily damaged if not handled carefully, or an extra DIN plug/jack assembly for connection between the Interface and the computer.

Installing the Power Supplies

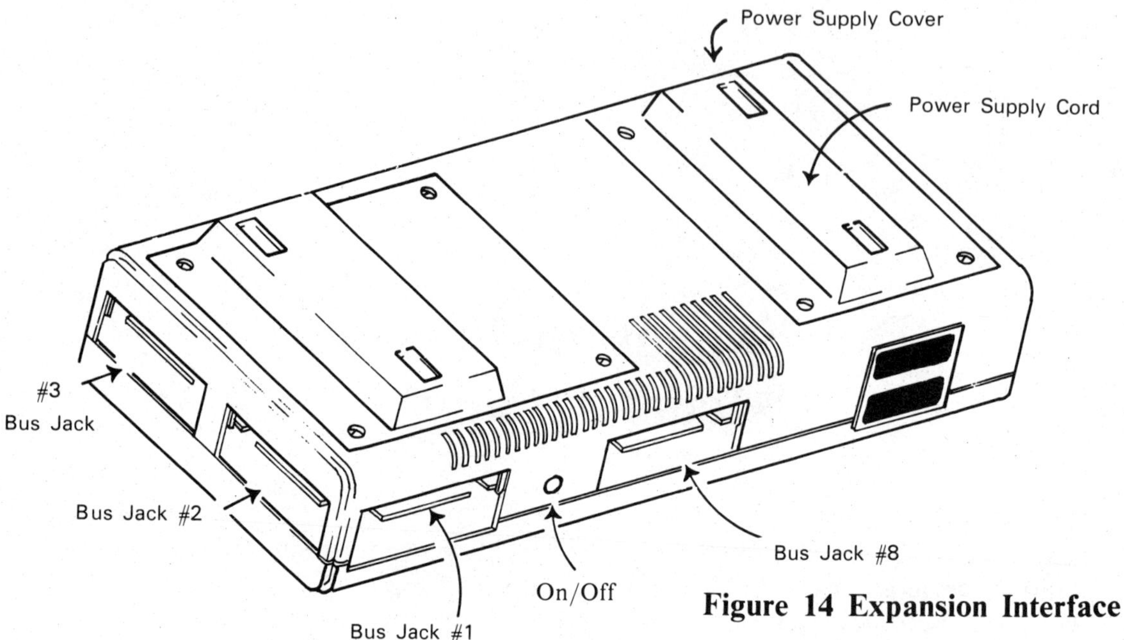

Figure 14 Expansion Interface

Remove the power supply compartment cover (located on the top right-hand side of the Interface as you face it) by removing the three Phillips-head screws. Connect one Power Supply cable's 5-pin DIN connector on the edge of the printed circuit board. Place this power supply inside the Expansion Interface, closest to the front.

Notice that space is provided in the Interface compartment for two power supplies. This enables you to place the computer's power supply out of sight along with the one for the Interface. If you choose to place the computer's power supply in this compartment, route its cable through the door cutouts in back. Connect the DIN plug to the power jack on the computer as usual. Replace the power supply cover door on the Expansion Interface, being careful not to damage the case by overtightening the screws.

Positioning the Expansion Interface

Place the Expansion Interface behind the TRS-80 computer with the identification plate facing the computer. The following tasks must be accomplished before plugging in A.C. power cables from the computer power supply, Expansion Interface power supply and any accessories.

Lift the little door covering the Expansion Port Connector on the TRS-80's left rear panel and slide it slightly to the right, then lift it up and away from the computer. (Be careful not to break the little tabs.) Attach one end of the Expansion Ribbon Cable to this Expansion Port. It is important that the ribbon cable extends downward, out the *bottom* of each edge connector.

Units supplied with the buffered cable have arrows on the Buffer Box indicating which connector to attach to the computer and which to the Expansion Interface. With nonbuffered cables you may use either end. Attach the curved door onto the computer case. It should close, allowing the ribbon cable to feed out between it and the case.

Finally, attach the Expansion Ribbon Cable connector to the bus jack located to the left of the push-button power switch on front of the Expansion Interface.

(#1 in Figure 14.)

Turning It On

After all connections have been made and double-checked, plug the A.C. power plugs from the two power supplies plus the Video Display unit into an A.C. outlet. If you spring for a 3-wire power strip with switch, pilot light and circuit breaker (about $20), you will find it to be a great convenience and well worth the money. Turn on the Video Display unit, Expansion Interface, and while holding down the ⟨ENTER⟩ key, turn on the TRS-80 computer.

If MEMORY SIZE? is not displayed on the video monitor, turn off the Interface. Power up the computer first, then turn on the Interface. The MEMORY SIZE? question should appear and you can respond to it as usual.

MEM SIZE? for new ROMS.

Another Gimmick

If you are not interested in using dual cassettes because you have no need for data storage, or you are using the Disk system, you can still make use of the cassette switching relay in the Expansion Interface as a noise generator for special effects. (Most expensive New Year's Eve noise maker in the house!)

Each time the computer switches from cassette number 1 to cassette number 2 and back again, you'll hear a clicking sound. By increasing the switching speed, the slight click sound becomes a buzz easily heard by all. Using the relay in this manner is not recommended if you intend to use the dual cassette feature in the future because you are reducing the life expectancy of the relay. Think of it as opening and closing your car door several hundred times each time you get in the car. Before long either the door hinges or your arm will fail. (More probably the smog devices!)

Now that you know the pitfalls, try this program to hear the "buzzer" in action. Before RUNning, be certain both recorders are disconnected from the Interface, to prevent possible damage to them, or a possible fusing together of the relay contacts.

```
10 REM BUZZER GENERATOR
20 PRINT "PRESS 'B' TO HEAR THE BUZZER"
30 A$=INKEY$: IF A$= "B" GOTO 50
40 GOTO 30
50 FOR X= 1 TO 50
60 POKE 14308,1
70 POKE 14308,0
80 NEXT X
90 FOR X= 1 TO 100: NEXT
100 GOTO 30
```

By setting bit 0 at address 14308 to 1, and then to 0 in lines 60 and 70, the relay in the Interface switches back and forth between cassette number 2 and cassette number 1, respectively. This sound can be "tuned" somewhat by changing the relay switching time in line 50 to generate the special effects used in game programs like Pong, Submarine, etc. . . .

Figure 14 shows the additional hookup points to the Expansion Interface. Note that connection point number 2 is used for hooking to Radio Shack's line printers. Smaller printers which can be hooked directly to the TRS-80 bus are connected at point number 2 which is a direct extension of the TRS-80 bus.

The DIN jacks in the back will be discussed in more detail in the chapter dealing with dual cassette operation. Point number 8, front and center, is used to connect to the optional RS-232 interface board.

Use the utmost care in hooking up to these ports. Triple check to see that the right end of the cable is being used and that the cable always feeds downward from the connector. I've seen these interfaces and peripherals "buy the farm" when the user was experimenting with what should go where, and how — with the power ON. (No, it wasn't me. . .this time!)

LLIST and LPRINT

These BASIC commands/statements are almost too easy.

> LLIST is typed at the command level when you want a listing on the printer.

> LPRINT is used in a program when you want the program to print something on the printer.

Both can be used either as statements or commands. If you want to print both on the screen and on paper, use duplicate program lines, with PRINT in the one for the screen, and LPRINT for the printer.

Enter any program of your choice and convert it to LPRINT the results on your printer. Make a "hard copy" LLISTing of it.

If you accidentally precede either PRINT or LIST with the letter L and don't have a printer connected, there may be trouble. It's especially easy to have a simple LIST turn into LLIST if the L key bounces. If an Expansion Interface is *not* connected, a simple RESET will make things OK again.

If an Interface *is* connected, it automatically assumes (right or wrong) that disk drives are also connected and won't let you do a simple RESET. You either have to hook up a printer and let it accept the information directed its way by the LLIST or LPRINT, or press RESET (with the `ENTER` key down), *losing your program in the process.*

If you have an Interface, you should do frequent dumps to cassette tape when developing new programs — *just in case.*

LPRINT TAB

We can only TAB as far as position 63 using LPRINT. To go beyond that point it is necessary to resort to devious means.

With the later ROM we can TAB to 127.

We can recall that PRINT STRING$ is used to repeat a number of characters or actions. We can use it to sneak around the above rule by having it repeat a number of spaces.   For example:

```
10 LPRINT STRING$(75,32);X
```

will "print" 75 blank spaces before printing the value of X. "32" is the ASCII code for a blank space.

Advanced LPRINT Capabilities

Five different ASCII codes are set aside for use with printers. Since different printers respond differently, we can only talk here in general terms, and learn how to test our own printer to see how it responds.   The five codes are:

10	line feed and carriage return
11	roll paper to top of next sheet
12	roll paper to top of next sheet
13	line feed and carriage return
138	carriage return and line feed

To see what all this means, hook up your printer (assuming you have one . . .if not, guess you can stay with us and read on).

```
1 CLS:PRINT
10 INPUT "ENTER A CODE NUMBER ";N
20 LPRINT CHR$(N)
90 PRINT : LIST
```

. . .and RUN.

Try each of the codes and see what happens. Some codes may do nothing. Your printer's manual may have additional (or replacement) codes.

There are no universal rules. Keep your test program simple and be aware that LPRINT with CHR$ is not always predictable when mixed on the same program line.

The "top of form" or "top of next sheet" feature is a necessary one for using the printer to prepare printed statements, or printing information which must always start at the top of a page. Users with "continuous roll" printers have little need for a "top of form".

When your computer is turned on, if it's going to do any printing, it automatically assumes it will be printing six lines per inch on sheets of paper 11 inches long, 66 lines per page. This information is stored in memory location 16424. Type:

```
PRINT PEEK (16424)
```

and we should get back the number:

```
67
```

That's one more than the number of lines to be printed.

If we use a different size paper, we can change the number of lines for that page by POKEing in a different number.

Suppose we are printing on paper that is 8 inches long. 8 inches times 6 lines per inch = 48. 48 + 1 = 49. We will:

```
POKE 16424,49
```

In order for the "top of page" feature to work, it is also necessary for the computer to keep track of how many lines have been printed on each page. This information is stored in memory location 16425. Let's PEEK:

```
PRINT PEEK (16245)
```

and we'll get a number, the size of which depends on how many lines have already been printed. That will vary with how much experimenting we've been doing, and with which code.

The difference between how many lines *can* be printed on a page (memory location 16424) and how many *have* been printed (memory location 16425) tells the computer how many have yet to be printed before starting the top of a new page. It's all very simple, in principle.

We can even POKE a 1 into location 16425 at the beginning of our program to initialize the counter. Each time we use a "form feed" code (11 or 12) the counter is reset back to 1 for a new page.

With a little experimenting, you will have your big printer doing what you paid to have it do.

Time Out

The Real Time Clock

The Expansion Interface has one additional feature − a Real Time clock. "Real Time" means "now" time. It contains a real clock, the time being controlled by an internal quartz crystal. In addition, that clock can be accessed (gotten to) by software (programs) and used to serve as an event-timer or master clock to control events. Up 'til now we've used simple FOR-NEXT loops to approximate times − satisfactory only over a short period.

The Level II ROM does not have the software built in to activate and control the clock. In order to use it, we must load in a machine language program from a tape furnished free by Radio Shack.

Winding Up The Big Machine

Tighten your belt and put on the helmet. We are going to RAM the line − with finesse.

To load the REAL TIME CLOCK program we'll need a cassette recorder connected to the keyboard. Power up the computer and Expansion Interface. Since this entire book is about Level II, what follows does not apply to the Interface when used with floppy disks. The disk system has its own DEBOUNCE ROUTINE which is activated automatically, as well as a clock routine that can be activated without going through what we are about to do.

When the computer asks:

```
MEMORY SIZE
```

answer with:

65400 if you have 48K of RAM

49016 if you have 32K of RAM

32632 if you have 16K of RAM

20344 if you have 4K of RAM

to leave room at the "top" of memory for both the DEBOUNCE and CLOCK routines. (Users with either 4 or 16K of RAM would obviously be using the Interface box for something other than to hold extra memory . . .there might be some of them, somewhere.)

The screen will verify we are in Level II BASIC and say:

READY
   >

We enter the Monitor mode by typing:

SYSTEM

and following the

*?

we type:

RELO

(the name of the machine language program we want to read from Radio Shack's tape).

Set up the recorder to play the KEYBOARD DEBOUNCE/REAL TIME CLOCK SYSTEM * RELO tape,

and press:

ENTER

After a time, the usual asterisks will appear in the upper right-hand corner, followed by another:

*?

to which we respond:

/   ENTER

The computer wishes to engage us in rather extensive dialogue, saying:

```
TRS-80 RELOCATING LOADER
BASE = (a hexadecimal number)
+
```

Ignoring it all, we charge blindly onward, and confidently press the single letter:

```
S
```

and watch the screen. The recorder rolls, and up comes:

```
KB DEBOUNCE ROUTINE.
```

plus another

```
+
```

to which we say:

```
L
```

(Doesn't really matter for now what all this means. That's for another time, place, and specialized book. There are some hints as we go along, but not enough to divert us from the main thing we're trying to learn right now.)

Persistent it is, and it chatters:

```
LOCATING RELOCATION DIRECTORY.
LOADING RELOCATABLE CODE.
RELOCATION COMPLETE, BASE =  (another HEX number).
```

This time we have to write down that HEX number since we will need to use it very soon. (If you have 32K of RAM, you should get the number BFC8.) Again we see a:

```
+
```

and with equal persistence we say again,

```
S
```

(meaning Search for the next machine language program).

It says "I found it, and its name is":

```
REAL TIME CLOCK
+
```

Again we say "don't just sit there using up juice, LOAD it" and type:

```
L
```

It repeats itself in a computer-like monotone, saying:

```
LOADING RELOCATION DIRECTORY.
LOADING RELOCATABLE CODE.
RELOCATION COMPLETE, BASE =   (another HEX number).
```

Yes, we have to write this HEX number down, too. Don't get the two mixed up! (32K RAM users should get BF7A.)

BFB1 with new ROM.

Seeing another

```
+
```

we decide we've had enough of this chatter, and elect to Escape to BASIC by typing:

```
E
```

and see the welcome

```
READY
  >
```

Whew! Another close scrape with machine language!

But there is more work to be done. We first have to *activate* the KEYBOARD DEBOUNCE routine.

Turning to our HEX number notes, we look up the BASE of the DEBOUNCE routine. What do you have? 32K users got BFC8. Going to the HEX-to-Decimal conversion chart on the next page, we convert BFC8 to a decimal number. Follow me through this example:

Working from left to right:

    B = 45056

    F =   3840

    C =   192

Add them all together and they spell:

    8 =   8
          ——————

       49096

Now if you don't see how we got that, STOP right now and don't go on until you figure it out. We can't continue without knowing how to make these conversions.

OK, the BASE of the KEYBOARD DEBOUNCE routine is at memory location 49096. We have to increase that number by one, then go back into machine language to activate the program.

HEX CODE	Most Significant Bytes		Least Significant Bytes	
	IV	III	II	I
0	0	0	0	0
1	4096	256	16	1
2	8192	512	32	2
3	12288	768	48	3
4	16384	1024	64	4
5	20480	1280	80	5
6	24576	1536	96	6
7	28672	1792	112	7
8	32768	2048	128	8
9	36864	2304	144	9
A	40960	2560	160	10
B	45056	2816	176	11
C	49152	3072	192	12
D	53248	3328	208	13
E	57344	3584	224	14
F	61440	3840	240	15

Figure 10
Hex-to-Decimal Conversion Chart
Decimal Value = IV + III + II + I

Living with real gusto, we leap at the keyboard and type:

```
SYSTEM
```

followed by:

```
*? /49097
```

Then flee to the safety of:

```
READY
>_
```

Closing in on the REAL TIME CLOCK, it's sweaty palms all the way. No way to avoid this machine language biz.

Look at the *second* HEX number you wrote down. It is the BASE of the CLOCK routine, and we must increase it by one, then get tricky. What number did you get? 32K users got BF7A. One number larger than BF7A must be BF7B. Look at the chart, if necessary.

For new ROM, BFB1 + 1 = BFB2.

Having made that startling discovery, we now have to split our HEX number into two parts — the *most* important, and the *least* important. (You know, things like this could easily give computers a bad reputation as being unnecessarily complex!)

Anyway, since the little numbers are always on the right, we say:

> 7B represents the *least* significant bytes and, by uncanny reasoning, we conclude BF must represent the *most* significant bytes.

Now we get to convert them separately to decimal. Sticking with our 32K RAM example (you do your own thing if you have 4K, 16K or 48K of RAM — the example here illustrates the principle):

$$LSB = 7B = 112 + 11 = 123 \text{ decimal}$$

$$MSB = BF = 176 + 15 = 191 \text{ decimal}$$

Terrific! What are we supposed to do with that? The fastest way to get the answer is to type in this program, study it carefully, then RUN it.

```
10 REM * REAL TIME CLOCK PROGRAM *
20 CLS : PRINT "WE HAVE TO START BY
                SETTING THE CLOCK" : PRINT
30 INPUT "WHAT IS THE HOUR "; H
40 INPUT "WHAT ARE THE MINUTES "; M
50 INPUT "WHAT ARE THE SECONDS "; S : CLS
100 POKE 16481,H        'POKES IN THE STARTING HOUR
```

```
110 POKE 16480,M          'POKES IN THE STARTING MINUTES
120 POKE 16479,S          'POKES IN THE STARTING SECONDS
150 POKE 16526,123        'SETS UP LSB FOR A CALL FROM USR
160 POKE 16527,191        'SETS UP MSB FOR A CALL FROM USR
200 X = USR(1)            'USR(1) STARTS CLOCK,USR(0) STOPS
300 PRINT@5,"HOURS","MINUTES","SECONDS"
500 PRINT@70,PEEK(16481),PEEK(16480),PEEK(16479)
9999 GOTO 500
```

See how our LSB and MSB fit in lines 15Ø and 16Ø? Memory locations
16479-81 hold the time, as seen in lines 1ØØ-12Ø.

Pretty slick, eh? It's a minimum sort of program, but its expansion is limited
only by your own imagination. As a starter, let's change line 5ØØ and add
51Ø:

```
500 H=PEEK(16481) : M=PEEK(16480) : S=PEEK(16479)
510 PRINT@70,H,M,S
```

    . . .and RUN.

The modified program assigns variables to the hour, minute and second, giving us a means to compare them against other numbers. Add these lines:

```
600 REM * USE OF LOGIC WITH REAL TIME CLOCK *
610 IF H = 12 AND M = 35 AND S = 52 THEN 1000
700 GOTO500
1000 REM * A ROUTINE NEEDED HERE TO THROW THE BIG SWITCH *
1010 PRINT "HYDROTURBINE #7 STARTUP SEQUENCE INITIATED"
```

    . . .and RUN.

Combining real time with program logic presents possibilities that boggle the
mind. (To learn how to actually "throw the big switch" see *Controlling The
World With Your TRS-80*. It is an entire book dedicated to designing, con-
structing and controlling hardware with BASIC software, and is made to
order for those interested in this sort of thing. Soon to be published by Com-
puSoft®. Same author. Ahem.)

RUN again, with this change:

```
1010 PRINT@54, "HYDROTURBINE #7 STARTUP SEQUENCE INITIATED"
```

But there's more! Add these lines:

```
2000 REM * LOGS ACTIVITIES ON CASSETTE TAPE *
2010 T=T+1:IF T>2 GOTO500 'ONLY ONE WRITE TO TAPE
2020 X = USR(0)        ' SHUTS OFF CLOCK
2030 C = 71            ' LET CODE 71 MEAN TURBINE #7 STARTUP
2040 PRINT#-1,C,H,M,S  'LOG EVENT AND TIME ON TAPE
2050 PRINT@648, "EVENT LOGGED ON TAPE"
2060 X = USR(1)        ' TURN CLOCK BACK ON
```

Now insert a blank tape into your recorder, set to record,

    . . .and RUN.

Refer to Appendix G for more information on PRINT#-1 and INPUT#-1.

Wow! Now we can maintain a log on tape of every event that occurs at the old powerhouse. It will be no problem at all to write a little program to IN-PUT that DATA back off tape and print on the screen or a printer.

You're wondering what lines 2020 and 2060 are all about? Well, the Real Time Clock, on both Disk and non-Disk systems, really screws up cassette operation. The clock *must* be turned off in order to do tape INPUTs and SAVEs. Don't try to CSAVE a program without first shutting off the clock (otherwise it won't take). Fortunately, the clock *can* be readily turned OFF and ON, both with program statements and at a command level by using:

```
X=USR(0)
```

to turn it off, and

```
X=USR(1)
```

to turn it back on.

In the process, some time is lost, and the clock will fall behind a bit. If every second is really that precious in your application, you could note that we lose about five seconds each time we log an event on tape. Can you think of an easy way to add five seconds to the time after such logging? Sure you can.

On the brighter side, if program execution is STOPped with a STOP statement or the **BREAK** key, the clock keeps running even though the time isn't displayed on the screen. Typing CONT will resume program execution and the clock will be right on time.

Since the clock does not reset to zero at the end of 12 hours, you might say it's a 24-hour clock. Since it doesn't reset at the end of 24 hours either, maybe it's more of an elapsed time clock. In any case, if you want these resets, they have to be accomplished in the program software — not a very difficult task.

The final Coup de Grace (our French-speaking readers like a little of that sort of thing. Wonder what it means?) for this chapter is the automatic logging of events on your printer. If you don't have a printer yet, beware of line 112Ø, since execution freezes until a printer accepts that line. Just put a REM there if you don't have a printer.

```
11ØØ REM * LOGS ACTIVITIES ON PRINTER *

111Ø N = N + 1 : IF N => 2 GOTO 5ØØ ' PRINT ONLY ONCE

112Ø LPRINT"TURBINE #7 STARTUP BEGAN AT ";H;M;S

113Ø PRINT@584, "EVENT LOGGED ON PRINTER"
```

So, cock the recorder, turn on the printer, set the clock at a little before 12:35:52, and stand aside.

49. . .50. . .51. . .52 KERCHUNK!!! There goes the big turbine. . .it's winding up! Ratatatata, the printer is getting it all down. Hmmmmmmm Hmmmmmm, round and round go the tape hubs. Yep. . .the video screen is reporting the action.

RUN it again, Sam. . .RUN it again! (As Wagner's euphoric "Ride of the Valkerie" swirls in our head.)

•
•
•

Breathes there a man with soul so dead, who never to himself has said. . .

•

•

•

"This must be how good the old sow feels wallowing in wet mud on a hot day."

•

•

•

Music: Up and out.

Dual Cassette Operation

With the Expansion Interface dual cassette feature, it is possible to Write and Read data to and from tape using two separate and independent cassette recorders. (A similar feat can already be performed without an Interface using one recorder and two cassette tapes, but it can be tedious to the point of being impractical.) Two recorders, one set to PLAY and the other to RECORD, provide a practical, reliable and economical way of using your TRS-80 to perform genuine "Data Processing".

Setting Up For Dual Cassettes

Connect the Tape Interconnection Cable (the one with a 5-pin DIN plug on each end) from the computer's TAPE jack to the Expansion Interface cassette INPUT/OUTPUT connector (the DIN connector located on the back panel *next to the power cables* — Point #7). Connect the DIN plug from a Cassette Recorder (designated as #1) to the DIN jack on the Interface back panel located *next to the Disk port* — Point #5. The other end of this cable should be connected to the cassette recorder as normal.

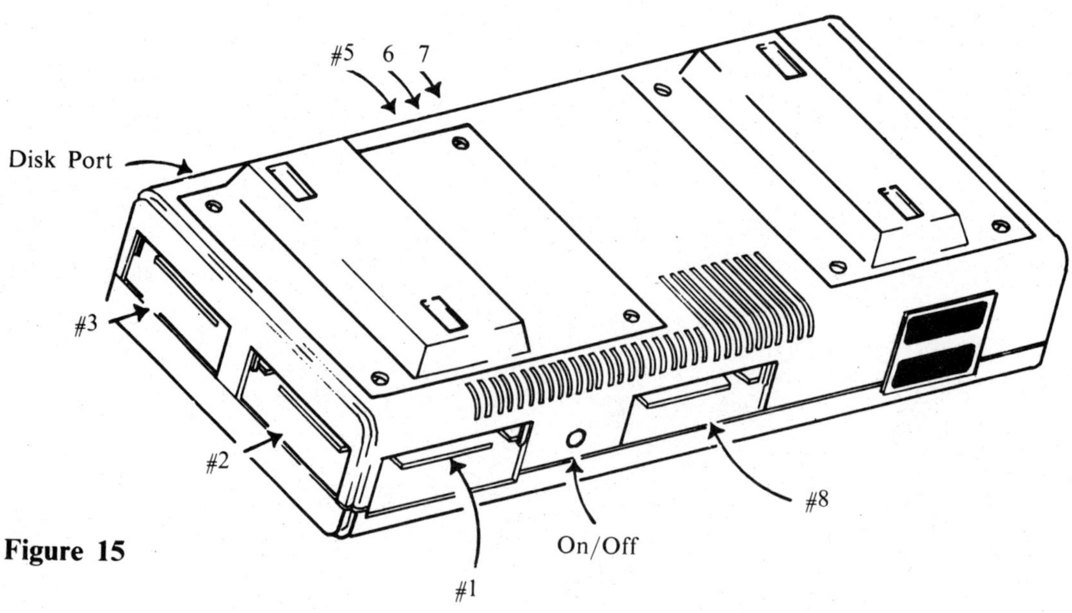

Figure 15

Connect the cable from the second Cassette Recorder (designated #2) to the remaining DIN jack on the Interface back panel (the *center* DIN jack, point #6).

Now that the dual cassette connectors on the Expansion Interface have been identified, attach stick-on labels to the back of the Interface case (above each connector) to save time trying to identify them again in the future.

Enter this program to verify that the two recorders are connected properly and are ready for use. Position the recorders with the access doors open so you can see the drive spindles. It helps to leave the cassettes out at this time. Press the PLAY key on each, and RUN.

```
10  REM * DUAL CASSETTE TEST *
20  CLS : PRINT "TYPE '1' TO RUN CASSETTE #1"
30  PRINT "TYPE '2' TO RUN CASSETTE #2"
40  N$ = INKEY$ : IF N$ = "" GOTO 40
50  IF VAL(N$) = 1 THEN PRINT#-1,1
60  IF NAL(N$) = 2 THEN PRINT#-2,1
70  GOTO 40
```

Refer to Appendix G for more information on PRINT#-1 and INPUT#-1.

Alternate between pressing the "1" key and "2" key. Watch the drive spindles on both recorders to see that each is operating as we have instructed. If you use CTR-80's, watch for the red light as well.

When using the Interface, the recorders can be addressed individually. Number 1 is identified as #-1 and number 2 is #-2. Any combination of both on PLAY, both on RECORD, one doing each, or both doing neither can be used.

New ROM Note: The cassette statements INPUT#, PRINT# and CSAVE# work as described on both recorders. CLOAD with the new ROM works only with recorder #1.

When CLOADing and CSAVEing, if neither recorder is specified, #1 is automatically assumed. The correct way to specify each is:

```
CSAVE#-1,"A"                or                CSAVE#-2,"A"
```

and

```
CLOAD#-1"A"                 or                CLOAD#-2"A"
```

To check for a good load, use either

```
CLOAD#-1,?"A"               or                CLOAD#-2,?"A"
```

CLOAD? by itself will automatically default to test for a good load on the first program encountered on Drive #1. In Appendix G we have a program for logging temperature and humidity. We're going to use it now — first to refresh our memory on how to use a single cassette, then modifying it to use twin cassettes.

The program is reprinted here for your convenience. If you already saved it on tape, CLOAD it in. If not, start typing.

```
10 REM * TEMPERATURE AND HUMIDITY RECORDING PROGRAM *
20 REM * DATA STORAGE MUST START ON THE 1ST DAY OF THE MONTH *
40 CLS : INPUT "WHAT DAY OF THE MONTH IS IT"; D
50 INPUT "WHAT IS TODAYS TEMPERATURE"; T
60 INPUT "WHAT IS TODAYS HUMIDITY"; H
70 PRINT : PRINT
80 IF D = 1 GOTO 430              'ON FIRST DAY IS NO PRIOR
DATA
100 REM * INPUTTING DATA STORED ON CASSETTE TAPE *
110 PRINT "WE MUST LOAD PRIOR DAYS TEMP & HUMIDITY FROM"
120 PRINT "THE DATA TAPE.  BE SURE IT'S REWOUND AND THE
RECORDER"
130 PRINT "IS SET TO 'PLAY'." : PRINT : PRINT
140 INPUT "PRESS 'ENTER' WHEN EVERYTHING IS READY TO
GO."; A$
```

```
160 CLS : PRINT "DATA IS NOW FLOWING INTO THE COMPUTER
FROM TAPE."
170 PRINT : PRINT : PRINT "DATE", "TEMP", "HUMIDITY" :
PRINT
180 FOR X = 1 TO D - 1
190 INPUT #-1, Y, Z                'BRINGS IT IN FROM TAPE
195 PRINT X, Y, Z                  'PRINTS IT ON THE SCREEN
200 B = B + Y : C = C + Z          'KEEPS RUNNING TOTALS
210 NEXT X
300 REM * MONTHS AVERAGES TO-DATE *
310 B = (B+T)/D : C = (C+H)/D      'COMPUTES THE AVERAGES
320 PRINT D, T, H
330 PRINT : PRINT "     **     THIS MONTHS AVERAGES     **"
340 PRINT TAB(7); "TEMP"; TAB(17); "HUMIDITY"
350 PRINT TAB(7); B; TAB(19); C
400 REM * STORING TODAYS TEMP & HUMIDITY ON TAPE *
410 PRINT:PRINT:INPUT "PRESS 'ENTER' WHEN READY TO
CONTINUE";A$
420 CLS : PRINT : PRINT
430 PRINT "TODAYS TEMPERATURE AND HUMIDITY WILL NOW BE
PRINTED"
440 PRINT "ON THE DATA TAPE.  BE SURE 'RECORD' & 'PLAY'
ARE"
450 PRINT "PRESSED.  DO NOT REWIND THE TAPE, YET." :
PRINT
460 INPUT "WHEN ALL IS READY, PRESS 'ENTER'"; A$ : CLS
470 PRINT "TODAYS DATA IS NOW FLOWING FROM THE COMPUTER
TO THE"
480 PRINT "TAPE.  WE WILL INPUT THIS PLUS THE EARLIER
DATA"
```

```
490 PRINT "TOMORROW." : PRINT
500 PRINT #-1, T, H                'PRINTS TODAY S DATA ON
TAPE
520 PRINT "TODAYS NUMBERS HAVE BEEN ADDED TO THE TAPE."
530 PRINT "REWIND THE TAPE IN PREPARATION FOR TOMORROW."
```

RUN the program through several days of arbitrary temperatures and humidity — enough to make a DATA tape.

Now let's modify the program and have cassette #1 act as the source of our historical DATA, and cassette #2 the place we will record the updated DATA. This means we will INPUT from #1 and PRINT to #2.

Fire up the EDITor and make the program read like this:

```
10 REM * TEMPERATURE AND HUMIDITY RECORDING PROGRAM *
20 REM * DATA STORAGE MUST START ON THE 1ST DAY OF THE MONTH *
40 CLS : INPUT "WHAT DAY OF THE MONTH IS IT"; D
50 INPUT "WHAT IS TODAYS TEMPERATURE"; T
60 INPUT "WHAT IS TODAYS HUMIDITY"; H
70 PRINT : PRINT
80 IF D = 1 GOTO 430                'ON FIRST DAY IS NO PRIOR
DATA
100 REM * INPUTTING DATA STORED ON CASSETTE TAPE *
110 PRINT "WE MUST LOAD PRIOR DAYS TEMP & HUMIDITY FROM"
120 PRINT "TAPE DRIVE #1.  BE SURE THE LATEST TAPE IS
REWOUND"
130 PRINT "AND THE RECORDER IS SET TO 'PLAY'." : PRINT
140 PRINT "PUT A FRESH TAPE IN DRIVE #2, AND SET TO
RECORD."
150 PRINT : INPUT "PRESS 'ENTER' WHEN EVERYTHING IS READY
TO GO."; A$
160 CLS : PRINT "DATA IS NOW FLOWING FROM DRIVE #1 INTO THE"
```

```
165 PRINT "COMPUTER, AND FROM THERE BEING RE-RECORDED ON
#2"
170 PRINT : PRINT : PRINT "DATE", "TEMP", "HUMIDITY" :
PRINT
180 FOR X = 1 TO D - 1
190 INPUT #-1, Y, Z              'BRINGS IT IN FROM TAPE
195 PRINT X, Y, Z                'PRINTS IT ON THE SCREEN
197 PRINT #-2, Y, Z              'PRINTS IT ON DRIVE #2
200 B = B + Y : C = C + Z        'KEEPS RUNNING TOTALS
210 NEXT X
300 REM * MONTHS AVERAGES TO DATE *
310 B = (B+T)/D : C = (C+H)/D    'COMPUTES THE AVERAGES
320 PRINT D, T, H
330 PRINT : PRINT "     **     THIS MONTHS AVERAGES     **"
340 PRINT TAB(7); "TEMP"; TAB(17); "HUMIDITY"
350 PRINT TAB(7); B; TAB(19); C : GOTO 470
430 PRINT "BE SURE THERE IS A FRESH TAPE IN DRIVE #2 AND"
440 INPUT "IT IS SET TO RECORD. PRESS 'ENTER' WHEN
READY"; A$
470 PRINT "TODAYS DATA IS NOW FLOWING FROM THE COMPUTER
TO DRIVE #2."
480 PRINT "WE WILL INPUT THIS PLUS THE EARLIER DATA FROM
DRIVE"
490 PRINT "#2, TOMORROW." : PRINT
500 PRINT #-2, T, H              'PRINTS TODAY S DATA ON TAPE #2
525 PRINT "RECORDING COMPLETE." : PRINT
530 PRINT "REWIND & STORE TAPE #2 IN PREPARATION FOR
TOMORROW."
540 PRINT "KEEP THE OLD TAPE AS A BACKUP FOR AT LEAST ONE
DAY."
```

RUN the modified program through at least five days temperature and humidity readings to get a good feel for how it works.

Pretty nifty, huh!? Be sure to CSAVE this program as we use it again in Appendix G.

This learning program is not an ideal model of programming technique for dual cassette operation. It was written to cause lots of relay clicking, turning on and off of motors, blinking lights and screen action, and help us *learn* what's going on. It contains far more explanatory verbiage than actual program logic.

Due to the chance of an error every time a relay is switched or motor started or stopped, in actual practice it's best to keep the mechanical action to a minimum. How can we do this?

Make the data dumps, both to and from the computer, as large as possible, each time a motor is actuated. Ideally, we might have only one dump from drive #1 to the computer at the beginning of a session, then only one dump from the computer to drive #2 at the end. The software and computer reliability are exceedingly high. Enhance the software as much as possible to cut down reliance on hardware. Got any ideas?

How about this one? Could we set up an array that is 31 days long by two pieces of data wide? Yes.

Could we then dump to tape the entire array, with all addresses initialized to zero? Yes.

Could we then bring in this "null array" in one tape-read, change the data for only one day, then unload the entire array in one dump? Yes. Could we even improve on this idea? Yes.

There you have it! Users who are serious about data processing with cassette tape have their assignment.

Precautions

Those who are serious about using ordinary cassette tape recorders for computer work should bear in mind that they were designed for recording talk and music, not digital data. We are only using them because they are inexpensive and available.

Only the very highest quality tape should be used. Certified tape, such as that sold at Radio Shack stores is a bit expensive, but required if you want high reliability. Quality is even more critical in DATA applications than for storing programs. We normally make only one recording of the DATA instead of multiple dumps, and only one READ, though that could be changed in the software.

Periodic maintenance is a must. Tape heads must be cleaned after every few hours use, and demagnetized frequently. The tape drives and tapes must be kept impeccably clean. Data processing is not the same as just "fooling around" with computers, and erratic tape systems will drive you to drink faster than any software bug. (Hic!)

If approached with purposeful diligence and an understanding of the level of technology we are dealing with, cassette systems can do the job.

Model II Special Features

Functions

LOGICAL OPERATORS — In addition to Model I and III BASIC's three logical operators AND, OR, and NOT, the Model II supports:

IMP — Result will be true unless first operand is True and second operand is False.

EQV — Result will be true if both operands are the same.

XOR — Result will be true if only one expression is true.

INPUT$ — This function is used in two ways:

INPUT$(length) limits the input of a string to be the number of characters specified by 'length'. Example:

```
AB$ = INPUT$(3)
```

INPUT$ is handy in password entry as the keystrokes do not show on the screen.

INPUT$(length, buffer-number) is the same as above except it inputs the string from a disk file. Example:

```
AB$ = INPUT$(10,1)
```

inputs up to 10 bytes from file buffer 1.

MOD − The MODulo function returns the remainder when one number is divided into another number. For example:

```
17 MOD 4
```

returns a 1 since 17/4 is 4 with a remainder of 1.

OCT$ − This function returns a string which represents the argument expressed in Octal (base 8). For example:

```
OCT$(49)
```

returns 61 since 49=(6*8)+1. The argument can be in the range -32768 to 32767.

SPACE$ − The Model II does not have space compression codes embedded in its ASCII set like the Model I and Model III computers. Instead, it has a function SPACE$ that allows the user to print from 0 to 255 blank spaces. For example:

```
PRINT "A";SPACE$(20);"B"
```

will print A and B with 20 spaces between them.

SPC − This is almost the same function as SPACE$, but it doesn't use string space. Example:

```
PRINT "A";SPC(25);"B"
```

prints 25 blank spaces between A and B.

TIME$ − Displays the time in 24-hour format. Use the TRSDOS command TIME to change the time. For example:

```
SYSTEM "TIME 22.45"
```

changes the time to 10:45 p.m. Then:

```
PRINT TIME$
```

will display the time.

Statements/Commands

FORMS – used to initialize a line printer, e.g., line length, page length, etc.

PRINT@ – Because of the 24-row/80-column Model II screen, the PRINT@ positions are numbered 0 through 1919. To convert Model I/III PRINT@ positions to Model II, try this formula:

```
INT(INT(P/64)*1.5)*80 + INT((P MOD 64)/64*80)
```

where P is the Model I/III position.

SWAP – This statement allows the exchanging of values of two variables of the same type. The variables must have previously assigned values. Example:

```
SWAP A,B
```

SYSTEM – Allows execution of DOS commands from BASIC. "High Memory Commands" may not be used. The command must be enclosed in quotes. SYSTEM by itself returns to DOS, losing the resident BASIC program.

Miscellaneous

EXPONENTIATION – The Model II uses a carat (^) instead of the right bracket or up arrow for exponentiation.

FLASHING CURSOR – This is similiar to the Model III's cursor except it is slightly lower on screen.

GRAPHIC CHARACTERS – The Model II uses codes 128-158 for graphic characters. These characters bear no resemblance to Model I/III graphic characters.

REVERSE CHARACTERS – The Model II can print black characters on a white background. CHR$(26) turns the reverse character mode on, and CHR$(25) turns it off.

Model II Video Display Worksheet

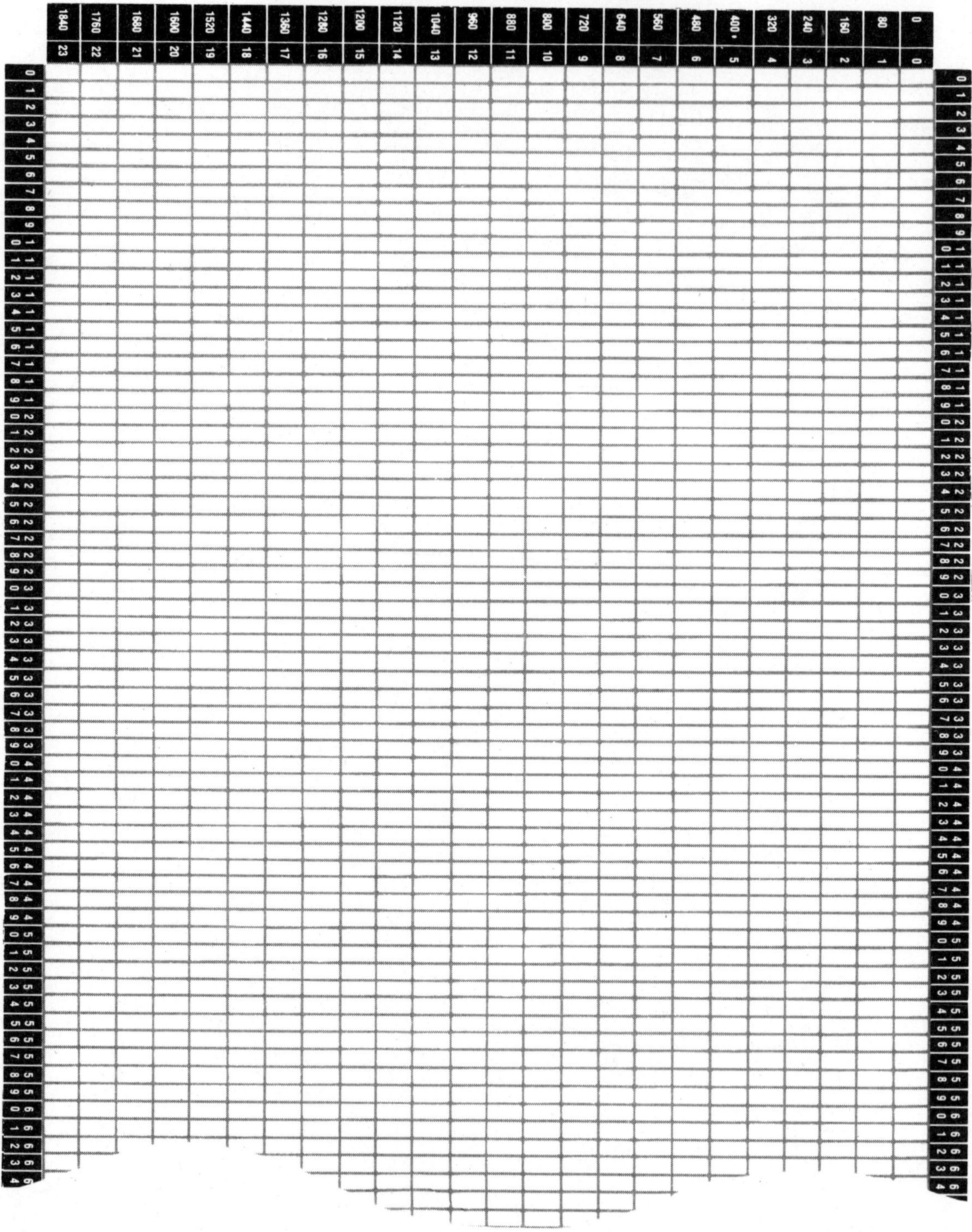

Model III Features

In this appendix, we note some of the unique features of the Model III computer.

Flashing Cursor

The Model III sports a flashing cursor. Users can choose the desired character by poking its ASCII code into location 16419. Location 16412 controls the blink status of the cursor:

$$0 = \rightarrow \text{blink}$$

$$1 = \rightarrow \text{no blink}$$

Exponentiation

The ⬆ key on the keyboard is used for exponentiation. On the screen, this character shows as a left bracket "[".

TIME$

TIME$ is a function that returns the date and time as a string. See your Model III Reference Manual to set the time.

Auto Repeat Feature

Every key has a built-in auto repeat feature. Hold down any of the keys. After a slight delay, the key will automatically repeat.

Cassette Speeds

The two cassette speeds supported are 500 Baud (same as Model I) and 1500 Baud. See Chapter 11 for help in changing speeds.

Screen PRINT

The Model III allows users to dump the screen to a line printer. The manual tells us to use SHIFT ⬇ with the "*" key, but newer Model III versions require that we   simultaneously press the S and P keys. One of these methods should work on your system.   Of course, graphics will not reproduce accurately, but this is a fast way to get hard copy of your screen.

Upper/Lower Case — Caps Only Switch

The computer starts out in caps only mode. Press SHIFT Ø to cause the computer to print upper and lower case like a typewriter. Use SHIFT Ø to switch between these two modes.

Models II and III Reserved Words*

*Many of these words have no function in LEVEL II BASIC; they are reserved for use in DISK BASIC. None of these words can be used inside a variable name. You'll get a syntax error if you try to use these words as variables.

@	DATA	FORMAT	LOF	POS	STEP
ABS	DEFDBL	FRE	LOG	POSN	STOP
AND	DEFFN	FREE	LPRINT	PRINT	STRING$
APPEND	DEFINT	GET	LSET	PUT	STR$
ASC	DEFSNG	GOSUB	MEM	RANDOM	SYSTEM
ATN	DEFSTR	GOTO	MERGE	READ	TAB
AUTO	DEFUSR	IF	MID$	REM	TAN
CDBL	DELETE	INKEY$	MKD$	RENAME	THEN
CHR$	DIM	INP	MKI$	RESET	TIME$
CINT	EDIT	INPUT	MKS$	RESTORE	TO
CLEAR	ELSE	INSTR	NAME	RESUME	TROFF
CLOCK	END	INT	NEW	RETURN	TRON
CLOSE	EOF	KILL	NEXT	RIGHT$	USING
CLS	ERL	LEFT$	NOT	RND	USR
CMD	ERR	LEN	ON	RSET	VAL
CONT	ERROR	LET	OPEN	RUN	VARPTR
COS	EXP	LINE	OR	SAVE	VERIFY
CSNG	FIELD	LIST	OUT	SET	
CVD	FIX	LLIST	PEEK	SGN	
CVI	FN	LOAD	POINT	SIN	
CVS	FOR	LOC	POKE	SQR	

Storing Data Files
On Cassette

Note: Not for Model II.

The material in this Appendix is optional and yet very important. The more practical programming you do, the more you'll appreciate your TRS-80's data file capabilities.   They allow you to go from the world of programming to the larger world of Data Processing.

> What we mean is, you'll be able to do lots more with larger quantities of information.

Up to now we've relied on Level II's numeric variables, string variables and DATA lines to store the data our programs need. This leaves us with two limitations:

1. The computer's memory may not be large enough to hold all the data we need (for example, an inventory list).

2. When we turn off the computer, the values of all variables are lost.

Cassette data files solve both of these problems. We can save huge quantities of information on tape and retrieve them later, just as we save and reload programs. Only instead of the commands CSAVE and CLOAD, we use the special statements PRINT# and INPUT#.

> To perform the exercises in this Appendix, you'll need to keep your tape recorder connected and set in the proper mode — RECORD, PLAY or STOP — as indicated in the text. Insert a blank cassette tape and set the tape counter to zero so you'll know where you started the data file.

Press RECORD and PLAY keys on your recorder at the same time, then type in the following lines and RUN:

```
50  A=1:B=2:C=3

100 PRINT #-1,A,B,C
```

This program causes three things to happen:

1. The tape recorder is automatically started (assuming you have it set in the RECORD mode).

2. The values of A, B and C are written onto the cassette.

3. The recorder is automatically stopped. (You should then press STOP on the recorder to disengage the recording head.)

You now have a permanent record which can easily be read back into the computer. Note that the variables A, B and C are *not* written onto the tape — just the *values* of those variables (in this case, 1, 2 and 3) are stored.

To read back the data from tape, you must first press REWIND on the recorder to rewind the tape to the point where the data file started. (You'll have to disconnect the REMote plug to gain manual control of the recorder. When you have rewound the tape to the starting point, reconnect the REMote plug.)

Not necessary with CTR-80 Recorder.

Type NEW to clear out the old program and enter these lines:

```
110 INPUT #-1,A,B,C

120 PRINT "THE DATA HAS BEEN READ FROM THE TAPE."

130 PRINT "A=";A, "B=";B, "C=";C
```

Now press PLAY on the recorder and type RUN.

If the data from the earlier program was stored and read properly, the computer should display:

```
THE DATA HAS BEEN READ FROM THE TAPE
A= 1             B= 2             C= 3
READY
```

Line 11Ø causes the recorder to start, loading three numbers into the variables A, B and C. When the three numbers have been read, the recorder motion is stopped.

Line 12Ø prints a reassuring message. This is important when the computer is using an external device such as a tape recorder. Print messages are also valuable as prompting instructions to the user regarding the control of the recorder. For example, before the computer executes a PRINT# statement, we can have it print a message telling the user to put the recorder in the record mode. Line 13Ø prints the data that was read from the tape.

NOTE: If the recorder is not in the PLAY mode (with proper connections made) when it executes an INPUT# statement, the computer will keep trying to read the tape until it gets something. To regain control of the computer, press BREAK (or press the RESET button).

One last word of advice: If you PRINT# a list of, say, 10 values onto tape, you should INPUT# a list of 10 values also. If you don't match up the number of PRINT# items with the number of INPUT# items, you'll end up either losing data or having to press BREAK to regain control of your system.

The following program demonstrates how a data file can be used to create a list of data items, process and update it. Study it carefully and think how similar programs might handle inventories, or any sequential lists.

```
REM  * TEMPERATURE AND HUMIDITY RECORDING PROGRAM *
REM  * DATA STORAGE MUST START ON THE 1ST DAY OF MONTH *
CLS : INPUT "WHAT DAY OF THE MONTH IS IT"; D
INPUT "WHAT IS TODAYS TEMPERATURE"; T
INPUT "WHAT IS TODAYS HUMIDITY"; H
PRINT : PRINT
IF D = 1 GOTO 430                'ON FIRST DAY IS NO PRIOR DATA
Ø REM * INPUTTING DATA STORED ON CASSETTE TAPE *
Ø PRINT "WE MUST LOAD PRIOR DAYS TEMP & HUMIDITY FROM"
Ø PRINT "THE DATA TAPE.  BE SURE IT'S REWOUND AND THE RECORDER"
Ø PRINT "IS SET TO 'PLAY'." : PRINT : PRINT
Ø INPUT "PRESS 'ENTER' WHEN EVERYTHING IS READY TO GO."; A$
Ø CLS : PRINT "DATA IS NOW FLOWING INTO THE COMPUTER FROM TAPE."
Ø PRINT : PRINT : PRINT "DATE", "TEMP", "HUMIDITY" : PRINT
Ø FOR X = 1 TO D - 1
Ø INPUT #-1, Y, Z                'BRINGS IT IN FROM TAPE
5 PRINT X, Y, Z                  'PRINTS IT ON THE SCREEN
Ø B = B+Y : C = C + Z            'KEEPS RUNNING TOTALS
Ø NEXT X
Ø REM * MONTHS AVERAGES TO-DATE *
Ø B = (B+T)/D : C = (C+H)/D    'COMPUTES THE AVERAGES
Ø PRINT D, T, H
Ø PRINT : PRINT "    **    THIS MONTHS AVERAGES    **"
Ø PRINT TAB(7); "TEMP"; TAB(17); "HUMIDITY"
Ø PRINT TAB(7); B; TAB(19); C
Ø REM * STORING TODAYS TEMP & HUMIDITY ON TAPE *
```

```
410 PRINT:PRINT:INPUT "PRESS 'ENTER' WHEN READY TO CONTINUE";
420 CLS : PRINT : PRINT
430 PRINT "TODAYS TEMPERATURE AND HUMIDITY WILL NOW BE PRINTE
440 PRINT "ON THE DATA TAPE.  BE SURE 'RECORD' & 'PLAY' ARE"
450 PRINT "PRESSED.  DO NOT REWIND THE TAPE, YET." : PRINT
460 INPUT "WHEN ALL IS READY, PRESS 'ENTER'"; A$ : CLS
470 PRINT "TODAYS DATA IS NOW FLOWING FROM THE COMPUTER TO TH
480 PRINT "TAPE.  WE WILL INPUT THIS PLUS THE EARLIER DATA"
490 PRINT "TOMORROW." : PRINT
500 PRINT #-1, T, H                    'PRINTS TODAY'S DATA ON TAPE
520 PRINT "TODAYS NUMBERS HAVE BEEN ADDED TO THE TAPE."
530 PRINT "REWIND THE TAPE IN PREPARATION FOR TOMORROW."
```

Line 19Ø reads back all the previous days' numbers, two at a time.
When all the information is read in, the average temperature and
humidity are calculated (using the current day's info as well). Line
5ØØ then writes the current day's information at the end of the list.

For a sample run of the program, assume it is the first day of the month.
Enter plausible temperature and humidity figures. Continue running the
program until you've got a cumulative listing for several days. Getting the
feel for data files?

Suggestions for Further Use of Data Files

1. Teaching/Testing. Write a program that gives a multiple-choice test,
   for example, a vocabulary test. Include ten questions. The program
   should write the student's name and all ten responses onto a cassette
   data file. Design the program so that any number of students may take
   the test in sequence. Include instructions about when to use the
   RECORD, PLAY and STOP keys.

   Write a grader program that uses the data file created above to read
   each student's name and responses, grade the test, and then read the
   next student's test. Be sure to leave time for the teacher to mark down
   the names and grades in his or her little black book.

2. Inventory. Write a program that sets up an array in which you store the following information about a group of cars:

   License No., Engine Size, Color Code, and Body Style.

The program should then store the array in a data file.

Write another program which:

1. Asks you which car you're interested in (you enter the license number).

2. Reads the data file until it comes to the correct license number.

3. Prints out all the information about that particular car.

TRS-80 BASIC ERROR Messages

Model I and III

Code	Abbreviation	Explanation
1	NF	NEXT without FOR
2	SN	Syntax error
3	RG	Return without GOSUB
4	OD	Out of data
5	FC	Illegal function call
6	OV	Overflow
7	OM	Out of memory
8	UL	Undefined line
9	BS	Subscript out of range
10	DD	Redimensioned array
11	/O	Division by zero
12	ID	Illegal direct
13	TM	Type mismatch
14	OS	Out of string space
15	LS	String too long
16	ST	String formula too complex
17	CN	Can't continue
18	NR	NO RESUME
19	RW	RESUME without error
20	UE	Unprintable error
21	MO	Missing operand
22	FD	Bad file data
23	L3	Disk BASIC only

Explanation of Error Messages

NF   NEXT without FOR: NEXT is used without a matching FOR statement. This error may also occur if NEXT variable statements are reversed in a nested loop.

SN   Syntax Error: This usually is the result of incorrect punctuation, open parenthesis, an illegal character, or a misspelled command.

RG   RETURN with GOSUB: A RETURN statement was encountered before a matching GOSUB was executed.

OD   Out of Data: A READ OR INPUT # statement was executed with insufficient data available. The DATA statement may have been left out or all data may have been read from tape or DATA.

FC   Illegal Function Call: An attempt was made to execute an operation using an illegal parameter. Examples: square root of a negative argument, negative matrix dimension, negative or zero LOG arguments, etc. Or USR call without first POKEing the entry point.

OV   Overflow: The magnitude of the number input or derived is too large for the computer to handle. Note: There is no underflow error. Numbers smaller than $\pm 1.701411E\text{-}38$ single precision or $\pm 1.701411834544556E$ double precision are rounded to 0. See /O below.

OM   Out of Memory: All available memory has been used or reserved. This may occur with very large matrix dimensions, and nested branches such as GOTO, GOSUB, and FOR-NEXT loops.

UL   Undefined Line: An attempt was made to refer or branch to a non-existent line.

BS   Subscript out of Range: An attempt was made to assign a matrix element with a subscript beyond the DIMensioned range.

DD   Redimensioned Array: An attempt was made to DIMension a matrix which had previously been dimensioned by DIM or by default statements. It is a good idea to put all dimension statements at the beginning of a program.

Explanation of Error Messages

/0   Division by Zero: An attempt was made to use a value of zero in the denominator. Note: If you can't find an obvious division by zero check for division by numbers smaller than allowable ranges. See OV above.

ID   Illegal Direct: The use of INPUT as a direct command.

TM   Type Mismatch: An attempt was made to assign a non-string variable to a string or vice versa.

OS   Out of String Space: The amount of string space allocated was exceeded.

LS   String Too Long: A string variable was assigned a string value which exceeded 255 characters in length.

ST   String Formula Too Complex: A string operation was too complex to handle. Break up the operation into shorter steps.

CN   Can't Continue: A CONT was issued at a point where no continuable program exists, e.g., after program was ENDed or EDITed.

NR   No RESUME: End of program reached in error-trapping mode.

RW   RESUME Without ERROR: A RESUME was encountered before ON ERROR GOTO was executed.

UE   Unprintable Error: An attempt was made to generate an error using an ERROR statement with an invalid code.

MO   Missing Operand: An operation was attempted without providing one of the required operands.

FD   Bad File Data: Data input from an external source (i.e., tape) was not correct or was in improper sequence, etc.

L3   DISK BASIC Only: An attempt was made to use a statement, function, or command which is available only with the Disk system.

Model II Error Messages

Code	Abbreviation	Explanation
1	NF	**NEXT without FOR.** NEXT is used without a matching FOR statement. This error may also occur if NEXT variables are reversed in a nested loop.
2	SN	**Syntax.** This is usually the result of incorrect punctuation, an illegal character or a misspelled command.
3	RG	**RETURN with GOSUB.** A RETURN statement was encountered before a matching GOSUB was executed.
4	OD	**Out of data.** A READ statement was executed with insufficient data available. The DATA statement may have been read.
5	FC	**Illegal function call.** An attempt was made to execute an operation using an illegal parameter. Examples: square root of a negative argument, negative array dimension, negative or zero LOG arguments.
6	OV	**Overflow.** The magnitude of the number derived or input is too large for the data storage type assigned to it. The integer range is $[-32768,32767]$; other numbers can be in the range $[-1\text{x}10^{+38}, -1\text{x}10^{-38}]$ or $[+1\text{x}10^{-38}, +1\text{x}10^{+38}]$. **Note:** There is no underflow error; numbers smaller than $+/-1.701411\text{E-}38$ (single precision) or $+/-1.70141834544556\text{E-}38$ (double precision) are rounded to 0.
7	OM	**Out of memory.** All available memory has been used or reserved. This may occur with large array dimensions and nested branches such as GOSUB and FOR/NEXT loops.
8	UL	**Undefined line.** An attempt was made to reference a non-existent line.
9	BS	**Bad subscript.** An attempt was made to assign an array element with a subscript beyond the dimensioned range.

Code	Abbre-viation	Explanation
10	DD	**Double-dimensioned array.** An attempt was made to Dimension an array which had previously been created with DIM or by default statements. ERASE must be used first.
11	/0	**Division by zero.** An attempt was made to use a value of zero in the denominator. **Note:** If you can't find an obvious division by zero, check for division by numbers smaller than allowable ranges (see OV above).
12	ID	**Illegal direct.** An attempt was made to use a program-only statement like INPUT in an immediate (non-program) line.
13	TM	**Type mismatch.** An attempt was made to assign a number to a string variable or a string to a numeric variable.
14	OS	**Out of string space.** The amount of string space allocated was exceeded. Use CLEAR to allocate more string space. 100 bytes is the default string space allocation.
15	LS	**Long string.** A string variable was assigned a string which exceeded 255 characters in length.
16	ST	**String too complex.** A string operation was too complex to handle. The operation must be broken into shorter steps.
17	CN	**Can't continue.** A CONT command was given at a point where the command can't be carried out, e.g., directly after the program has been edited.
18	UF	**Undefined user function.** An attempt has been made to call a USR function without first defining its entry point via a DEFUSER statement.
19	NR	**No RESUME.** During an error-trapping routine, BASIC has reached the end of the program without encountering a RESUME.
20	RW	**RESUME without error.** A RESUME was encountered when no error was present. You need to insert END or GOTO in front of the error-handling routine.

Code	Abbre-viation	Explanation
21	UE	**Undefined error.** Reserved for future use.
22	MO	**Missing operand.** An operation was attempted without providing one of the required operands.
23	BO	**Buffer overflow.** An attempt was made to input a data line which has too many characters to be held in the line buffer.
24-49	UE	**Undefined error.** Reserved for future use.
50	FO	**Field overflow.** An attempt was made to Field more characters than the direct-access file record length allows. The record length is assigned when the file is first Opened. The default length is 256.
51	IE	**Internal error.** Also indicates an attempt to use EOF on a file which is not Open.
52	BN	**Bad file number.** An attempt was made to use a file number which specifies a file that is not Open or that is greater than the number of files specified when BASIC was started up.
53	FF	**File not found.** Reference was made in a LOAD, KILL or OPEN statement to a file which did not exist on the diskette specified.
54	BM	**Bad file mode.** Program attempted to perform direct access on a file Opened for sequential access or vice-versa.
55	AO	**File already Open.** An attempt was made to Open a file that was already open. This error is also output if a KILL statement is given for an Open file.
56	IO	**Disk I/O error.** An error has been detected during a disk read.
57	FE	**Undefined** in Model II BASIC.
58	UE	**Undefined error.** Reserved for future use.

Code	Abbre-viation	Explanation
59	DF	**Disk full.** All storage space on the disk has been used. Kill unneeded files or use a formatted, non-full diskette.
60	EF	**End of file.** An attempt was made to read past the end of file.
61	RN	**Bad record number.** In a PUT or GET statement, the record number is either greater than the allowable maximum or equal to zero.
62	NM	**Undefined** in Model II BASIC.
63	MM	**Mode mismatch.** A sequential OPEN was executed for a file that already existed on the disk as a direct access file, or vice versa.
64	UE	**Undefined error.** Reserved for future use.
65	DS	**Direct statement.** A direct statement was encountered during a load of a program in ASCII format. The load is terminated.
66	FL	**Undefined** in Model II BASIC.

Section E

Index

Index

COMPUSOFT
PUBLISHING

A DIVISION OF COMPUSOFT, INC., SAN DIEGO

NOTICE

Thank you for purchasing the Second Edition of *LEARNING TRS-80 BASIC*.

Every book that deals with the rapidly changing field of personal computers requires updating. *LEARNING TRS-80 BASIC* is no exception. We at CompuSoft Publishing want to be certain that you are informed of any changes, updates or errors. If you will send us your name and address we will send you the latest UPDATE MEMORANDUM without charge.

Mail to: CompuSoft Publishing, Inc.
Dept. T-2
P. O. Box 19669
San Diego, CA 92119

For Additional Copies
of
Learning TRS-80 BASIC

Contact your local Computer, Electronics or Book Store

or

Send $19.95 each + $1.00 Postage & Handling
(California addresses add 6% sales tax)

Foreign Orders
Payable in U.S. funds on a U.S. bank
Surface: Send $19.95 + $2.50
Allow 6 to 8 weeks for delivery
Air: Send $19.95 + $10.00

To

COMPUSOFT® PUBLISHING
P.O. Box 19669
San Diego, CA 92119

Dealer inquiries welcomed

Educational discounts available for quantity purchases.

Write for details.

ISBN 0-932760-08-2

Library of Congress # 81-70768